LEAVE ANY INFORMATION AT THE SIGNA
WRITINGS, INTERVIEWS, BITS, PAGES
ED RUSCHA
EDITED AND WITH AN INTRODUCTION BY ALEXANDRA SCHWARTZ

Ed Ruscha is among the most innovative artists of the last forty years. He is also one of the first Americans to introduce a critique of popular culture and an examination of language into the visual arts. Although he first made his reputation as a painter, Ruscha is also celebrated for his drawings (made both with conventional materials and with food, blood, gunpowder, and shellac), prints, films, photographs, and books. Though often associated with Los Angeles as a Pop and Conceptual artist, Ruscha tends to regard such labels with a satirical, if not jaundiced, eye. Indeed, his work is characterized by the tensions between high and low, solemn and irreverent, and serious and nonsensical, and it draws on popular culture as well as Western art traditions.

Leave Any Information at the Signal not only documents the work of this influential artist as he rose to prominence but also contains his writings and commentaries on other artistic developments of the period. The book is divided into three parts, each of which is arranged chronologically. Part one contains statements, letters, and other writings. Part two consists of more than fifty interviews, some of which have never before been published or translated into English. Part three contains sketchbook pages, word groupings, and other notes that chart how Ruscha develops ideas and solves artistic problems. They are published here for the first time. The book also contains more than eighty illustrations, selected and arranged by the artist.

Ed Ruscha is an internationally acclaimed artist based in Los Angeles. Alexandra Schwartz is a doctoral candidate in art history at the University of Michigan, where she is writing her dissertation on Ed Ruscha's work from 1960 to 1975. She lives in New York City.

An OCTOBER Book

LEAVE ANY INFORMATION AT THE SIGNAL

LEAVE ANY INFORMATION AT THE SIGNAL

WRITINGS, INTERVIEWS, BITS, PAGES

ED RUSCHA
EDITED BY ALEXANDRA SCHWARTZ

AN OCTOBER BOOK

THE MIT PRESS
CAMBRIDGE, MASSACHUSETTS
LONDON, ENGLAND

This book was set in Bembo by Graphic Composition, Inc., Athens, Georgia, using Quark XPress and was printed and bound in the United States of America.

Library of Congress Cataloging-in-Publication Data

Ruscha, Edward.
  Leave any information at the signal : writings, interviews, bits, pages / by Ed Ruscha ; edited and with an introduction by Alexandra Schwartz.
    p.   cm.
  "An October book"
  Includes bibliographical references and index.
  ISBN 0-262-18220-3 (hc. : alk. paper)
  1. Ruscha, Edward—Interviews. 2. Artists—United States—Interviews. 3. Ruscha, Edward—Notebooks, sketchbooks, etc. I. Schwartz, Alexandra. II. Title.
N6537.R87 A35   2002
760′.092—dc21
                                                                                    2001045039

CONTENTS

INTRODUCTION AND ACKNOWLEDGMENTS   xiii
Alexandra Schwartz

PART ONE   WRITINGS   1

STATEMENT IN "'WEST COAST STYLE': SOMETHING
ABOUT LOS ANGELES," COMPILED BY HENRY HOPKINS   3

STATEMENT IN "THE ARTIST AND POLITICS:
A SYMPOSIUM"   4

"SOME OF THE '654 THINGS . . .' LIST"   6

STATEMENT IN HENRY HOPKINS, *50 WEST COAST
ARTISTS*   10

STATEMENT IN "PICASSO: A SYMPOSIUM"   12

A PROPOSAL BY EDWARD RUSCHA FOR THE
CIRCULAR RING AND FOR THE LUNETTES OF THE
NEW MIAMI-DADE PUBLIC LIBRARY, APRIL 1985   14

A PROPOSAL BY EDWARD RUSCHA FOR THE
ARCHWAY LUNETTES OF THE SECOND AND THIRD
FLOORS OF THE MIAMI-DADE PUBLIC LIBRARY,
APRIL 1987   16

Contents

"The Witness"   18

Statement in "What Artists Like about the
Art They Like When They Don't Know Why,"
Compiled by Paul Gardener   19

PART TWO   INTERVIEWS   21

"Concerning *Various Small Fires:* Edward
Ruscha Discusses His Perplexing Publications"   23
John Coplans

"From Common Scenes, Mr. Ruscha Evokes Art"   28
Douglas M. Davis

"Ed Ruscha Discusses His Latest Work with
Christopher Fox"   30
Christopher Fox

Interview with Titia Tybout, May 27, 1971   34

"Art: Interview with Ed Ruscha"   35
Robert Colacello

"Ruscha as Publisher [or All Booked Up]"   40
David Bourdon

"'My Books End Up in the Trash'"   46
A. D. Coleman

"'I'm Not Really a Photographer'"   51
A. D. Coleman

Contents

"Words with Ruscha"   55
Howardena Pindell

"' . . . A Kind of a Huh?': An Interview with
Edward Ruscha"   64
Willoughby Sharp

"Feature Interview: Edward Ruscha"   73
Diane Spodarek

"A Conversation with Ed Ruscha"   82
Trina Mitchum

Interview with Edward Ruscha in His
Western Avenue, Hollywood Studio   92
Paul Karlstrom

"Ed Ruscha: An Interview"   210
Henri Man Barendse

*L.A. Suggested by the Art of Edward
Ruscha*   220

"Ed Ruscha, Young Artist: Dead Serious
about Being Nonsensical"   225
Patricia Failing

"Catching Up with Ed Ruscha"   238
Lewis MacAdams

"A Conversation with Edward Ruscha"   242
Robert Landau and John Pashdag

Contents

An Excerpt from "Art: L.A.R.T.: Edward Ruscha"   247
Joan Quinn

"Interview with Edward Ruscha"   250
Bernard Brunon

"Premeditated: An Interview with Ed Ruscha"   252
Jana Sterbak

"A Few Words with Ed Ruscha"   257
Vicki Sanders

"Ed Ruscha: Goodbye to Vistas and All That"   259
Ralph Rugoff

"Ed Ruscha"   262
Fred Fehlau

"Rebel with a Canvas: Ed Ruscha's Original Art Is Drawing Attention"   269
Chris Hunter

"The Sentimental Musical Tastes of Ed Ruscha"   272
Kristine McKenna

"Ed Ruscha"   274
Bill Berkson

"Ed Ruscha"   281
Thomas Beller

Contents

"Hot Property"   286
Victoria Lautman

"An Interview with Edward Ruscha"   288
Bonnie Clearwater

"The Last Word"   296
Ralph Rugoff

"Conversation with Ed Ruscha"   300
Bernard Blistène

"Getting a Read on Ed Ruscha"   309
Suzanne Muchnic

"A Conversation between Walter Hopps and
Edward Ruscha, Who Have Known Each
Other Since the Early 1960s, Took Place on
September 26, 1992"   312
Walter Hopps

"An Interview with Ed Ruscha," June 17, 1994   329
Elizabeth Armstrong

"Pronounce His Name Rew-shay"   332
Guy Cross

"Panoramic Art at Library Elusive but
Impressive"   336
Steven Rosen

"Library Muralist Slow to Praise . . ."   338
Steven Rosen

Contents

"ART MUSEUM, LIBRARY TO FEATURE 'WORD'
ACCORDING TO RUSCHA"   339
Mary Voelz Chandler

"HOLLYWOOD DECKS THE HALLS: ED RUSCHA"   341

"THE RETURN OF A NATIVE SON: PAINTER
ED RUSCHA RESURFACES IN L.A."   342
Michael Duncan

"CONFESSION IN CHELSEA"   344
Jeffrey Hogrefe

"LIGHTENING UP THE GETTY"   345
Kristine McKenna

"FROM RUSCHA WITH LIGHT"   353
Reed Johnson

"SEEING THINGS AGE IS A FORM OF BEAUTY:
A CONVERSATION WITH ED RUSCHA"   355
Tracy Bartley

"COLLECTING OUR THOUGHTS"   361
Ralph Rugoff

"THE WEATHER OF PRINTS: AN INTERVIEW WITH
EDWARD RUSCHA," JULY 16, 1998   362
Siri Engberg

CONVERSATION WITH EDWARD RUSCHA IN HIS
STUDIO, VENICE, CALIFORNIA, OCTOBER 29, 1999   370
Alexandra Schwartz

Contents

"Profile: The Paintings of Ed Ruscha"   379
Susan Stamberg

Part Three   **Bits and Pages**   383

Notes   431

Additional Sources   437

Credits   441

Index   447

———

INTRODUCTION AND ACKNOWLEDGMENTS

Alexandra Schwartz

"AN ATTEMPT TO SET UP A RIDDLE"

—*Ed Ruscha, "Bits"*

Ed Ruscha has a history of refusing to play along. Over the course of his career, which began in the early 1960s, he has worked in an enormous range of media, experimenting with painting, drawing (both with conventional art supplies and with food, blood, gunpowder, and shellac), printmaking, photography, film, and books. He has long cultivated an interest in written language and typography, and many of his images consist mainly of words. He maintains a careful distance from the East Coast art establishment; the fact that he has never lived in New York indicates a certain reluctance to participate in the frenzy of posturing and politicking that characterizes the Manhattan art world. Instead, he belongs to a group of Los Angeles–based artists (including Billy Al Bengston, Joe Goode, and Jerry McMillan, among others) who, though never enjoying the superstar status of some of their New York counterparts, dominated the California scene in the 1960s and into the 1970s. As historians reevaluate the production of artists who came of age during that era, Ruscha's work has risen to prominence. In the last five years alone, he has had two major museum retrospectives, earned several large public art commissions, and been the subject of several books.

The idea for this anthology developed out of my own scholarly work on Ruscha; my objective in initiating it was to introduce a comprehensive account of his art—and that of the often-underestimated Los Angeles community in which he has played so crucial a role—into the art historical literature. While entirely supportive of this project, Ruscha has also been eager to subvert expectations of what such a book should be like, to ensure that the end product is not just informative but provocative and amusing. The resulting anthology comprises a diverse collection of documents dating from every phase of the artist's career. Spanning the years 1960 to 2000, these texts address subjects ranging from his stance on the political potential of art, circa 1970 ("Statement in 'The Artist and Politics: A Symposium' "), to his dream about an uncanny Manhattan hotel populated primarily by artists ("Nightmare of June 1, 1984," in "Bits"). A large number of these texts have never before been published. Others, I discovered, have until now been scattered throughout various magazines, journals, and books, many of which proved difficult to locate or have never before been translated into English. I unearthed documents in libraries and archives from Los Angeles to Washington, D.C. to Paris, and also worked closely with the artist in choosing selections from his extensive personal holdings. Ultimately, I included those that best testified to both the intellectual currents influencing Ruscha's work and the historical developments shaping his career. While some selections relate to specific artworks, others speak to broader issues in contemporary culture.

The anthology is divided into three parts: "Writings," "Interviews," and "Bits and Pages." The first two chapters primarily contain occasional pieces: statements requested by magazines, interviews conducted around the time of exhibition openings, and other such texts. Part One includes writings penned by Ruscha throughout the course of his career. They range from a 1974 proposal— never before published in the United States—for a public art project in France (ironically called "234 Things from the United States"), to a reflection on the Museum of Modern Art's Picasso retrospective of 1980 ("Statement in 'Picasso: A Symposium' ").

Over the years, Ruscha has been interviewed by many prominent figures in postwar American art. These texts appear collected together for the first time in Part Two, and include interviews by critics and curators such as Walter Hopps, Henry Hopkins, and John Coplans; artists such as Howardena Pindell, Douglas Davis, and Jana Sterbek; and art journalists such as Willoughby Sharp for *Avalanche* and Robert Colacello for *Inter/View: Andy Warhol's Movie Magazine*. Part Two also features Ruscha's previously unpublished account of the 1960s Los Angeles art scene, as told to Paul Karlstrom for the Archives of American Art California Oral History Project. Archival photographs, selected and arranged in consultation with the artist, appear throughout Parts One and Two. While some of these pictures complement specific texts, others serve as records in their own right, providing important visual testimonies to the artist's working and creative processes.

Part Three, "Bits and Pages," is quite different. Rather than choosing simply to photograph or transcribe pages from his sketchbooks, Ruscha has compiled and transcribed a collage-like collection of notes he's jotted down over the years: some in journals, some on napkins, some on the nearest scrap of paper he could find while driving his car (ideas often come to him on the road). The typographical notes are called "bits," and the notebook leaves reproduced in their entirety are called "pages." Collected together, the documents in all three chapters form an artistic and intellectual autobiography, the artist telling his story in his own words.

One of the most profound aspects of all these texts is their testimony to the ways in which the very quality that first impressed me about Ruscha's work—its refusal to conform to expectations, its intentional marginality—guides almost every aspect of his production. His contentiousness (often sly, sometimes taunting, always good-humored) comes through in his earliest writings as well as his most recent interviews. It's also all over his work; this is, after all, the artist who gave us the grand-scale oil entitled *The Los Angeles County Museum on Fire* and adorned the catalog of his first major museum retrospective with a drawing called *I Don't Want No Retro Spective*. In pictures such as these, Ruscha delights in teasing an art world that, he is well aware, has treated him extremely well. There can be no question that he is a provocateur. But it is this kind of tension, this discomfort, this refusal to let anyone predict how he will act and what sort of art he will make, that both defines Ruscha's work and gives it its greatest strength.

Ruscha chose the title of this book, *Leave Any Information at the Signal*. It's a riddle, and intentionally so. If the book is supposed to elucidate Ruscha's thought processes, then the apparent obscurity of its title might be construed as a gesture toward covering them back up again. He is loath to let us get too confident in our understanding of his work and, just as the words in many of his paintings glimmer with a touch of the nonsensical, so too does the title of this book. Nevertheless, it is precisely *because* this title is cryptic that it ultimately works. For if we can get past its initial trick—the odd, rather absurdist turn of phrase that sends us reeling off-track—we realize that by choosing it, Ruscha has laid before us his long-standing dilemma: his ambivalence about embracing the roles he is assigned by the art world.

But if the publication of this book testifies to his acceptance into the art historical "establishment," then his naming it after his answering-machine greeting demonstrates his resistance to that establishment and all that it implies. He balks at our expectations of what a scholarly book is supposed to be—just as, in the past, he has disrupted our notions of what an artist's book or an oil painting is supposed be. Here, as before, his playfulness belies another, graver purpose stirring just below the surface. The tension between his ever-competing impulses—gravity and levity, resistance and complicity—is what generates the power behind his art.

I am indebted to numerous people who have helped to guide this book to completion, but there are a number who must be thanked by name. First and foremost, my thanks go to Ed Ruscha. His energetic cooperation and assistance with all aspects of the project have been extraordinarily generous. I would also like to thank to Mary Dean, Paul Ruscha, Pat Poncy, Jessica Nesmith, and everyone else who was so helpful at the studio and office.

Tremendous thanks go to the writers and artists whose work is included in this volume, and who allowed their contributions to be reprinted without charge or for a nominal fee. I am deeply grateful for their generosity and enthusiasm.

———

This project could not have happened without the without the help and support of my teachers at the University of Michigan and Harvard University. I am particularly indebted to Yve-Alain Bois and Maria Gough, whose advice and encouragement from start to finish was invaluable. This book was made possible in part through grants from the Henry Luce Foundation and, at the University of Michigan, the Department of the History of Art and the Horace H. Rackham Graduate School; I am grateful to Celeste Brusati and Elizabeth Sears for their help and resourcefulness in securing this funding. My thanks also go to Howard Lay for his suggestions on the manuscript and his ongoing support and encouragement. I am greatly indebted to Roger Conover at the MIT Press, for his good judgment, support, and expertise; and to my research assistant, Kevin Smith, for ably helping me with all the nuts and bolts.

Finally, I am profoundly grateful to the friends and family who have assisted with various aspects of the project and have supplied support and solidarity during the time it has been in the works. There are too many to name, but I'd like particularly to thank Anne Duroe, Rita Hao, Kelli Patton, Steve Petersen, Mike Rosenbaum, and Vicky Solan; Jane Carpenter, Chris de Fay, and Carmen Higgenbotham; and especially my grandparents, my brother, and my parents.

Ed Ruscha, Mojave Desert, 1962. Photo: Patty Callahan.

PART ONE

WRITINGS

In Parts One and Two, dates of artworks by Ruscha are indicated in square brackets, following the first time each work is mentioned.

Throughout the following interviews, all of Ruscha's words appear in roman type. Other writers' and speakers' words appear in italic type.

In their original forms, the writings and interviews in Parts One and Two sometimes repeat each other, the same topics having been discussed on different occasions over the years. Such repetitions have been largely deleted. These and other editorial cuts are indicated by ellipses within square brackets. When these bracketed ellipses are printed in roman type, the deletions include remarks by Ruscha. Ellipses not in square brackets appear in the original texts.

STATEMENT IN "'WEST COAST STYLE': SOMETHING ABOUT
LOS ANGELES," COMPILED BY HENRY HOPKINS

Questions asked of the artists: What influence or effect has Los Angeles had on your work?
What are you doing now?

Being in Los Angeles has had little or no effect on my work. I could have done
it anywhere. I don't see any independent trends here. The climate isn't that con-
ducive to painting. Right now I'm working on some unfinished paintings in the
realm of "still life" and on my fourth book, called *Sunset Boulevard,*[1] which is a
continuous series of photographs from one end of the boulevard to the other.
When it is completely finished it will be about three-quarters of a mile long.

Originally published in *Art Voices,* v. 5, n. 4, fall 1966, pp. 61, 68.

STATEMENT IN "THE ARTIST AND POLITICS: A SYMPOSIUM"

The symposium question that follows was sent to various artists . . .

A growing number of artists have begun to feel the need to respond to the deepening political crisis in America. Among these artists, however, there are serious differences concerning their relations to direct political actions. Many feel that the political implications of their work constitute the most profound political action they can take. Others, not denying this, continue to feel the need for an immediate, direct political commitment. Still others feel that their work is devoid of political meaning and that their political lives are unrelated to their art. What is your position regarding the kinds of political action that should be taken by artists?[2]

Draping works of art in black as a protest is ridiculous. It testifies to its own meekness and becomes an invisible statement. The withdrawing of art from exhibits sponsored by the United States government is not much better. Both acts are like shutting up shop and turning out the lights. It's like not growing wheat for some purpose or other or pantomiming what should actually be yelled about. What can finally be accomplished by not doing things?

The United States government does not need artists to maintain its cultural image to the world and won't be hurt when artists refuse to cooperate. The sooner

Originally appeared in *Artforum,* v. 9, September 1970, pp. 35–39.

artists are on to this, the better. I cannot seriously believe that art is the stooge of politics. How can artists, with all their works, compete with the moonshot?

I have excluded political science from my program. As an artist, I lean towards natural things rather than those created by people, which include forms of government, economic patterns, and national policies. An objective attitude is one which makes all world events neither bad nor good but only so much data to play with or not play with. I isolate myself and my work continues smoothly with no involvement in any issue. As an American citizen though, I have no trouble seeing how bad things are. And I don't think the American public necessarily needs to be alerted to how serious it is. It knows. The facts alone are staggering and become a protest in themselves.

The most natural reaction to an injustice is a physical response. Don't people raise hell when they are mistreated? It seems to be a staple in American history and has accomplished most in American history and always gets government consideration before anything else. The plain truth behind the Watts riots is that the riots themselves were good and beneficial and healthy regardless of loss of life.[3] The Watts riots nationalized sympathy for a gigantic racial injustice.

If silent dissent is going to continue and be a success, it can't be handled on a part-time basis. It needs meat behind it, so it has to enlist even those who are only remotely in agreement with its ideas. And only when its actions are unanimous will it be effective, if at all.

I don't think an artist can do much for any cause by using his art as a weapon.

[Draft for a submission to "Propositions for a City," a competition to create an original artistic policy for the redeveloped Défense district, Paris. Sponsored by L'Établissment Public de la Défense, Départment des Arts Plastiques Documentations, L'Établissment Public du Centre Beaubourg. The proposal went through several versions and the list was eventually reduced to 234.]

1. CLOTHING
   suits—men's, women's and children's, shoes, socks, t-shirts, hats, raincoats, gloves, women's wig, etc.

2. NON-PERISHABLE FOODS
   instant, powdered, and imitation foods, etc.

3. MEDICINES AND CHEMICALS
   aspirin, cold tablets, first-aid kit, safety goggles, hot water bottle, ice pack, etc.

From a project for a stone time capsule containing "popular products immediately available to all American consumers of the year 1974," 1974.

4. PERSONAL ITEMS

toiletries, shaving gear, hair spray, briefcase, hand-gun, scissors, flashlight, greeting cards, etc.

5. HOUSEHOLD ITEMS

garden supplies, kitchen equipment, cleansers, broom, American flag, Revere ware, folding beach chair, roach powder, etc.

6. BUILDING MATERIALS AND HARDWARE

tools, automotive goods, cans of oil, hammer, nails, screws, screw driver, hand saw, car tire, blender, bricks, glue, electrical equipment, etc.

7. OBJECTS OF INFORMATION

current newspapers and magazines, best-seller books, best-seller phonograph records, typewriter, stationery, radio, camera, clock, adding machine computer, bible, music sheets, burglar alarm (that works!), etc.

8. OBJECTS OF ENTERTAINMENT

toys, sporting goods, games, playing cards, baseball hat, yo-yo, checkers, monopoly, camping equipment, football, musical instruments, basketball, bowling ball, tobaccos, etc.

Ed Ruscha, "A Time Capsule of American Products for the Defense, Paris, France" (unbuilt), *234 Things from the United States*. 1974. Pencil on paper. Photo courtesy Ed Ruscha.

EDWARD RUSCHA, 1024¾ N. WESTERN AVENUE, HOLLYWOOD, CALIFORNIA 90029 (213 463-7057)

"234 THINGS"

PROPOSAL FOR A TIME-CAPSULE MONUMENT
CONTAINING MANY OBJECTS OF EVERY DAY
USE MANUFACTURED IN THE UNITED STATES.
TO BE CONSTRUCTED OF CLASSIC STONE AND
PLACED WITHIN A PEDESTRIAN AREA OF THE
DEFENSE. MONUMENT COULD BE OPENED
EVERY 100 YEARS FOR INSPECTION AND
RE-CLOSED. A SMALL BOOK COULD BE
PRINTED LISTING ALL CONTENTS WITH A
PHOTOGRAPH AND DESCRIPTION OF EACH
OBJECT.

THE FACING OF THE MONUMENT TO BE
MADE OF STONE "PLATES" LEAVING THE
INSIDE HOLLOW FOR SHELVES TO HOUSE
THE OBJECTS. THE NUMBER "234" IS
ARBITRARY AND DEPENDS ON THE FINAL
NUMBER OF OBJECTS TO BE PLACED IN
THE MONUMENT.

Edward Ruscha

Ed Ruscha, "234 Things" (artist's statement). 1974. Ink on paper. Photo courtesy Ed Ruscha.

Sometimes this art business is beyond the range of human comprehension, since the viewer is part of the experience. This makes it open to anyone's indulgence and the individual work falls or rises depending on who's looking at it.

The hardest thing to accept is that the number one rule is that there are no rules. This leaves it open-ended and makes the teaching of art impossible. It's maddening, isn't it?

No matter what style an artist operates under, he or she is still a little soldier to art history. If he were born fifty years earlier he wouldn't do the same things as he does today. Artists are so vulnerable that, despite the tough exterior, they are influenced by trivia that they would consciously reject. I find myself using things that once scared me stiff. So a visual artist has the right to never be questioned about what he does. Isn't this what they call "artistic license"?

As it stands, what do I know about silicones or sideburns or accidents? Not much except that I am committed to collecting thoughts and potential issues. The result can be vague if it wants to be. It's not important. The important thing is to create a sort of itch-in-the-scalp [. . .].

Originally published in *50 West Coast Artists: A Critical Selection of Painters and Sculptors Working in California,* edited by Douglas Bullis (San Francisco: Chronicle Books, 1977), pp. 112–113.

I was born in Omaha in 1937 and moved to Oklahoma at age five. The word "cartooning" had a powerful strength at around age eight. Whenever I saw the word I would get excited. I knew that I wanted to be a cartoonist, if not an artist. Oddly enough, the word itself kept me going. India ink somehow played a big part in the tools-of-the-trade instinct.

Spike Jones influenced me in his stage style. When I was ten I got a gofer job with his band, running for things like a dozen eggs, which Spike would then grab and throw at his musicians. I was very impressed.

It was only natural, then, that I gravitated to the discovery of the Dada movement—another subject that can be appreciated by name alone. I hated "sketching." Images were more important to me than rendering. I left high school and Oklahoma in 1956 to go to art school in California. New York was too cold and intellectual.

On arriving I immediately realized that I had to unlearn everything, including the Catholic Church. At Chouinard Art Institute I got the one lesson I probably would not have gotten elsewhere. I learned to be dedicated to my work. I was not running scared, because making money in art was the last thing that mattered.

The painting of a target by Jasper Johns was an atomic bomb in my training.[4] I knew that I had seen something truly profound. Johns was unknown and so was his kind of art. The teachers said it was *not* art. Twenty years later, of course, what does their art resemble? Enough said.

The time I did at Chouinard was helpful, but less from the instruction than from my fellow students. I also became aware of the art of movies. I would forget the story but remember the emotion. I began to believe that it is not so much what you say that matters, but how you say it. This ruled out so-called emotional painting. Everything should be preplanned.

Statement in "Picasso: A Symposium"

[Participants[5] were asked about their impressions of the exhibition.]

On entering the museum, I was determined not to be overwhelmed by the force of this colossal art figure. I found myself continually checking years in which works were made. Eight conclusions presented themselves:

1907: Exhaustive

1914: Brilliant

1921: Hot

1934: Cold

1937: Pretty Good

1958: Shameful

1973: Self-redeeming

His greatest work? *Glass of Absinth* (1914). Who would argue?

Originally published in **ART IN AMERICA** Magazine, Brant Publications, Inc., December 1980 (v. 68, n. 10, pp. 9–19). Published on the occasion of the exhibition *Pablo Picasso: A Retrospective* at the Museum of Modern Art, New York.

Pablo Picasso, *Glass of Absinth*. Paris (spring 1914). Painted bronze with absinth spoon, 8½ × 6½ × 3⅜″ (21.6 × 16.4 × 8.5 cm); diameter at base 2½″ (6.4 cm). The Museum of Modern Art, New York. Gift of Mrs. Bertram Smith. Photograph © 2001 The Museum of Modern Art, New York. © 2001 Estate of Pablo Picasso / Artists Rights Society (ARS), New York.

Arthur G. Dove, *Goin' Fishin'*. 1925. Collage on wood panel. 21¼ × 25½″. Acquired 1937. The Phillips Collection, Washington, D.C.

A Proposal by Edward Ruscha
for the Circular Ring and for the Lunettes
of the New Miami-Dade Public Library,
April 1985

In act III, scene iii of William Shakespeare's *Hamlet,* the King utters, "Words without thoughts never to heaven go." This noble quotation is as timeless as it is poetic. It is a quotation that is profound and yet simple. For me, it burns with curiosity.

A philosophical thought of this nature, as subject matter in a mural painting, will be a striking and perfect embellishment for the Library. As one enters and approaches the overhead ring, the eye meets a series of eight connecting oil-painted panels, the most obvious and straight ahead one containing the first word of the quotation. This central panel, by its nature encouraging a person to read, will lead the eye to the right to gain attention to the remaining seven panels, one word per panel, with the last panel containing no word and thus acting as a divider. The person enters reading WORDS, then WITHOUT, then THOUGHTS, until the entire quotation is observed. It is my intent to separate the words by enough space as to cause the viewer to not only observe the thought as a whole, but to reflect for a moment on each word as an individual word and each picture as an individual picture. Thus the mural is a composite of eight separate yet harmonious pictures. The power of the complete quote cannot be denied, but the attention will also be focused on each single word.

I propose to have canvas mounted on aluminum panels, each to fit up to the outside edges of the ring. The panels will be neatly and smoothly joined. Colors will sometimes seem to blend through from one panel to another, and occasionally be abrupt. A combination of fastening methods will be followed. One technique is a method of hanging the panels from metal brackets that are attached to the wall, with attention to keeping the panels completely circular in form. Another method under study is that of fastening the panels with bolts, with occasional spot adhesives added where necessary. A system of furring strips may also be used. A flexible molding of wood or plastic will be used horizontally, top and bottom. No molding will be used where the panels touch vertically.

The archway lunettes, also being rather high above a person's line of sight, offer a unique opportunity to carry an aesthetic theme throughout the entire Library. Since there are 140 of these rather large areas to consider, my proposal is to approach this part of the project by means of the mass production technique of silkscreen printing. Each image would be different from the next, but an overall pictorial similarity would exist, since the backgrounds would be printed by the same methods. A more or less black and white effect of streaking and blending would be my theme, with bits of pure color added as accents from panel to panel. The strokes of the colors would vary between being horizontal and diagonal. Upon each panel would then be hand painted a word or words referring back to language itself, with occasional single alphabetical letters by themselves. Words such as HOWEVER, WHEREAS, IF and AND could be abrupt and isolated units in certain combinations in the Library, each playing off its neighbor in a provocative and abstract way, to challenge the mind of the viewer.

Both the circular ring and the archway lunettes are site-specific concepts that will be inspired by observations gained within the Library itself. I would like to think of this work as being a companion piece to the architecture that surrounds it, with its literary and artistic connotations lending credible and enthusiastic support to the Library.

A Proposal by Edward Ruscha
for the Archway Lunettes
of the Second and Third Floors
of the Miami-Dade Public Library, April 1987

The archway lunettes throughout the Miami-Dade Public Library present a unique architectural situation. These lunettes, while being separate from one another, become a powerful force in their groupings within the various departments of the entire building. Some are singular while others reside in series. Certain groups are partially obscured from a person's line of sight by shelving or lighting tracks, while others are completely open and inviting to the eye. The lunettes offer an opportunity to combine the vision of the Library with the vision of artistic expression.

After spending much time in the Library I see that painting all 138 lunettes would be excessive and unnecessary. For this reason I propose to paint up to forty-five, but not less than forty, of those that have the most meaningful and direct locations. These lunettes would be painted on canvas and then adhered without molding to their precise positions in the setback of the archways. I envision thematically similar images. Backgrounds of pure black and pure white blended together in diagonal strokes would reflect the spirit of black ink printed on white paper. Over these backgrounds in various colors would be words such as those seen in the model of the archways. I see a running side-by-side series incorporating the words "WHO," "WHAT," "WHEN," "WHERE," "WHY," "HOW," all reflecting their duty to the nature of linguistics and the English language, and perhaps each diminishing in size to echo the same pictorial direction as the circular mural of the reception area of the Library. Other lunettes, appropriately placed, would echo certain singular alphabetical letters, such as a simple "E" or an "S." A series of three could possibly contain "A" and "B" and "C." The foreign characters of "ñ" and "ç" are also choice possibilities and could even be placed in relation to the section of the Library for foreign languages. I see dynamic possibilities with respect to the various combinations of these lunettes and how they appear together in side-by-side rows. Singular lunettes also offer opportunities for visual punctuation.

I would like to repeat the statement "WORDS WITHOUT THOUGHTS NEVER TO HEAVEN GO" within one or possibly two archways side-by-side in a more remote area of the Library (enclosed is a transparency of that image).[6] The style of the letterforms would echo that of the circular mural, so that each complements the other. Each lunette would play off its neighbor in a provocative way to challenge the mind of the viewer.

I have researched the various materials and installation methods and am anxious and available to begin on this project immediately.

———

"THE WITNESS"

It's all just rape of the land for profit these days. It's fairly sick. Southern California is all just one big city now. But what do you say about progress? Birth control? Everybody wants to have a large family and the best in life. So something's got to give, and the landscape's the first thing that gives. On the other hand, I'm not just looking for pretty flowers to paint. There is a certain flavor of decadence that inspires me. And when I drive into some sort of industrial wasteland in America, with the themeparks and warehouses, there's something saying something to me. It's a mixture of those things that gives me some sense of reality and moves me along as an artist.

Originally published in *Esquire,* v. 109, June 1988, pp. 190–191.

Statement in "What Artists Like about
the Art They Like When They Don't Know Why,"
Compiled by Paul Gardener

When I was a baby to art I was disarmed by Arthur Dove's 1925 painting *Goin' Fishin'*. His unorthodox materials—the use of collage—drove home some point I never expected. So did Alvin Lustig's book-cover illustrations for New Directions Press back in the '50s. I had a terrific initial response but I didn't try to ponder it.

Art has to be something that makes you scratch your head.

Originally published in *Art News,* v. 90, n. 8, October 1991, p. 117.

Part Two

Interviews

———

"Concerning *Various Small Fires:* Edward Ruscha Discusses His Perplexing Publications"

John Coplans

JC: This is the second book of this character you have published?

ER: Yes, the first, in 1962, was *Twentysix Gasoline Stations.*

JC: What is your purpose in publishing these books?

ER: To begin with—when I am planning a book, I have a blind faith in what I am doing. I am not inferring I don't have doubts, or that I haven't made mistakes. Nor am I really interested in books as such, but I am interested in unusual kinds of publications. The first book came out of a play with words. The title came before I even thought about the pictures. I like the word "gasoline" and I like the specific quality of "twenty-six." If you look at the book you will see how well the typography works—I worked on all that before I took the photographs. Not that I had an important message about photographs, or gasoline, or anything like that—I merely wanted a cohesive thing. Above all, the photographs I use are not "arty" in any sense of the word. I think photography is dead as a fine art; its only place is in the commercial world, for technical or information purposes. I don't mean cinema photography, but still photography; that is, limited edition, indi-

Originally published in *Artforum,* v. 5, February 1965, pp. 24–25.

vidual, hand-processed photos. Mine are simply reproductions of photos. Thus, it is not a book to house a collection of art photographs—they are technical data like industrial photography. To me, they are nothing more than snapshots.

JC: You mean there is no design play within the photographic frame?

ER: No.

JC: But haven't they been cropped?

ER: Yes, but that arises from the consciousness of layout in the book.

JC: Did you collect these photos as an aid to painting, in any way?

ER: No, although I did subsequently paint one of the gasoline stations reproduced in the first book—I had no idea at the time I would eventually make a painting based on it.

JC: But isn't the subject matter of these photos common to your paintings?

ER: Only two paintings. However, they were done very much the same way I did the first book. I did the title and layout on the paintings before I put the gasoline stations in.

JC: Is there a correlation between the way you paint and the books?

ER: It's not important as far as the books are concerned.

JC: I once referred to Twentysix Gasoline Stations *and said, "it should be regarded as a small painting"—was this correct?*

ER: The only reason would be the relationship between the way I handle typography in my paintings. For example, I sometimes title the sides of my paintings in the same manner as the spine of a book. The similarity is only one of style. The purpose behind the books and my paintings is entirely different. I don't quite know how my books fit in. There is a whole recognized scene paintings fit into. One of the purposes of my books has to do with making a mass-produced object. The final product has a very commercial, professional feel to it. I am not in sympathy with the whole area of hand-printed publications, however sincere.

One mistake I made in *Twentysix Gasoline Stations* was in numbering the books. I was testing—at that time—that each copy a person might buy would have an individual place in the edition. I don't want that now.

JC: To come back to the photos—you deliberately chose each subject and specifically photographed them?

ER: Yes, the whole thing was contrived.

JC: To what end? Why fires and the last shot, of milk?[7]

ER: My painting of a gas station with a magazine [*Standard Station, 10¢ Western Being Torn in Half* (1964)] has a similar idea. The magazine is irrelevant, tacked onto the end of it. In a like manner, milk seemed to make the book more interesting and gave it some cohesion.

JC: Was it necessary for you, personally, to take the photographs?

ER: No, anyone could. In fact one of them was taken by someone else. I went to a stock photograph place and looked for pictures of fires, there were none. It is not important who took the photos, it is a matter of convenience, purely.

JC: What about the layout?

ER: That is important, the pictures have to be in the correct sequence, one without a mood taking over.

JC: This one—I don't know quite what it is—some kind of fire, looks rather arty.

ER: Only because it is a kind of subject matter that is not immediately recognizable.

JC: Do you expect people to buy the book, or did you make it just for pleasure?

ER: There is a very thin line as to whether this book is worthless or has any value—to most people it is probably worthless. Reactions are very varied; for example, some people are outraged. I showed the first book to a gasoline attendant. He was amused. Some think it is great, others are at a loss.

———

JC: What kind of people say it is great—those familiar with modern art?

ER: No, not at all. Many people buy the books because they are curiosities. For example, one girl bought three copies, one for each of her boyfriends. She said it would be a great gift for them, since they had everything already.

JC: Do you think your books are better made than most books that are marketed today?

ER: There are not many books that would fit into this style of production. Considered as a pocket book, it is definitely better than most. My books are as perfectly made as possible.

JC: Would you regard the book as an exercise in the exploration of the possibilities of technical production?

ER: No, I use standard and well-known processes; it can be done quite easily, there is no difficulty. But as a normal, commercial project most people couldn't afford to print books like this. It is purely a question of cost.

JC: Do you know a book called Nonverbal Communication *by Ruesch and Kees?*

ER: Yes, it is a good book, but it has a text that explains the pictures. It has something to say on a rational level that my books evade. The material is not collated with the same intent at all. Of course, the photographs used are not art photographs, but it is for people who want to know about the psychology of pictures or images. This IS the psychology of pictures. Although we both use the same kind of snapshots, they are put to different use. *Nonverbal Communication* has a functional purpose, it is a book to learn things from—you don't necessarily learn anything from my books. The pictures in that book are only an aid to verbal content. That is why I have eliminated all text from my books—I want absolutely neutral material. My pictures are not that interesting, nor the subject matter. They are simply a collection of "facts"; my book is more like a collection of "readymades."

JC: You are interested in some notion of the readymade?

ER: No, what I am after is a kind of polish. Once I have decided all the details—photos, layout, etc.—what I really want is a professional polish, a clear-cut machine finish. This book is printed by the best printer west of New York. Look how well made and crisp it is. I am not trying to create a precious limited edition book, but a mass-produced object of high order. All my books are identical. They have none of the nuances of the hand-made and crafted limited edition book. It is almost worth the money to have the thrill of 400 exactly identical books stacked in front of you.

"FROM COMMON SCENES, MR. RUSCHA EVOKES ART"

Douglas M. Davis

[. . . Ruscha has] a cool, dry, sly humor that obscures his point of view as completely as do his books.

Despite that, his conversation—also like his books—touches profound cultural issues. "I'm losing money as a publisher," *he says.* "But I'm getting to the point now where it's starting to give me enough return so the loss isn't too great. I mean, it's not a profit-motive thing, but I do have a budget for each book and that limits the edition. I mean, I could print a hundred books each and sell them at $50 apiece as great works of art. But I don't want to do that. I want to get the price down, so everyone can afford one. I want to be the Henry Ford of book making." *[. . .]*

[. . . There] is almost no selection involved [in making the books], no attempt to seek out the most "picturesque" gas stations, parking lots, and pools available. "I'm not even interested in Americana," *he says,* "not even in that. I took sixty or seventy photographs of gas stations between here and Oklahoma City. Well, the eccentric stations were the first ones I threw out. I didn't want to have the look of variety to it, necessarily. I wanted the book to be severe." *[. . .]*

Originally published in the *National Observer*, July 28, 1969, p. 1.

[Royal] Road Test *[1967] is simply a series of photographs of a typewriter thrown out of a speeding car onto the desert.* "It's like a police report," *Mr. Ruscha says proudly.* "What a police photographer would produce in a report on how somebody was killed." *[. . .]*

"The intent of the book," *Mr. Ruscha says about* Gasoline Stations, "is to be out front there, and let people judge for themselves." *Then, again:* "I don't have any message about the subject matter at all. They're just natural facts, that's all they are."

———

"Ed Ruscha Discusses His Latest Work with Christopher Fox"

Christopher Fox

Edward Ruscha is an artist from Los Angeles of growing interest and reputation. [. . .] Recently, at Editions Alecto, he has been working on a project through the use of silk-screen process. Or rather, through a personal and inventive employment of that process of print-making: foodstuffs, crushed flowers, syrups, and sauces have been used in place of the conventional inks. [. . .]

"Right now, I am out to explore the medium. It's a playground or a beach, so I'm going to send as much sand up in the air as I can! I think the next time I'll print with iodine. I have to be in control of the medium. The organic elements have to combine satisfactorily. What I'm interested in is the possible range; also in the use of a *processed* media." *Ruscha does not narrowly contrive the possible effects of his project; rather, he wishes to cut to a minimum the number of possible accidents. It is the control in the unpredictable area which he enjoys. But control for him does not mean rigidly transposing a preconceived image in print; the latitude for chance* "goes hand in hand with it." *Yet within this latitude he will cast aside effects which he finds pleasing if they contain a slight flaw. He views his project modestly:* "It's like a juggling act," *he explains.* "We were here week after week—proofing and proofing; then I could *feel* I had organized the elements." *He listed the disappointments that occurred:*

———

Originally published in *Studio International*, n. 179, June 1970, pp. 281, 287.

"Carnations did not pull. The paste separated from the liquid—so carnations are out. . . . Let's see what else. . . . Certain brands of mustard turned to dust, and chicory syrup similarly. A cream was not very satisfactory because it left slimy deposit. It's very difficult to look at colors and guess what they will turn out like. Tomato paste, for instance, dries to gray dust. For one reason or another I just rejected it because there were six prints; but I kept it to refer to. Also pastels on paper give effects which I don't like. A lot of bother went into simply finding the results of printing."

Yet even in listing these apparent failures he was intoxicated by the event, by the sense of discovery. He followed by explaining the full title of the projects: News, Mews, Pews, Brews, Stews & Dues *[1970]. The fact of being in London dictated the title:* "England's the only country that has Mews; and it also sounds very English. It's awful you see just to say it; the full six words that is. It has a corny and irritating sound to it. Language gets into my work. Country gets into my work. The type style relates to England; it's an Old English type-set." *The most striking thing about Ruscha was the feverish delight of his response to London:*

"Greens here are very beautiful. The green of Hyde Park I noticed immediately coming over on the plane. And the greens here around the plates are marvelous. The greens also on some of the large trucks are beautiful. . . . I was very impressed by that."

In view of his responses, it is not difficult to understand why he uses a conventional medium in an inventive way; it is because he has a fundamental trust in his own feelings and allows them to direct his concerns; his judgements are also personal and intuitive: "I don't like . . . I reject the kind of art which self-consciously attaches itself to history. I'm not abstaining . . . I simply can't relate to it. Pressures on artists today are extreme. They feel obliged to push things as far as they will go. I find that very unnatural. It's funny that—people keep pushing and pushing. I feel comfortable; that's the rules. I get satisfaction from my work, I really do."

The satisfaction for him is in combining incongruous elements. One print of which he was most pleased was Brews: "The pleasure of it is both in the wit and the absurdity of the combination. I mean, the idea of combining axle grease and caviar!" *He listed the other five:* "News *is blackcurrant preserves blended with*

———

salmon roe and the letters are blank, *Mews* is a combination of egg, which forms letters, and solid pasta sauce; *Pews* is a mixture . . . sixty percent chocolate syrup and forty percent coffee mixture—the letters are squid in ink. *Stews* has no background: the letters here are of baked beans blended with daffodils, chutney, tulips—leaves and stalks—caviar and cherry-pie filling. *Dues* is combined pickle letters printed over solid pickle background."

Ruscha's wit is essentially affable. He does not use it didactically; it is something which is combined with the "naturalness" of his responses to things; it hovers around his concerns like an atmosphere. He does not make a distinction between "serious" art and that which contains wit: "Oldenburg's best works are good as art and also very funny."

Prior to this project at Editions Alecto, Ruscha compiled a collection of stains [Stains, 1969]: "The book of stains is a kind of documentation, though my interest in doing it was not biological or scientific. It is a shallow box of black needle-finished leather. It has a Church look and quality about it . . . a kind of coffin!"

The mock-solemnity of this excites him: "The minute somebody hangs one of these things on a wall they miss the point entirely. There are seventy-six stains: number sixty is yellow pepper; forty-five is egg-yolk; twenty-seven is sulfuric acid; fourteen is gunpowder. Most of them were just applied. Some are invisible. An eyedropper was used to apply the liquids. I've done ten books altogether. You could say if you want to categorize me that I'm a Surrealist; but I don't attach myself to a label. New mediums encourage me. I still paint in oil paint. But what I'm interested in is illustrating *ideas*. I'm not interested in color; if color suits me I use it intuitively . . . either it works or it does not work.

"I'd prefer my painting to come to an end. I'd be satisfied to paint myself into a corner, and then just give it up. It's not a vocation. I just use painting. Painting for me is a tool. All the things that I achieve through it become obsolete. I'm terrified to think I'll be painting at sixty."

Yet Ruscha also clearly feels he learns through art: "I don't know . . . maybe, there's a great deal of satisfaction through learning. I don't worry about what I'm about to do. I don't even make that a question in my life; I may, in time, turn towards science . . . art and science are very alike. Many artists work their entire lives worrying whether their work is important. They just get too involved with what's around them.

"The important thing is to believe in what you are doing, even if it's absurd. Most people's rational consciousness prevents them from doing what they should have blind faith about.

"I want people to be able to look at these prints—chocolate and syrup—and see the way that they come out as important, and to be able to discern that I wanted it to be this."

Interview with Titia Tybout, May 27, 1971

[Ruscha was one of a group of artists brought to the Netherlands as a part of Sonsbeek 71, *an international exhibition of new art, to create a work of art on site and show it in a group exhibition. The book* Dutch Details *[1971] was Ruscha's contribution, and this interview appeared in the show's catalog.]*

I had no idea what I was going to do until I came to this country, and when I came over on the plane the pilot said that he did not know what the weather was like in Amsterdam, but he'd let us know the details very soon. And that just clicked in my mind, this word "details," and so I let that be something to guide me on this project and then I immediately thought: Dutch Details, and that got me moving on the whole project. [. . .]

   I don't want people to go look at these photographs after they are enlarged and they see them on a wall in museum, maybe under the auspices of a museum, and consider them to be like a painting, for instance. I have done paintings before that I would sell, but I could never sell these photographs because these photographs are only representations of some project that I participated in. The book [*Dutch Details*], in the end, will be a closer representation to the project.

Originally published in *Sonsbeek 71, Sonsbeek buiten de perken*, Part 2 (Arnheim: Centrum Park Sonsbeek), p. 53.

———

"ART: INTERVIEW WITH ED RUSCHA"

Robert Colacello

RC: Have you been working on some graphic series lately?

ER: Yes, I'm doing some little insect graphics.

RC: I heard that you were going to give up painting altogether.

ER: Well, I haven't painted for two years, over two years now. I hit the bottom of the bucket, I guess. I just could not work any more. I stopped for several reasons. I was doing a few other things and I wanted to work on that movie and I worked on a lot of drugs. I just could not paint.

RC: Why was that?

ER: I don't know . . . something happened. I was kind of glad; I told everybody about it and proclaimed I couldn't paint and that I wouldn't start again.

RC: Do you think you just ran out of ideas?

ER: Not exactly. I'm pretty facile and I can do a lot of things. But I did not like the paintings. I still don't. I'd like to find some other way to make images.

Originally published in **INTERVIEW** Magazine, Brant Publications, Inc., March 1972 (n. 20, p. 42).

RC: Do you think there is still a place for the creation of objects?

ER: Oh yes, sure.

RC: I think so too, but there seem to be some people—you know, especially conceptual artists—who don't.

ER: Oh, but most conceptual artists are visual artists. You know, when you think about it, they all have some kind of product that you can see. Like Joseph Kosuth had a reproduction in a magazine that showed chairs next to clocks, and that's visual art. If it was totally conceptual, the artist would not allow you to look at any picture at all—no photos, no images, nothing. The only pure conceptual artist I know is Larry Weiner. He has things that he just transmits by word of mouth. It's like poetry, you know.

RC: You've been painting since when? Early '60s?

ER: Yes.

RC: And who were you influenced by at that time? Did you know what the Pop artists were doing in New York?

ER: Oh no, I thought I was the only person in the world doing that kind of paintings. But then I came back here on a trip and someone told me, "Come and have a look at my back room"—it was Ivan Karp—and he had a lot of Roy Lichtenstein's work . . . and I thought, Oh God. What it is, is that a lot of different people in different parts of the country are actually doing the same thing, because it is inevitable.

RC: What do you think of this new thing, photographic realism?

ER: It's interesting. But it's not my language. Actually, all I've seen of it are reproductions in magazines, which is part of the art. For instance one of the artists that most influenced me, Jasper Johns—I had never seen any of his work before I saw a photograph in a magazine . . . and I thought if he had a photograph in a magazine, he had to have some kind of power.

RC: Does your film have a title?

———

ER: *Premium* [1970].

RC: May I ask you why you did it, because I didn't get much point out of it?

ER: Well, I wanted to tell a story and not only see the end product, but mix it up with producing a movie.

The movie is not like an artistic statement to me. Not at all. I just wanted to tell a story. I did not very cleverly put things in there connected to my art work, I just borrowed all the techniques I had seen on TV and just did it.

RC: How long did the whole movie take you to do?

ER: It took five days of shooting, and then I had it edited in L.A. I didn't do any of the shooting myself, I hired a crew. The actors worked for free.

RC: How much did that salad cost you?

ER: Very cheap actually. You wouldn't believe it, but I used the same all the time. We kept it in a refrigerator with crushed ice. Just about $20—I think.

RC: Do you see any big difference between the California art scene and the New York art scene?

ER: I don't know really. It's kind of unified now. I don't see any difference except that there are a lot of palm trees out there . . . that's about all.

RC: One always hears that Californian art is cooler and slicker. . . .

ER: No, there is very little difference really.

RC: What do you see as the purpose of art? Do you think people really need it?

ER: Yes, I think they do. Any time it becomes too much of a commodity, it's really confusing, for everyone involved. The least so for the collector, but more for the galleries. When an artist gets a lot of calls for his work, it changes his whole attitude.

RC: Is that what happened to you?

ER: No, not really. I've had a few shows around and all that, but I really don't know where my work is.

RC: *I've been told you're in demand, though.*

ER: Maybe in some ways I am, I don't know.

RC: *I heard you really sell very well.*

ER: Well, all I know is I had a lot of success in Texas and in Oklahoma.

RC: *What do you think of movies, moviemakers?*

ER: I've always liked Stanley Kubrick. And Don Siegel . . . he did *The Killers,* which I think is one of the greatest movies of all times. And the guy who did *Seconds,* Frankenheimer.

RC: *They're all American.*

ER: I like some foreigners too. . . . I can't think who. Marcello Mastroianni is pretty good.

RC: *I was thinking of directors.*

ER: Oh . . . there aren't too many foreign directors I like. I like Antonioni, I guess. He's solid.

RC: *I like Visconti.*

ER: Visconti? I can't stand him. If there is anybody I dislike, it's him.

RC: *Why?*

ER: I don't know. I was insulted by looking at that movie called *The Damned.*

RC: *Have you seen* Death in Venice*?*

ER: No. Maybe I should though. I heard it's a beautiful picture. Have you ever seen my books?

RC: *No, I haven't.*

———

ER: My books have always been underground underground. I don't mean popular underground. I'd like to get them out in the open, but it's pretty hard. I've done fourteen books.

RC: Do you have them printed yourself?

ER: Yes, I started my own publishing company.

RC: Do you consider them a form of poetry?

ER: Well, I don't really know what that means. It's a heavy word . . . sure they are.

RC: But they have things written in them?

ER: No, just pictures with captions.

RC: How do you choose the words you do paintings of?

ER: Well, they just occur to me; sometimes people say them and I write down and then I paint them. Sometimes I use a dictionary.

———

―――――

"RUSCHA AS PUBLISHER [OR ALL BOOKED UP]"

David Bourdon

[. . .] *Ed Ruscha first came to attention in the early 1960s, with stylized paintings of gas stations, which identified him as one of the West Coast's prime exponents of Pop Art. [. . .] He started out as a painter, and had his first one-man show of paintings in 1963 at the Ferus Gallery in Los Angeles. But in the last couple of years he has painted almost nothing at all.* "I can't bring myself to put paint on canvas," *he says;* "I find no message there anymore." *The bulk of his recent work has been in the field of prints and drawings, many of which have been shown widely in this country and in Europe. This month he will be showing about 100 prints, drawings and books in his first one-man museum show at the Minneapolis Art Institute.*

Ruscha's books are probably the best known and most widely admired of all his works, a situation that pleases the artist immensely. "If there is any facet of my work that I feel was kissed by angels," *says Ruscha,* "I'd say it was my books. My other work is definitely tied to a tradition, but I've never followed tradition in my books. The books are just neuter gender, and that's what I like about them. That's why I feel so free when I do them. They're the easiest thing to do, and sometimes the best. I like the idea of spending $2,000 on something that's just totally

――――――――――――――――――――――

Originally published in *Art News*, v. 71, April 1972, pp. 32–36, 68–69.

frivolous and spontaneous. When I start on one of these books, I get to be the impresario of the thing, I get to be majordomo, I get to be creator and total proprietor of the whole works, and I like that. It's nice. And I'm not biting my nails over whether the book is going to hit the charts or not."

Ruscha has published fourteen books in the last ten years. All of them are picture books, containing nothing but snapshot-like photographs (usually by Ruscha) and minimal copy (frequently just one-line captions). Most of the publications have straightforward, no-nonsense layouts, and are handsomely printed, often with sewn-bound pages and white paper covers that are protected by glassine dustjackets. All of the publications are well-made, professional-looking books that rival in printing quality the products of large commercial publishing houses. Although most of the books were initially published in limited editions, Ruscha has decided that such imposed rarity is irrelevant. "All are reprintable, and that's the way they should be." *[. . .]*

Ruscha's first book, Twentysix Gasoline Stations *[1962], contains photographs of twenty-six different (but not so individual) gas stations in California, Arizona, New Mexico, Oklahoma and Texas; each station is identified by a one-line caption giving name and location.* "I had a vision that I was being a great reporter when I did the gas stations," *Ruscha says.* "I drove back to Oklahoma all the time, five or six times a year. And I felt there was so much wasteland between L.A. and Oklahoma City that somebody had to bring in the news to the city. It was just a simple, straightforward way of getting the news and bringing it back. I think it's one of the best ways of just laying down the facts of what is out there. I didn't want to be allegorical or mystical or anything like that. It's nothing more than a training manual for people who want to know about things like that.

"I had the title, *Twentysix Gasoline Stations,* even before I took the photographs," *Ruscha says.* "The titles are not always first, but the title is very important. Then it was a simple matter of just going out and taking the pictures." *For the first word of his titles, he prefers either a specific number, because it sounds so factual, or a word that connotes vaguer quantities, such as "various," "some," or "a few." The title is all that appears on most covers, usually laid out in capital letters in three, evenly spaced rows against a white background.* "Type always gives it a manual look," *he notes;* "it has that factual kind of army-navy data look to it that I like." *[. . .]*

The artist holding *Various Small Fires* (1964). Photo: Unknown. Courtesy Ed Ruscha.

More gas stations and more apartment buildings turn up in another context in Ruscha's most famous book, Every Building on the Sunset Strip *[1966]. Although it is the same size (7 by 5½ inches) as the preceding books, it is unique among Ruscha's publications in that the photographs are printed on a single, accordion-folded sheet that can be pulled out to its full length of twenty-seven feet. Each side of the street is shown in its entirety (the photographic image is only 1⅝ inches high), and the paired panoramas face each other on one side of the sheet, the reverse being blank. [. . .] Ruscha photographed the Strip in the harsh light of high noon, making it appear just as dull and tacky-looking as a Midwestern Main Street, except that it has a few more rent-a-cars and motor lodges.* "All I was after was that store-front plane," *he says.* "It's like a Western town in a way. A store-front plane of a Western town is just paper, and everything behind it is just nothing." *[. . .]*

A book that offers an even more startling perspective on a commonplace subject is Thirtyfour Parking Lots *[1967], which, oddly enough, has only thirty-one photographs of vacant parking lots, shot on a Sunday by a professional aerial photographer in a helicopter. The aerial pictures reveal surprising variety in parking lot shapes and patterns.* "Architects write me about the parking lots book," *says Ruscha,* "because they are interested in seeing parking lot patterns and things like that. But those patterns and their abstract design quality mean nothing to me. I'll tell you what is more interesting: the oil droppings on the ground." *And he points out with relish how the largest and most saturated oil spots indicate which spaces are the most favored and parked upon.*

In the brochure in which Ruscha advertises his books, this volume is described as containing a "Strange Foldout." It is scarcely noticeable, appearing at the end of the book alongside a double-page photograph of a blocks-long parking lot on Santa Monica Boulevard; the right-hand page has a tiny, tipped-on photograph, only 1⅜" wide, which nonsensically opens out to reveal a few more parking places. "I like the idea of a little flap coming out like that," *Ruscha says.* "I worked very hard at that little thing at the end, and it cost a lot of extra money to put that little thing in there."

A surprise ending also appears in Nine Swimming Pools *[1968], Ruscha's only book with color photographs. The pools, which come in a variety of sizes and shapes, are all sun-dappled and invitingly empty; but the last picture is a staged photograph, showing a broken drinking glass lying on a blue sheet of glass, providing a jarring conclusion to an otherwise placid sequence. One of the curiosities of this sixty-four-page book is that the ten color plates are sprinkled with seeming randomness amid a few dozen blank pages.* "This was the cheapest way to have the color printed so I just let the blank pages fall as they did," *Ruscha explains.* "I could have added one or two more swimming pools at no extra cost, but I wanted the thing to be 'nine' swimming pools rather than 'eleven.'"

Real Estate Opportunities *[1970] is especially original because its subject is a seldom noticed street scene that Ruscha makes glaringly visible. The book contains twenty-five photographs of vacant lots—residential, commercial, on hillsides, on corners, with palm trees, with weeds; nearly all have signs advertising them for sale. Unlike the architectural subjects in the previously mentioned books, the vacant lots are negative spaces, unattractive cavities eventually to be filled with buildings. Again, most of the pictures have been photographed from the opposite side of the road; consequently, the lower half of each picture shows nothing but an empty, paved street, making the lots look relatively messy and cluttered.* "Sometimes the ugliest things have the most potential," *Ruscha says.* "I truly enjoyed the whole afternoon while I shot those pictures. It's a great feeling to be on self-assignment, out looking for subjects. I went off in the car and I went down to these little towns, to Santa Ana, Downey, places like that. I was exalted at the same time that I was repulsed by the whole thing." *[. . .]*

Ruscha, who does not want to be thought of as a professional photographer, also strives for "styleless" compositions and, in doing so, has achieved a recognizable style. "I like the anonymity of photographs," *he says,* "but you can never achieve it. Years from now people will know that they were done in the 1960s."

One of the most baffling aspects of Ruscha's work is the relationship of the photographs to the paintings, drawings, and prints. He has made a dozen or so finished drawings of apartment buildings, and several paintings and prints of gas stations, all based on his own photographs. But the works that are based on photographs are in many ways significantly different from the source, and implicitly different in attitude. [. . .]

Ruscha's stylistic discrepancy is most apparent in the painted and screen-printed images of gas stations, all of which derive from a single photograph of the Standard station in Amarillo, Texas that appears in Twentysix Gasoline Stations. *The gas station in the photograph is ordinary and rather puny; but the same station in the subsequent paintings and silk-screen print is streamlined, glamorized and idealized. In transforming the subject, he flopped the image, dropped from an eye-level to a worm's-eye view, elongated the canopy over the pumps and eliminated all the pennants, parked cars and display signs. The final result, shown in exaggerated perspective and non-naturalistic lighting, resembles a highly stylized architectural rendering. Although the subject derives from a photograph, the composition derives from a 1962 painting (of an altogether different subject), in which the picture is diagonally bisected from the upper-left to the lower-right corners.* "I didn't care what the subject matter was," *Ruscha says,* "but I wanted it to have that lower-right, upper-left diagonal to it. So I just fit this building to that painting."

Photographs also played a part in Ruscha's largest (11 feet wide) and most ambitious painting, The Los Angeles County Museum on Fire *[1965–68], which is shown in aerial view.* "I had gone over the art museum in a helicopter, kind of by mistake, and took a lot of pictures of it," *Ruscha explains.* "Also, there was an aerial photograph of the museum on the cover of the telephone book; it was really a nice picture, with a beautiful background to it, so that kind of moved me in that direction too." *The combined photographs enabled him to work out the final composition. In Ruscha's idealized view, the museum's confectionery pavilions and reflection pools are afloat in an atmospheric, non-specific type of space; Hancock Park and the La Brea Tar Pits have been converted into murky-looking greenery, and Wilshire Boulevard has shrunk to a narrow, untrafficked path. The chief difference between the actual museum and its portrait is that Ruscha has set one of the pavilions ablaze, with wind-whipped flames leaping from the far side of the building.* "I knew at the time that I started the picture that I was going to assault that building somehow," *he says.* "It wasn't the idea of it being an art museum, because there were several other buildings I could have worked on." *[. . .]*

" 'My Books End Up in the Trash' "

A. D. Coleman

Los Angeles—"After a book leaves here, it's for whatever anyone wants to use it
for. I'd love to have the facts on where my books are. . . . I had a daydream once
not long ago about an imaginary person known as the Information Man, and I
wrote it down. Let me read it to you.

  " 'The Information Man is someone who comes up to you and begins telling
you stories and related facts about a particular subject in your life. He came up to
me and said, 'Of all the books of yours that are out in the public, only 171 are placed
face up with nothing covering them; 2026 are in vertical positions in libraries, and
2715 are under books in stacks. The most weight on a single book is sixty-eight
pounds, and that is in the city of Cologne, Germany, in a bookstore. Fifty-eight
have been lost; fourteen have been totally destroyed by water or fire; two-hundred
sixteen books could be considered badly worn. Three hundred and nineteen books
are in positions between forty and fifty degrees. Eighteen of the books have been
deliberately thrown away or destroyed. Fifty-three books have never been opened,
most of these being newly purchased and put aside momentarily.

  " 'Of the approximately 5000 books of Ed Ruscha that have been purchased, only thirty-two have been used in a directly functional manner. Thirteen

Originally published in the *New York Times*, v. 121, n. 41, 854, August 27, 1972, p. D12.

of these have been used as weights for paper or other small things, seven have been used as swatters to kill small insects such as flies and mosquitoes, two were used as a device to nudge open a door, six have been used to transport foods like peanuts to a coffee table, and four have been used to nudge wall pictures to their correct levels. Two hundred and twenty-one people have smelled pages of the books. Three of the books have been in continual motion since their purchase; all three of these are on a boat near Seattle, Washington.'

"Now wouldn't it be nice to know these things?"

It is early afternoon and we are in the bright, spacious, white-walled studio of Ed Ruscha (pronounced Rew-Shay, as his business card indicates) on North Western Avenue. A punching bag hangs on one wall; a motorcycle sits in another room; there are paintings on the wall, and a framed photo of Bela Lugosi with cigar. Several cowboy hats hang from the edge of an unframed mirror resting on an easel. From the radio comes a mixture of rock, jazz, and cowboy yodeling.

Ruscha, a transplanted Oklahoman who has already established a hefty reputation as a painter, is also the creator and publisher of a unique series of photographic books. The first of these, Twentysix Gasoline Stations, *was issued in 1962; it has been followed by thirteen more, making a sizable set of works altogether.*

In addition to Twentysix Gasoline Stations, *the entire canon consists of:* Various Small Fires, *1964;* Some Los Angeles Apartments, *1965;* Every Building on the Sunset Strip, *1966;* Thirtyfour Parking Lots, *1967;* Royal Road Test, *1967;* Business Cards, *1968;* Nine Swimming Pools and a Broken Glass, *1968;* Crackers, *1969;* Real Estate Opportunities, *1970;* Babycakes, *1970 (part of a set of multiples and not for sale separately);* A Few Palm Trees, *1971;* Records, *1971; and* Dutch Details, *1971.*

For the most part, they are simple little volumes which show exactly what the titles indicate. Thirtyfour Parking Lots *is a set of aerial photographs of same;* Nine Swimming Pools—*the only one which employs color photographs—includes photographs of nine swimming pools and a broken glass. A few are more elaborate in format:* Sunset Strip *consists of two sets of "continuous motorized photos" printed on an accordion fold which expands to twenty-seven feet in length;* Dutch Details *is made up of foldouts. All in all,*

Ed Ruscha and Mason Williams examine Royal typewriter, from *Royal Road Test* (1967). Photo: Patrick Blackwell. Courtesy Ed Ruscha.

they form an impressive, cryptic, and funny collection of photographic works by an artist who does not even consider himself to be a photographer.

Many of the photographs in the books, in fact, were not even made by Ruscha himself, but by such collaborators as Joe Goode, Patrick Blackwell, Art Alanis (the aerial photos of the parking lots) and Jerry McMillan. "It's not really important who takes the photographs," asserts Ruscha. "I don't even look at it as photography; they're just images to fill a book."

Are they equivalent to drawings then?

"No, no, because the drawing gives a touch of the hand to it that I didn't want at all. The camera is used simply as a documentary device, the closest documentary device; that's what it's all about . . . Drawings would never express the idea—I like facts, facts, facts are in these books. The closest representation to an apartment house in Some Los Angeles Apartments is a photograph, nothing else, not a drawing, because that becomes somebody else's vision of what it is, and this is the camera's eye, the closest delineation of that subject."

Asked if he has been influenced by the work of other photographers, Ruscha replies, "None. I have no interest in photography as a medium. I mean, I like to look at photographs, I really find them intriguing, especially when they have a documentary sense to them. I like Mathew Brady, just because I get to look at all those soldiers and look at the way life was back then; and At-get—how do you pronounce it? Atget?—I love his work just because it's like going on a little trip, a little storybook trip, and that's what I like about it."

If, as Henry T. Hopkins has written, Ruscha's creation of these books "undoubtedly stems from some deep-seated hoarding instinct developed in childhood," Ruscha has sublimated such motivation beyond recognition. "I know," he says, "that my books are not thought of in the same way as my paintings are. People take a painting and they put it back in a vault somewhere, but these books they'll just throw on a shelf and that amuses me, the fact that it just turns over and it affects people, people get the pictures and look at the pictures and they put it away and eventually somehow it just kind of ends up in the trash, which is OKAY—that's all right with me, it doesn't bother me that much, that they might decompose, or not be thought of as 'objects of art,' because they're definitely not.

"I've shown them, I had a show in Germany of these, in Munich. I went to the gallery, and we had a lot of frames there, and I couldn't think of a better way of displaying them than just putting them in these little pop-in frames and putting them up on the wall. But then I also put a table there and put books out, for people to sit down in chairs and look at them, too. So I was just *showing* the covers of them; but people would come in and say *[sotto voce]* 'Psst—how much is that?' and I'd say, 'Psst—three dollars . . .'" *He laughs.*

"'I'm Not Really a Photographer'"

A. D. Coleman

"It's a playground, is all it is," *says Ed Ruscha.* "Photography's just a playground for me. I'm not a photographer at all."

Despite this disclaimer, Ruscha's fourteen small books of photographs have found much of their audience among people interested in contemporary photography. They were among the first of the new wave of privately published photography books; they also pioneered in the use of photography as a basic tool of conceptual art. Quite aside from their historical significance, these books have a consistency and a charmingly mystifying ambiguity which results from their very literalness. They seem—at this admittedly early stage—to be remarkably durable works, Ruscha's fear of their eventual "quaintness" notwithstanding.

Ruscha indicates that he began working with photographs out of "a combination of desires." *One was to, first of all, make a book.* "I wanted to make a book of some kind. And at the same time, I—my whole attitude about everything came out in this one phrase that I made up for myself, which was 'twenty-six gasoline stations.' I worked on that in my mind for a long time and I knew that title before the book had even come about. And then, paradoxically, the idea of the photographs of the gas stations came around, so it's an idea first—and then I kind of worked it down. It went hand in hand with what I felt about traveling. . . .

Originally published in the *New York Times,* v. 121, n. 41, 868, September 10, 1972, p. D35.

"I just barely got my feet wet with gas stations," *he continues.* "Then I just had a lot of other things come out. Fires have been a part of my work before too, I've painted pictures of fire, and there've been little things about fire in my life— not an experience, not in a negative way, there's been no catastrophe as far as fire goes, but the image of fire has always been strong in my work and so it just culminated in this little book here *[*Various Small Fires, *which contains sixteen images—burning pipes, cigars, cigarettes, a flare, a cigarette lighter aflame].* It's probably one of the strangest books—it kind of stands apart, a lot of people have even mentioned that to me about how it stands apart from the others because it's more introverted, I guess; introverted, less appealing, probably more *meaningless* than any of the other books, if you know what I mean."

I mention finding, in a Fourth Avenue used-book store, a copy of a catalog from one of his exhibitions, the cover of which was charred by fire. "Charred by fire?" *Ruscha laughs.* "Everything gets its due, right? Bruce Nauman took a copy of *Various Small Fires* and burned it ceremoniously, took a picture of each page, and made a big book out of it, which is an extension of that. I think he liked *Various Small Fires.*

"Some of them look like *capers,*" *Ruscha adds.* "Like *Business Cards* looks like a caper, which it is. . ." *Or* Crackers?

"*Crackers* is a caper; *Sunset Strip* is a *visual* caper; *Royal Road Test,* yeah. . ." *This is a significant distinction, especially in light of the slight note of dissatisfaction which Ruscha applies to the term "caper." All four of these books hinge on something other than the images themselves, being thus more specific and conceptually limited (though also, perhaps, more accessible) than the rest.* Sunset Strip *depends on its accordion-fold format and the inclusion of every building on the Strip; the other three are tied to staged events.*

Royal Road Test *documents the results of heaving a Royal typewriter out the window of a 1963 Buick Le Sabre traveling at ninety miles per hour; it stars Ruscha himself as Driver and singer-songwriter-humorist Mason Williams as Thrower. Williams wrote the story on which* Crackers—*an improbable and somewhat misogynistic narrative in stills—is based. (Ruscha, working on a Guggenheim Fellowship, recently turned this into a movie titled* Premium.*) And* Business Cards *records a business card exchange between Ruscha and Billy Al Bengston and a presentation dinner in celebration thereof.*

The latter book is also one of the two signed editions Ruscha has published, a practice from which he has since veered away. "I decided I don't want anything like that, I just want to get the book out. And the books will compete with any other books on the paperback market; they'll just be my style of books, you know? . . . Most of my books should be of unlimited quantity. I don't want people to come up to me and say, 'Boy, I'm going to save this because some day it's going to be a work of art.' That's not it—you missed it . . . "

Ruscha, who feels that he's "just scratching the surface" *with his books so far, indicates that* "It's not only photography that interests me, it's the whole production of the books. . . I just use that thing *[the camera—he works with a Yashica, by the way]*, I just pick it up like an axe when I've got to chop down a tree, I pick up a camera and go out and shoot the pictures that I have to shoot. I never take pictures just for the taking of pictures; I'm not interested in that at all. I'm not intrigued *that* much with the medium . . . I want the end product; that's what I'm really interested in. It's strictly a medium to use or to not use, and I use it only when I have to. I use it to do a job, which is to make a book. I could never go through all my photographs I've taken of different things and make a book out of it." *Do you mean, I ask, that you can't conceive of a* Greatest Hits of Ed Ruscha, *with two parking lots and one swimming pool and three palm trees?* "Well, no, I wouldn't say that . . ." *He laughs.*

Having run out of questions and tape, we begin to pack up. Ruscha answers a knock at his door and admits Billy Al Bengston, resplendent in a bright red hat, looking—somewhat studiedly—like a refugee from an Al Capp panel. Ruscha gives Bengston a box of trout flies, a belated Christmas gift. Then he inquires as to whether I like anchovies and, upon receiving an affirmative response, gives me two tubes of anchovy paste and two cans of rolled filets of anchovy with capers. He explains that he hates anchovies, and had used a number of these same tins and tubes to surround a present for his wife, who despises them equally.

I accept the anchovies and ask Bengston if he considers Ruscha to be a photographer. "Oh, sure," *Bengston replies.* "He's a fine photographer. Ed's made pictures that don't look like anyone else's I've ever seen." *He flashes an evil grin, and chortles.*

Of those anchovies, one tube of paste has been sent to Van Deren Coke, author of The Painter and the Photograph, *for his collection; one can of rolled filets has been sent to Peter Bunnell as a contribution to the collection of Princeton University. The second can of filets has been reserved for personal consumption at some future date, and the second tube is in the brown paper bag Ruscha offered them in, sitting in a cabinet outside my work-room, marked "Gift of Ed Ruscha."*

Now isn't it nice to know these things?

"Words with Ruscha"

Howardena Pindell

[. . .] HP: Is there any particular process in printmaking you like?

ER: I've never made an etching. I think I just got into the habit of making prints in the past two, three years. Printmaking is glorified as a great art at the expense of people knowing it's a fantastic marketable item. But it produces some of the best results in any form of making anything a multiple—my books included because they are printed offset.

HP: Are you in it for the money?

ER: No, but if you make prints, you're around people—artists who make prints and people who buy prints. It confuses me how prints can be whipped around and turned over so quickly. You know, they literally sell like pancakes. They're so marketable it's confusing, but I've always liked it. I've always had a good time making prints, and the people I've worked with have always been very interesting. I'm just frankly tired of doing it. Tired of the whole act, so I don't consider myself a printmaker with a capital *P.* I like Artist with an *A.*

Originally published in *Print Collector's Newsletter,* v. 3, n. 6, January–February 1973, pp. 125–128.

HP: Why did you start making organic prints and does it bother you that the prints decompose?

ER: It was a spinoff of my *Stains* book, an edition of boxed sheets of 100 percent rag bond paper, each containing a single stain dropped at random, middle of each sheet. In the prints, instead of using ink, I filled the empty shape areas with organics or anything that would allow itself to print. There's been no decomposing of my prints, but two failed the "100-year-total sunlight-absorption test" and this produced some insignificant color-fading.

HP: I noticed in the catalog for your exhibition in Minneapolis[8] last spring a list of words. Do you keep lists of words?

ER: No, the curator Gus Foster and I thought of listing all the words I've used since I started working while doing the catalog. So I had to go back and dig out the records. I had to get out all my old diaries and look up all the words.

HP: You keep diaries?

ER: Yeah. I had to go back and compile *all* that stuff. It's just possible there are one or two words that are left out, but I doubt it.

HP: I can't imagine having time to keep a diary.

ER: Well, it's not a diary where I say, "July 40, 1972. Today I. . . ." It's things that strike me funny. You know, like I heard somebody say, "It's your baby. You rock it." Well I just *ran* to my book with that.

HP: Do you play Scrabble?

ER: Scrabble? Scrabble intrigues me. Here's what I thought—sooner or later I can take all my words and maybe make a sentence, except that I don't have any contractions with the exception of "won't."

HP: Why don't you like contractions?

ER: I like "Crescent Technology" better than "Crestek." But I did the word "won't" once. "Won't" just seemed tighter packed than "will not."

———

HP: Why are you attracted to specific words like "Annie," "carp," "lisp," "sing"?

ER: Because I love the language. Words have temperatures to me. When they reach a certain point and become hot words, then they appeal to me. "Synthetic" is a very hot word. Sometimes I have a dream that if a word gets too hot and too appealing, it will boil apart, and I won't be able to read or think of it. Usually I catch them before they get too hot. I have, though, caught words in the dictionary instead of had them come to me via flashes.

HP: How do you decide to render a word in liquid or ribbon letters?

ER: I move with the particular mood I'm in rather than the word I happen to choose. But there are, for reasons of classical painting, yes's and no's. I can't do a painting of a ribbon word, because ribbons belong only with drawings. Liquids have not been used in my drawings for a long time—liquids are for prints and paintings only. These media are good for only certain techniques.

HP: Why do you use insects in your work? They're repulsive.

ER: Because I had a jillion cockroaches around my studio. I love them but I don't want them around.

HP: I recently saw photographs of two 1959 Duchamps in a Paris publication—a plaster cast of a foot with flies and a marzipan sculpture of vegetables with flies.

ER: Of all the work I've seen of Duchamp, I've never seen those.

HP: Did you see the Duchamp exhibition at the Pasadena Museum in 1964?

ER: Oh sure, I met him when he came there. His work influenced me much before I met him or actually saw his work. See, it's the kind that can be transmitted through the media, through magazines. His work goes very well that way. Most artists' don't. . . . People will say it's better to see their work than it is pictures of their work. I don't believe this. He's really influenced me.

HP: Any specific work?

ER: *The Chocolate Grinder* . . . and some other things I could never figure out.

HP: Did Magritte influence you?

ER: Yes, Magritte did influence me, but it came the other way around—what I call 360-degree influence. That's influence from a person's thoughts and force and not from his pictures, which the person being influenced has not seen, until later on. The same with Dalí. I've been influenced by Dalí, but it's been through other sources. Because I'll go back, and I'll be working on something and I'll see a picture of Dalí's I've never seen before, and *there is my work.* Jasper Johns is the person who actually got me working as an artist.

HP: What was it that influenced you? Johns's recognizable subject matter or his words?

ER: It was the fact his paintings did not look like paintings. I saw *American Flag* [*Flag*, 1954–55] and *Targets* [*Target with Four Faces,* 1955]. Those two paintings were the reason for my being an artist.

HP: Did any other artists or friends influence you?

ER: Yes, but less what my work is like and more the kind of person I am.

HP: Why have you confined your documentation to the West?

ER: Oh, for no particular reason. I think if I lived in New York I'd do things about New York. I'm sure it would work that way.

HP: What about the trips you've been taking? You go back and forth to Oklahoma . . . and your trip to Paris? Do you pull information from these experiences?

ER: I traveled to Europe in 1961, and I really learned nothing. I thought I was going to, you know, the History of Art. . . . I just yawned a lot.

HP: The reason I asked—the catalog for your Minneapolis exhibition reproduces a head of Mussolini by Bertelli.

ER: Oh yes, that's the one piece that affected me while I was in Europe . . . more than any piece in the Louvre or the Prado or any museum I went to. That's the piece that sort of popped the top off of the can. I've never seen another by him.

R. A. Bertelli, *Continuous Profile of Mussolini*. 1933. Ceramic, 19¼″ (height). Imperial War Museum, London.

An artist should be lucky to have done one piece like that in his entire life. It's one of the greatest works of art in the twentieth century.

HP: *Was it the lettering?*

ER: No, I just liked the piece itself, and the method, you know, the method of doing it . . . I guess he spun it out on a potter's wheel.

HP: *But you haven't brought anything from your travels into your work in terms of documenting where you have been or are.*

ER: Now you're talking like you read a book on concept art. You're talking like there are thousands of artists, hundreds of thousands of artists who do that and it's a kind of style. You're talking about a kind of style, and you're asking me why I haven't done that style. You've seen my *Royal Road Test*? I guess you could say it is the closest thing to documenting something that happened, you know, in a one-two-three fashion; on the desert, etc.

HP: *I don't really mean it in terms of concept art at all. I think destroying a typewriter in the desert is storytelling anyway. I mean, you use the Standard Oil station and the Hollywood real estate sign, but there hasn't been another "monument" that's seemed important enough to you to use it in your work.*

ER: Oh, I see what you mean by document. No, I don't think there is, but there are other things that worked their way into being documents, monuments, like the swarm of ants could be a monument. I also did a painting of the 20th Century Fox trademark [*Large Trademark with Eight Spotlights,* 1962] and after that a painting of the Los Angeles County Museum [*Los Angeles County Museum on Fire,* 1965–68].

HP: *Burning?*

ER: Yes.

HP: *Why did you select small fires, swimming pools, and parking lots as subjects for your books?*

———

ER: Purely for areas of concentration in my life. *Small Fires* came at a time when I needed to come inside. It's my only interior book. The rest are all exteriors, with the exception of *Records,* which is neuter. *Pools* came when I was swimming every day and *Parking Lots* when I felt like being aerial.

HP: I noticed in Banks, Tanks, Ranks[9] *a photograph of Captain Medina. Was there a reason?*

ER: No. It was just a quick way of saying "rank," but no political note intended. I don't care what he did, as far as my art goes. Again it was a photo of a photo and not a photo of a person which is important.

HP: But Medina's the only person in your work with the exception of your friends in Royal Road Test. *You use banal monuments, the swimming pool, the gas station, parking lots, whatever is used and left behind by humanity, but not people themselves. People are incidental.*

ER: Oh yeah, people *are* incidental. I've avoided having people in the pictures in all my books, because they're . . . because that's not the subject. Very distracting. People are very distracting anyway. Once, though, I painted a picture of a dead man, but it was actually a magazine cover with a painting of a dead man on it. So I not only painted a person who was not alive, but it was a painting of a painting. But you have to know when to say, "OK, no people." And so I had to do that in my books, too.

HP: What about your new book Colored People?

ER: I did say people were distracting but this is the first time that I've used the word "people" in anything. The objects in the book were affectionately called people—people "in color." The title was a primary motivation in the creation of the book. I have blind faith in the title and blind faith in the pictures, and the two seemed to come together so compatibly in this instance. The plants may appear to be more Mexican than Negro but they *are* colored people, yes?

HP: Why photographs of parking lots or palm trees and not prints?

ER: I could never make a drawing of a palm tree and I could never paint a picture of a palm tree, and I don't know why I can't but I can tell you that I absolutely could never do this. For the same reason I could never mix media. I could never use a photograph, say, in making a lithograph or a silkscreen print. I could never do a collage with photographs or a montage with photographs of my book in a print or a painting. I have special reservations about the limits of the photograph, and I couldn't cross it into any other medium. [. . .] The book is the look, not the photograph.

HP: I think some people may get confused though; for example, Camera *magazine did an article on you in their June 1972 issue.*[10]

ER: Oh, I'll always give people photographs if they want to run a reproduction in the magazine. That's fine. But anytime someone wants to take one of my photographs, buy it or frame it, or something like that, that's not . . . that's outside the limits of my art. If they're going to show my photographs, they're going to have to show the whole book. [. . .]

HP: What do you consider to be the limits of photography?

ER: There are no limits to anything. If some photographers said photography should be limited to fine art and others said it should be limited to functional or commercial art, then it would naturally be both. But the master of the issue should be the person doing it, not the critics or the public. Artists will tell people about art, not the other way around.

HP: Do you think you will do any more movies?

ER: I'd like to do a feature if I could, but I have no idea what I'd make it on. I should have an idea before I make a movie, shouldn't I?

HP: You don't have to. I would think so many things would strike you as you work.

ER: Have you seen my movie *Premium* [1970]?

HP: Yes.

―――――

ER: It's a pretty hard movie to distribute, and it doesn't fit any categories. If it was a movie of me standing against the wall or doing push-ups or doing concept art things, it would be one thing. But it doesn't fit the artist-statement category. Some artists make films that are an end in themselves, you know, they're statements. Mine's not like that. I don't want people to look at the film like it's a deep statement on my part. It's just an excuse, the story, to make a movie. I wanted to be able to tell a story. I don't know where the movie fits in anywhere, and I can't place it in my art at all.

HP: How do you react if people place you in a category—Pop or any category that delineates your work?

ER: No category fully encompasses someone's art. They're all outside what the artist does anyway—they're after the fact. All categories are made for the convenience of people to delineate someone's work. It shouldn't make that much difference, but it can affect someone's career more than it can someone's work . . . because it's on the street level, it's the business side of things, it's the desire to wrap someone up. All I know is I've kind of escaped all the labels because I started painting in 1961 . . . and my work wasn't in any of the Pop Art shows, with the exception of one. That was the *New Painting of Common Objects* at the Pasadena Museum in 1962.[11] I wasn't even called a Pop artist until lately, and I'm sure that's because I live on the West Coast. Some people have put my work in with Conceptual Art. But I think anybody's out of Conceptual Art who makes any kind of image in his work, which I do. I'm surprised I've gotten as much mileage out of my work as I have. I've been working for ten years now. A lot of artists don't stay around that long. Artists are getting more like athletes. . . . Their production is limited to a shot, to a real quick shot. They don't like to look at it that way—painters become old and they still work. But I've always questioned that. I've left it open. If it happens I ever run out of work to do or the desire to do it, even though I'm making a good living, I always think of the possibility of just dropping art, of going on with something else . . . like working in a restaurant.

HP: Working in a restaurant? I did it the other way around.

" ' . . . A KIND OF A HUH':
AN INTERVIEW WITH EDWARD RUSCHA"

Willoughby Sharp

WS: What interests me most about your books is the particular sensibility, the kind of ironic take you have on ordinary things.

ER: Mmmm. Yeah. That's going to be hard to get at because what it amounts to is a style of living and the taste of things . . . filtering the taste with the style of living and then coming up with statements.

WS: Like what?

ER: Like *Colored People*. That's a product of everything I think about, and everything I do, and everything I buy, and every way I live. All that stuff goes into the funnel and comes out as *Colored People*. That's what's funny, that's what's curious . . . don't you think? [. . .]

WS: Was Twentysix Gasoline Stations *your first book?*

ER: Yeah, months went into the planning of that. I could have saved myself a lot of trouble by loosening up. You know, not gotten so concerned with how I wanted the thing to look. I changed the format about fifty times at the printer's.

———

Originally published in *Avalanche*, n. 7, winter–spring 1973, pp. 30–39.

I couldn't decide what I wanted. I just won't jump right in and do something spontaneously. I'm talking about making a work of art, not about anything else.

WS: It seems you have a very serious attitude towards . . .

ER: Well, yeah, I am serious about it. I'm dead serious about everything I make.

WS: That's part of your humor, though, isn't it?

ER: Yeah, to have something come across as humor you have to be methodical about it. It has to be planned carefully. [. . .]

WS: You relate somehow to a lot of work that started much later which has a conceptual basis. It seems to me that this approach is something you pioneered with Twentysix Gasoline Stations *precisely because the idea had priority over the execution, which you made as anonymous as possible. You shot fifty stations and pared them down to twenty-six so the original idea carried. I'm interested in your reaction to that.*

ER: I realized that for the first time this book had an inexplicable thing I was looking for, and that was a kind of a "Huh?" That's what I've always worked around. All it is is a device to disarm somebody with my particular message. A lot of artists use that.

WS: Give me some examples of "Uh."

ER: I don't know, somebody digging a hole out in the desert and calling it sculpture. You know, it's a surprise to people.

WS: Would Duchamp be the first "Uh" artist?

ER: I think that would be spelled H–U–H, with a question mark. [. . .] I just use that word to describe a feeling that a lot of artists are attempting to bring out, and some are doing it very well.

WS: Yes.

ER: The entire collection of my books just doesn't have that feeling of "Huh?" When you go through the whole collection it begins to make some sense; it shows more about the attitude behind them than one of them does. One of them will kind of almost knock you on your ass.

WS: Nine Swimming Pools does that. . . . I see you have a book on Vermeer here.

ER: Well, I was curious about Vermeer's life and some of those pictures. The paintings in that book are all the ones he ever did, aren't they?

WS: Yes, I think he only did thirty-six. . . . Would you say that you pioneered the book form as an artwork?

ER: Oh, I don't know. It's just that traditionally the book has not been accepted as a work to be put in an art gallery.

WS: I can't think of anyone else who used the book medium as an art vehicle.

ER: Well a lot of poets have done it but it hasn't been called gallery art art.

WS: Have your books been getting more frequent?

ER: Well last year I did three but *Colored People* is the only one I've done this year. Everything in the media is paced for people's pace. *Time* magazine comes around once a week and that's about the time you've forgotten the last one. Or *Popular Mechanics* or what have you. A newspaper. I've gotten into the style of reading a newspaper in the morning for a couple of hours after I wake up. All the media are filtered that way to the cycles we live in. You know, we live in daily cycles, we live in weekly cycles, we live in monthly cycles so once a year an artist has a show; he might make ten shows a year but they'll be in different cities. It's all paced out. It's very natural the way all those things happen.

WS: Does that apply to your own work?

ER: The way to produce art is the same way as the media, to sort of go with that rhythm. That's why I don't do twelve books a year, because other people aren't ready for it and neither am I. I'm not ready to make twelve statements a year. I *could,* and possibly I could push my craft much further because I'm dedicated to this whole publishing thing. I really owe a lot to it. It's a responsibility, it's my baby. I have to develop it. When I did the books I had a complete feeling of creation in the same sense that a woman would have a child. I even wrote that down: "These books are my children." But when I got *Colored People* back from the press, I yawned, I just yawned.

WS: Was there a point in your career when you started losing interest in making things with your hands?

ER: Yeah, definitely. About three years ago, I just didn't have the desire to work with my hands, make a painting. I didn't want to take the time. Then it occurred to me that a way out was to find somebody who could paint and have him do it.

WS: Have you ever rejected anything that was already printed?

ER: Mmmmm. I've had practically a cardiac arrest over the reprint of one of my books, *[Every Building on] the Sunset Strip*. I had to go get a lawyer. The original printer finished the job and it was gonna go to the bindery but they cut and folded the whole job wrong. Then I showed them the dummy so they could see that it was not folded right and I said, "You'll have to do this over," and they started to argue with me and I just broke out in hives. I really had spots on my face; I was ready to have a heart attack on the spot and I got a lawyer and they finally did the job over again. They had to pay for the cost of the paper and printing and all that. I've run into all kinds of problems working with people like that and I've had to buy color separations and other things on the outside.

WS: Then isn't it desirable to find a medium that doesn't even . . .

ER: No, no, unless I just want to sit back . . . painting a picture is a very simple thing to do. You don't have to rely on other people; you're in total control. But you don't pick a particular medium so you can have total control over it. If you can't work, with those people, you're not going to get a good product.

WS: How could you make a better book?

ER: Better? I don't know how it can be better. I'm satisfied with the results that I've gotten so far. There are technical problems that I need to. . . .

WS: Like?

ER: It's a job making sure the thing gets delivered properly and that they keep on schedule. For example, *Colored People* had to be finished in time for the November opening at Castelli and it was pretty close to the wire. I got them about four days before I left for New York.

WS: *That book was your one-man show, but do you really need a gallery context for it?*

ER: Uh, well, I don't know whether I need a gallery for the books to survive or not.

WS: *No, no, what I meant was your book becomes a one-man show no matter where it is.*

ER: Absolutely.

WS: *You don't rely exclusively on the gallery situation to show your work. It passes into the culture as a product first. It isn't tied to a place. Most of the most significant works of the '60s were made for specific places. And by putting your art in a book you've transcended. . . .*

ER: Not transcended, no. Just traveled away from. . . .

WS: *. . . the problem of trying to fit art into a gallery context which is limited by its physical environment and its inability to reach other people who might benefit from it.*

ER: The books are definitely not works of art in the same sense as paintings, but I wouldn't call them traveling works of art. They're tied to place in the sense that they're tied to a bookshelf.

WS: *Well, that's like a painting in a storage room. But what about the multiple aspect of your books? When you make a painting there's only one, but your books are printed in editions of thousands. You're adapting a medium that exists very pervasively in the culture into something which is beginning to be classified as art. And it's a work of yours that people can buy for six bucks. Now some people might construe that to be a rather revolutionary idea. I can't think of any artist of the '60s who could produce something he could call his art for a couple of bucks.*

ER: Oh, you mean they always sold for much greater prices? *[Laughs.]*

WS: Is there a relation between your work and Salvador Dalí's?

ER: Yeah, more so now than I think I knew before.

WS: Does he have that "Huh"?

ER: No, he doesn't really have it.

WS: No. It seems to me that the thing that we have to talk about is the special kind of sensibility in your work and particularly its irony.

ER: Everything possesses irony. Nothing gets away from it. You know, that chair being right there. The way it's broken. It's ironical how that picture got up on the wall. Irony is everywhere.

WS: That's a surprise. Is there a certain surprise element in it?

ER: No, no. I don't look at irony as though it's a surprise. Irony to one person is not irony to another. It's an extremely personal . . .

WS: The obvious and the ironic.

ER: Yes. I mean, you can go through here and look at this room and it can just be a belly laugh, the way everything is placed in here . . .

WS: We haven't laughed much though, have we?

ER: No. *[Laughs.]*

WS: Let's take Colored People. . . . *There aren't any people in it.*

ER: It's blind faith in two separate things. One is the term "Colored People," the two words together, and the photographs of the cactus is another [. . .].

WS: The title is independent of the book?

ER: In some ways. My amusement with the whole project was being able to use them together through thinking that they weren't really too similar. . . . I've always tried to keep people out of my books.

WS: Why?

———

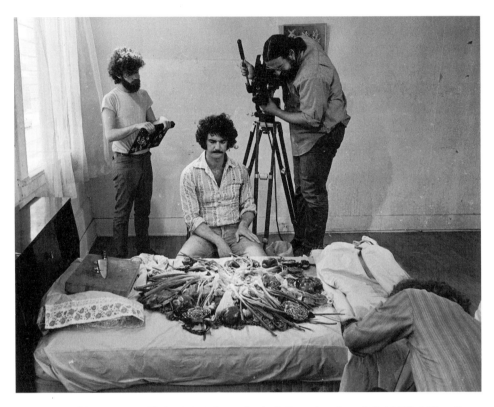

Production still from *Premium* (film). 1970. Left to right: Attila Domokos, Larry Bell, Neil Reichline, Bryan Heath (crouching). Photo: Danna Ruscha.

ER: I don't know. Just to eliminate the unnecessary human aspect. The first thing Andy [Warhol] said when he saw my book—I gave him *Twentysix Gasoline Stations*—was "How do you get all these pictures without people in them?" and I hadn't even thought about it before, but there aren't any people in them. Every once in a while you'll spot one. I seem to unconsciously eliminate people from them and I've never . . . I don't like imagery of people. Instead of using people, I'll use something else. But I've painted a picture of a dead man—it was actually a painting of a magazine cover that had a dead man on it. So I was painting a painting of a painting.

WS: A painting of a photograph of a magazine cover?

ER: No, it wasn't a photograph; it was a painting on the cover of a magazine. There's a ten-cent novel with a painting on it of a Texas Ranger walking out of a bank who's just shot a guy for trying to rob the bank, and the guy's dead over in the corner. So that's the painting I did.

WS: All the same, your movie has a cast. . . . Leon Bing, Tommy Smothers, Larry Bell and Rudi Gernreich.

ER: *Premium,* yeah.

WS: It's based on the same story as your book Crackers *[1970; co-authored with Mason Williams]. Were they both done at the same time?*

ER: No, *Premium* was done two years after the book.

WS: Really.

ER: I'm considering pulling the book off the market. I just don't think it's very good. Maybe I thought it was all right when I did it, but then the film negated it.

WS: In what way?

ER: The film told the story so much better and that's what I was after in that little act, telling the story.

WS: What struck me was that your attitude to the film was similar to your attitude to the book, kind of directorial.

ER: Well, in a sense I was impartial because I felt it was an opportunity to be a raconteur and I subjugated everything else to that function. I've always wanted to tell a story in another medium, rather than to tell it to someone as they're sitting next to me. The film was not my ultimate artistic statement, not that I know what my ultimate artistic statement is. It's not autobiographical. It's Mason Williams's story.

WS: How did you get Tommy Smothers to be in the film?

ER: He's a friend and I asked him to be in the book and he was interested in that. When I told him I was doing a movie he wanted to do it too.

WS: How long did it take to do?

ER: Oh, there were five days of shooting. Not consecutive, two and then three. It would have been impossible to shoot five days in a row. The whole thing was just gargantuan, because there weren't really enough people working on it.

WS: What enabled you to do the film?

ER: I got $13,000 from the Guggenheim Foundation.

WS: For that film?

ER: No, my project was to do a book and also to eradicate the bookworm which I've been having problems with. [. . .]

———

"FEATURE INTERVIEW: EDWARD RUSCHA"

Diane Spodarek

[. . .] DS: Can you talk about the film Premium *that you showed today?*

ER: I needed an excuse to make a short film so I took a story of a friend of mine who also inspired the book, *Crackers.* The story was by Mason Williams and was called "How to Derive the Maximum Enjoyment from Crackers." I didn't want to be too serious about it because I don't think film is the greatest art form. You can't excel in it as often as you choose—I think it's a real difficult medium. I have a few ideas for a feature length film in the future. Film is a do or die thing because there is so much money and people involved in the production, but it can show some of the greatest facets of what you choose to say. It's so different from a painting or drawing.

DS: Who is your audience for film?

ER: Anyone who is an audience for my work—it's the same. The films usually stay with the art crowd or people of college age because the films are not in a distribution set-up. And that's the frustrating part of the medium—it's limited—just a few people see it and so I'd like to work in an area for more people to see it.

———

Originally published in *Detroit Artists Monthly*, v. 2, n. 4, April 1977, pp. 1–5.

DS: Isn't there more of a possibility for people to see your films than your prints, drawings, and paintings?

ER: But not books. Books are a medium for people in the street to enjoy. They're made to compete with other machine-made items and other paperbacks. There isn't an "art price" on them with the exception of two that are a limited edition.

DS: I noticed in some of your books that you have printed more editions with each year. Is this because of a demand for them?

ER: Yeah. I get low in one area, one particular title, and I want to get it back up because people are interested in them and that has to do with the whole production of all the books.

DS: Do you find the area of film and books, which involves a lot of other people in the production who are not artists, affecting the outcome of the work?

ER: No, those people will never really understand what the director is up to because it's such a private thing of the whole medium. Other people fulfill this fantasy of the director and that's where I see creative potential—in the director. I don't see the people in the production seeing it in the same way as the director. To be able to say something so simple and yet see exactly what has to be done to reach this final result on film, is such a scary gap because on one hand, it's just a private little idea and you want to make sure it flows together, but then you see somewhere down the line, that you might not have enough money to make a particular shot.

DS: In an Avalanche *interview[12] you said you just yawned when you finished the book* Colored People. . .

ER: Did I say that?

DS: Yes, what were you referring to? To me it seemed possible that other people affected the outcome differently than you expected or intended.

ER: I think what I really meant, if I said that, was that I was not as surprised with the product as I thought because that's always happened with each project I do.

74

I sort of drop a medium and go back to it five years later or something. I may have just been disappointed for a moment. I may have felt on the down side about producing a book because I haven't done one in four to five years. Personally I like the idea of working with books because it deals with an almost non-existent audience. I wanted to make a product for a non-existent audience. That was what I really was after.

DS: Non-existent in what way?

ER: The attraction would be that they would be worthless to people. It's like doing something for no reason—or doing something as a great exercise, as I look at it. I wanted people to see it but I wanted it to be almost too hot to handle and be very open for all its ramifications. If someone buys a tour guide they want it to be right—they want all the listings to be accurate. That's a specific book for a specific purpose. Someone who writes novels writes for an audience that reads novels. I wanted it to be something that was not exactly construed as a work of art. I wanted it to be ambiguous. That's really what I was after—ambiguity.

DS: That seems to come out of your interest in the kinds of paintings, prints, and drawings you were doing before the books. During the lecture today you mentioned that the titles in the prints and paintings were intuitive, but to me they seemed to be a direct result of things you were very much interested in communicating about the culture.

ER: You could say art is intuitive—the cultural aspect could be intuitive. I like all those specifics—*Twentysix Gasoline Stations*. I don't know how you would categorize it, but if you are a writer or an historian, how do you categorize something that is a work of art made by an artist who knew what the title was going to be before he did the product? I knew it was going to be *Twentysix Gasoline Stations* and I'm not falling back on any kind of Zen Buddhism either.

DS: Would you say then that your work is "American"?

ER: Yeah, sure—very American. But if you want to historically examine things, people will see the strain of Europe or they may see China—that's global village. It's really American art—happening in America, things that have taken place in this continental United States.

DS: Was Colored People *directly related to a gallery show?*

ER: No, but there was one done in Holland about six years ago for the Community Government Project.[13] They had artists come in and do different things and they took me to a canal where I lived for a week. I took photographs (snaps) across a canal and the result of the project was the book. It was called *Dutch Details* and the pages folded out. I was approaching a building on the opposite side of the bridge as I walked across. The book was produced and people were interested but the publisher disappeared and recently I heard they destroyed the edition.

DS: Sunset Strip *also folded out. The mechanics of the book are interesting—perhaps more so than the actual images. There are two sides to the street and two sides to the layout of the book. For me, that is more appealing, and I have no desire to look at different images all the way through the book and turn it around to see the images on the other side of the street.*

ER: If you can hear an idea about something, or hear someone explain it, or see something written about it that is supposed to exist, you may never have to see the thing itself and somehow, that plays an important part in what I do in my work. I can't say "for example," because it's just that idea.

DS: Then you accept my approach to the book and you're not concerned that I don't really look at all the images?

ER: First of all, you almost have to say in that case, what interests you the most? You can say some of this is interesting and some isn't. You can say that about everything and yet I wonder what the interest really is. The individual pictures themselves went along with the idea and I wouldn't take one and transpose it because that's not my idea of the arts. My ideas are being factual, so my direction with the production of the thing was to keep factual. . . .

DS: But I never doubted that.

ER: But that's a disparity, maybe in the work, that I do as an artist. The stories in the movies are not true, not factual, but the books are, as far as the subject matter goes.

———

DS: I was also thinking about Twentysix Gasoline Stations. *I personally like the book but was never concerned if you in fact traveled a specific route to arrive at an "order." Eleanor Antin in an article about your work in* Art in America *[November–December 1973] said that that information was important to understanding the book.*

ER: I remember making the book very clearly. It was a difficult one because it was the first one I did. I wanted to establish for myself using a format of a particular size, number of pages, and all that. I had this classical idea of book making. I went to libraries and looked at old books and artists considered them a serious form of expression and I did too. So it was a difficult book because I wanted to be sure everything was right and that gave me a feel for the medium. The first five or six times I did it I considered the business part of it an art form.

DS: Weren't you involved with Seth Siegelaub in gallery shows with your books?

ER: Yes, but he's not doing that anymore.

DS: Isn't he credited with getting books of your type into a gallery space?

ER: In about 1967 there were artists making books in New York and he got these groups together and had shows of their work. You might call it book concept. That was the beginning of concept art. Then he started publishing and a few years later I got into it and he started distributing my books, in a small way, because it was an unpopular medium. People didn't grasp to it and didn't see it as a potential medium.

DS: How do you see it in terms of popularity now?

ER: Well, I've seen offshoots of it commercialized. Commercialized offshoots that are sometimes pleasing to look at. I have seen books that I have personally inspired, end up next to the cash register—people buy them by the thousands. There are a number of photographers who work now in a commercial book format that they never did before. It's a growing medium and photography was not there before.

DS: Do you see yourself as contributing to creating a market for them?

———

ER: There are several types of books. Some can be construed as poetry. Lawrence Weiner can be construed as pure poetry and people can read it as that. Other people have worked in other areas within the book format and it all comes across different. I guess people just didn't see the potential as an art form.

DS: *Do you think they are now?*

ER: I think they always will be. I'm not speaking of it as though it's a movement in art. I'm speaking of it in very general terms because it's going to take its own direction no matter how we care to see it.

DS: *What was the Hollywood sign project about that you did? The painting was on the cover of* Artweek *[v. 8, n. 8, February 19, 1977].*

ER: I did a painting with a friend of mine. I painted this huge billboard with two air compressors in an old Columbia movie studio. Someone offered billboards to a number of artists and the idea intrigued me. It's been done before a lot in L.A. The concept was that the artist painted it in the studio and they would show it in two places and the artist gets the painting back. It was amazing how simple the production was. There was a moving wall to work on and a machine pulled the stretched canvas up twenty feet and down to the floor; you could work on any area.

DS: *Did you know the locations the work would be displayed in before doing the painting?*

ER: No, I didn't care.

DS: *But the article in* Artweek *said that you could see the board in your rearview mirror, which righted the word "Hollywood." That seems carefully planned.*

ER: Well, I sort of did it in that spirit.

DS: *That seems to fit your interests in reaching a non-specific public.*

ER: Someone may look at it that way but I don't make throw-away art. If I make anything, I want it taken care of. Obviously there has to be a limit to how the work is handled. It's a problem with making anything.

———

DS: There's an underlying amount of humor in your work. Miracle [1975] is a really funny film, but in your other work, humor is more subtle.

ER: I think some of the things I've done in my movies have been more obvious, maybe. Action humor or things I may find in working with someone who is an actor (not a professional actor but someone playing a particular part), and see the actions that come out of these people, sometimes are humorous themselves and may not have been intended by me. In my films, I have more of an obvious reaction-type of humor, maybe.

DS: Don't you have to know the people quite well in order to got this spontaneous look to the film?

ER: I think that's strictly a style of filmmaking because the action is not that closely plotted and I wanted it to be that way. I wanted it to be simple and still be spontaneous. I think we did one rehearsal for each take we made. And the rehearsal was lightly structured so you had an idea of what you had to convey to the other actor. But I was after something that was not structured at all. I didn't want to say, walk into the room, deliver these lines, wait for reaction; it wasn't like that—it had to be fluid and simple. It was really common sense so you would not get the idea that it was just a production. So when people say to me, did you plan that rat there, did that girl know she was going to get thrown in the salad, I want to say, God, it's Hollywood. That's the great illusion about working with the medium of film.

DS: Are you interested in Hollywood films?

ER: I think it's a great medium. The films they make are a different story. Every so often there are pretty good things said in the medium. I recently saw *The Man Who Fell To Earth* and thought, "that was my movie." But that could have been because I suppose I was influenced by the same director that made the film [Nicolas Roeg]. It's a simple history. Everybody is influenced by people.

DS: Your name is pretty well known in the art community; I don't suppose you submit your films to competitions.

———

Costume change progression for *Miracle* (film). 1975. Lower right corner: sculpture by Jim Ganzer. Photo: Ellen Fitzpatrick. Courtesy Ed Ruscha.

ER: I don't, but why not? My name is not known in the film world. But my films are not films in many ways. I want to make a film and that is it. If someone else wants to distribute it, fine. The medium is not only in the production of the thing, it has to do with a finished product—film—and you have to go out and do something with it—try to get people to see it. I understand totally the concept of Hollywood films and how they're made. With all the vulgarity of Hollywood and the movie cinema industry and everything, it's still a great medium to use—it's an expressive medium despite all those things. So when I've produced a movie I'm finished with it. I don't want to have to go distributing my film around. I'm not interested in that. I'd like to do another one and I'd like to have it seen. It's not a big deal though. If some people can see it, that's fine. That's why I like to do any kind of visiting artist lecture program like this one; I like to show the films.

DS: When did you produce the film Miracle? *I was aware of* Premium *before I saw it but was not aware of* Miracle. *Personally, I like both movies but* Miracle *had something more to it.*

ER: *Miracle* was shot in January 1975, and came out in July. It's more like a blend and I like blends of things. The blend of things between one thing and another to me is like incompetency and almost a spiritual success, and all the blendings between, that's my film, that's "miracle."

———

"A Conversation with Ed Ruscha"

Trina Mitchum

[. . .] TM: For ten years I have been wanting to ask you about the business card you gave me to cure me of calling you "Edward Rooshka." Did it have something to do with the book you did with Billy Al Bengston?

ER: Yes, it was the card that Billy Al designed for me as part of *Business Card Exchange*. It started as a joke but then we decided to go through with it. We took four months to produce a book and we each designed and produced a business card for the other in secret. I wrinkled the one I made for him all up like [one of his "Dento" paintings]. We had a dinner at the Bistro in Beverly Hills and after dinner we had a very dramatic business card exchange which Larry Bell photographed with his Polaroid and good judgment. Later the book of photographs came out.

TM: That book sounds very much like Crackers *in that it tells a story in pictures.*

ER: They both had theatrical antics to do with them. That's the closest I could ever get to really directing anybody, except in my movies, so the movies and those books have something in common. In each case there's some harebrained story that I'm acting out.

Originally published in *Los Angeles Institute of Contemporary Art Journal*, January–February 1979, pp. 21–24.

I like the idea of having an excuse to do something, so in a sense the films were excuses. It has a lot to do with people getting together and acting out ideas.

TM: Which is fun.

ER: Yes.

TM: But to convey a story properly on film requires a great deal of preparation and precision. I loved both your films. Premium, *which was actually based on* Crackers, *was very good, but I was also very impressed by your second movie,* Miracle, *which was an original idea of yours. Why don't you show it?*

ER: It's hard to show because it's a half-hour movie. Its only real place is in film festivals and that's too costly.

TM: Couldn't you show it in galleries?

ER: You'd never see it properly in a gallery; people would be in and out. Movies can't be seen that way.

TM: The showings could be controlled. People usually expect to spend half an hour in a gallery anyway if they're serious about looking at the work. You could arrange for specific showings all day long and be strict about it. You just have to let people know what to expect.

ER: Well, perhaps it would work with a large collection of films. People wouldn't go to a gallery to see a thirty-minute film.

TM: I would.

ER: I would too.

TM: Lots of people would.

ER: Good, I'll see you there!

TM: I hope so. Are you going to make more films?

ER: I'm not thinking about making movies now. Creatively I'm thinking two-dimensionally, not three-dimensionally. It's not that I'm not thinking about movies, though, because I love to see what other people are involved with in movie-making. I go to see most movies, but I've been so disappointed recently that I haven't found any inspiration in films. There are no messages in most movies today; either that or they carry inflated messages. They're not really what they're cut out to be.

TM: It just isn't a practical art form for the individual artist. It's too expensive and so hard to orchestrate.

ER: Yes. Plus you're so public when you're making a movie. Everyone is knocking on your door. It's so draining.

TM: In 1965 you made the statement that photography is dead as a fine art.

ER: I meant that hand-crafted photographic prints are dead as a fine art. I think that the real fine art of photography is in picture-making. The making of an impression of a negative onto photographic paper is not as important as the actual picture value of the image which could be reproduced in a magazine, a newspaper, or a ten-cent Xerox. What makes the medium so fine is that anybody can go out and just go "snap." Still, artistry can be made by the single person behind the camera.

TM: I saw the photography show at the Museum of Modern Art in New York this summer and your book Every Building on the Sunset Strip *was displayed there.*

ER: A review came out in *Newsweek* magazine that said that my book had been edited down to nine feet for the show, so you didn't see the whole thing.

TM: I didn't realize that. How long is the whole book?

ER: Twenty-seven feet. So I was outraged about the editing. It also said in the review that the show had a dark room with projections on the wall of photographs from my book *[Thirtyfour] Parking Lots*. They made slides out of photographs in the book and projected them as if they were a slide show! I wrote the director of the show and told him, "Take my work out of your show if you're going to edit it. Show it right or ask the artist." That's the best idea: ask the artist.

———

Galleries take liberties. I didn't intend to have my book seen as a slide show; that's not mine; you can't put my name on it. The book is the important thing, the handling of the book. [. . .]

TM: Do you still continue to document the Sunset Strip?

ER: Yes, once a year. It's so much work. I have all of the Sunset Strip for the last five years in 35mm still shots.

TM: When do you do it?

ER: I begin early on a Sunday morning when no one else is around. I use a 250 Nikon, change the film real fast and just go along and document. Later I go back and see it all in pictures. It's very funny and has changed quite a bit in the last five years.

TM: Do you have plans to show the entire series?

ER: I'm thinking of ways to present it. That's the big problem. Cutting the pictures apart and making them match up is really an impossible scheme, but possible at the same time.

TM: I have always wanted to know about the different food stains and various substances you have used in painting.

ER: I first came about that through the silk-screen process. I made some prints using salmon eggs and caviar and different kinds of greases, like axle grease, substances that would attack a paper and leave some kinds of remnants of themselves. It definitely has to do with my thoughts about time and the future. Because the substances I used are commonly thought to dissolve right away, people thought the colors would dry up and go away, but they don't do that.

I also like the common tactual experience of working with wet substances between my fingers; it's fun.

TM: Like finger painting.

ER: Right.

TM: *Did you want to be an artist when you were a little kid?*

ER: Not really. I was uncertain until I got to high school and saw that there was something to do beyond just drawing cartoons or funny pictures.

TM: *So you took art lessons in high school?*

ER: I took classes, but they weren't lessons. It was just "Illustrate this spark plug."

TM: *Illustrate this spark plug?*

ER: Joe Goode spent a whole semester on illustrating a spark plug for Champion Spark Plugs and I used to do lettering on travel posters. You could do anything you wanted.

TM: *How did you react to being asked to draw a certain subject?*

ER: I hated it. It presented a big obstacle that was too grandiose to climb over so I never climbed over it. I don't feel that I have become a teacher's definition of what an artist should be, someone to whom they can say, "Capture the essence of this table by making a quick sketch." It doesn't have to be done that way. Someone can take a picture of it.

TM: *And yet you are a great technician. If you wanted to make a quick sketch of that table you could. You could paint any subject.*

ER: Can you make a map to somewhere? Do you know your directions? When you're in a strange part of the city and someone says, "It's south of here," do you know which way that is right away? I think there's a link between knowing your bearings and being able to draw.

TM: *Yes, because it has to do with proportion, knowing how things are in relation to one another.*

ER: Do you think there are statistics about how many people who can draw know their bearings? Maybe we have a real discovery on our hands!

TM: *In addition to the paintings you're working on, what else have you been doing?*

ER: I just made this print for Jerry Brown's campaign. It's an edition of seventy-five prints.

TM: Does that mean you are a Brown supporter?

ER: I'd have to be, wouldn't I? But I'm no crusader for politics.

TM: Lowell Darling believes that politics is an art form. Do you agree?

ER: I went out of my way to go to the polls to vote for Lowell over Jerry Brown because I thought he would be the best governor.

TM: What did you like about his platform?

ER: I liked the kamikaze aspect of it. Because of his radical humor, the seriousness of the candidate is suspect, but I think Lowell would have snapped to, given the opportunity.

TM: But don't you think that no matter what the intentions of the candidate are the surrounding bureaucracy makes it very difficult for him to effect any real changes?

ER: It's almost impossible; it's like an exercise in futility.

TM: Have you made any other prints recently?

ER: I made some lithographs in Hartford recently but due to some technical problems they haven't been produced yet, so I haven't seen the fruits of my labors.

TM: That's terrible.

ER: Isn't it? But I'll survive.

TM: I expect you will.

ER: I'm planning on having a long shelf life.

TM: Is there a typical Ruscha collector?

ER: I can't tell you who the typical person is. I got a call from a man last night who said that I had to paint him a picture no matter what. He has lots of my work and he puts great emphasis on some of the things I have done, but I don't even know the man that well. He's a person I do not understand. I find big gaps between me and some of the people who collect my work. I don't always know that they have the same feelings towards my art that I have.

TM: What are your feelings?

ER: I try never to create a precious object that I cannot say "goodbye" to at some point. Although I have very fond feelings for all the things that I have made, once something is gone I'm not aching for it, because all the work I did goes to regenerate my shop time. If the departure of my work pays for what I can do tomorrow then I am glad.

However, there are things that I would never sell so I do have some feelings about that. Other artists have deeper feelings about their work and are very mother hen about it, but I am not so much that way. I've let entire periods of my work go without saving any of it, but then I've got other works that I have saved. But there is a line between what is accepted and what is not. I destroy a lot of things.

TM: Why?

ER: They are things that are not resolved, that I know are not going to work. Most of my work works though. In other words, I don't do fifty paintings and throw away twenty-five of them. I throw away maybe four or five out of fifty.

TM: I think destroying your own work is a very powerful act. It takes courage. It's also a very powerful thing to let a little piece of you, your creation, go out into the world.

ER: It is very strange. It's also the power of the printed word. I was more influenced by reproductions of paintings in magazines than I was by standing in front of the magnificent thing itself.

TM: Because one hardly ever gets to stand in front of a magnificent painting?

ER: Right. So influence gets to us in a popular manner, like in magazines. Some magazines with color reproductions will claim that they give you more than you would get from a black and white reproduction; but it's not true, is it? It's still a reproduction.

———

Ed Ruscha, Western Avenue and Melrose, Hollywood, 1977. Photo: Trina (Petrine) Mitchum.

TM: The real emotional experience of viewing great art is missing when you see even the best reproduction.

ER: That's because nothing is like the work itself. If you have a fondness or respect for a work, then the best thing to do is put yourself in front of it. However, in theory I feel that the greatest power that comes from an image can come in any reproduced form, but I'm not necessarily promoting someone seeing a reproduction of my work.

The real painting is what I have done and if you'd like to see it you should really stand in front of it. At times I've even felt like having no photographs taken of my work.

TM: You have talked of using media as a voice; do you feel that there is a consistent message in your work?

ER: No, I don't. I'm not broadcasting my voice to people who don't want to get my point. The viewers have to come to me. My real medium of exposure is the gallery so I have to rely on people going to the gallery to see my work. I can't take any one work of art and say, "This is what I'm trying to say," because it's a combination of a lot of things. I just let people attach their own meanings to the work.

For anything an artist does though, he must be ready to take the consequences. If an artist paints tits and ass he can't say, "I want my work to be seen only as a religious statement." He's got to realize that people are going to see something else. So if you paint something you've got to take the consequences for it; you've got to take other people's interpretations and readings of it.

[. . .] The best place for me to operate is this little free-for-all zone where I don't have any real restrictions and I can say what I want. If I can't hit upon something that puzzles and attracts me at the same time, then I've entered that area. A lot of my work is actually met with real head-scratching. For example, when I first did the book on gasoline stations people would look at it and say, "Are you kidding or what? Why are you doing this?" [. . .]

TM: When do you do your best work?

ER: I get a lot of work done after the sun goes down, during the quieter parts of the day. I can't really work with a lot of people around. If I shut myself off, lock the door, and don't answer the phone, I know I can get work done. Most of my work is done at night for that reason. If I'm doing something like a lithograph, where I have to be with a printer, I work out the personal aspects of it first, alone. The rest is just technical. But when I'm painting or doing anything that depends entirely on my own decisions, I can do it better when I'm alone, late at night, sometimes all night.

TM: *Who is your favorite artist?*

ER: Hieronymus Bosch. He hasn't had that much influence on my work, either.

TM: *Has anyone?*

ER: Munroe Leaf is somebody who has influenced me. He was a cartoonist who made big square books for kindergartners and first graders. The title would be something like *Good Morning* and you'd open the book up and there would be little stick figures inside going through their little routines of teeth brushing and so forth. Absolutely dry, simple stuff. Kids brushing their teeth, feeding their dog.

TM: *There is something wonderful about simple, commonplace things.*

ER: Yes. There's something so direct about simplicity. There's a lot of conviction in the misspelled grocery sign. It's got heart, but then there might be a grammatical mistake. It's like the difference between a musician who goes to a recording studio and does a very polished, professional recording job and the guy who is down in the subway singing with a rusty voice. There's something about that guy who sings alone.

———

INTERVIEW WITH EDWARD RUSCHA
IN HIS WESTERN AVENUE, HOLLYWOOD STUDIO

Paul Karlstrom

PK: You were born in 1937 in Omaha, Nebraska. I would like you to give us some idea of your family background.

ER: My father was born in 1891 in Billings, Missouri. His father was born about thirty years before that, somewhere in Missouri or Illinois. I think my grandfather had a different name—I think it was Rusiska at one time.

PK: What nationality is that?

ER: It's Bohemian/German extraction.

PK: So that's your ethnic background.

ER: Yes, that's my father's background. I think my great-grandfather changed the name to Ruscha at some point. As I understand, it was changed to rhyme with the town, Chickasha, Oklahoma, where I guess someone was at that time. That's an Indian name, maybe Seminole Indian. Now, my mother was born in

California Oral History Project, Archives of American Art, Smithsonian Institution; October 29, 1980; March 25, 1981; July 16, 1981; October 2, 1981. This interview is published here for the first time and has been edited for inclusion in this volume.

Chicago in 1907, and her name was Dorothy Driscoll. Her father was Patrick James Driscoll, and he was born, I believe, in Washington, D.C. I knew Pat Driscoll, my grandfather. His father, which would be my great-grandfather, came from County Cork, Ireland, and their name could have been O'Driscoll at one time and then shortened to Driscoll. My mother and father met about 1935. My father was in the First World War in Camp Polk in Arkansas. He had a desk job, so he didn't have to go into combat. He was almost twenty-eight years old. Then he had some odd jobs from time to time, and he eventually got a job with the Hartford Insurance Company. He was an insurance auditor for about twenty-five years. He died in 1959 in Oklahoma. My mother's still alive.

PK: Living where?

ER: In Oklahoma City, the same house that we bought in 1941. She was just here last week; she's pretty healthy. She's seventy-three now. But my father was burdened with this responsibility of raising his brothers and sisters. My grandfather and his wife were real hard working; Teutonic class. Maybe his wife was born in Germany, but I'm not really sure. Her name was Durer. Either she or her father was born in Germany. They had a real tough life. My grandfather had a grocery store in Springfield, and also in Billings at the time, so they stuck pretty close to home and they were real strict Catholics. They were all raised that way and, naturally, I got this legacy of Catholicism that I eventually had to get smart and back away from.

PK: You've been fighting it ever since.

ER: I fought it until I was about eighteen. But anyway, I have a lot of pictures that he'd taken back in Missouri, family pictures. It was always real funny because the kids were all lined up, going to mass. Then my uncle Paul—who died of leukemia around 1900 or so—was a *Saturday Evening Post* delivery boy. There's a lot of rich old tradition.

PK: Real Middle America.

ER: Real Middle America. At the same time, not Protestant Middle America; it was definitely Catholic. But from farm stock and all that. Grandmother was real reserved and stoic, she'd mind her business. Traditional turn-of-the-century lifestyle for a mother at that time. But my mother had somewhat of an interest in art—not a mercenary interest in life. My father was more rigid in his thinking, much more rigid.

PK: A strong Catholic.

ER: Yes, right. Also he was thinking business and figures and so he had no time, really, for his children to go off and study anthropology like my sister did. I have a sister, Shelby, who is a year older, and a brother, Paul, who is five years younger than me. My father was profession-oriented and strict in his ways. He wasn't really that "touchy" with us; he was not emotional, not demonstrative. Rarely, I'd go to a baseball game with him or something. But I loved him as a father and I felt close to him. He was not around the house a lot. He would travel. He'd be gone three or four days out of the week, and so a lot of the time was spent with my mother. Dad would come back and then we'd do things, but it was not a real close relationship.

PK: But I gather with your mother, quite close.

ER: Yes, real close. My father made very little money, but he had a modest expense account and a company car, so we took this car once a year and would travel. I got to see the Grand Canyon and I got to come to California. I never went East.

PK: When did you first come to California?

ER: I would say it was around 1949.

PK: You did the standard tourist things, I suppose?

ER: Oh yes. The ocean, the trees. At that time the Driscolls, my grandparents, were living up in Boulder Creek, which is near Santa Cruz. I loved it up there. We would go up there every summer and visit them. Sometimes my sister and brother and sometimes the whole family would make these trips. They were all pretty good. But we couldn't do things like kids do today; you know, go into a toy shop. There was not much chance of that.

———

Ed Ruscha before his first Holy Communion, Oklahoma City, April 8, 1945. Photo: Simon Hughes. Courtesy Ed Ruscha.

PK: Now you're better off.

ER: Yes. Well, I feel like I got raised, shall we say, properly, despite all the psycho this and that involved in growing up. I think that I got distorted feelings about morality, maybe, and things that were put on me by the Catholic Church.

PK: Most of us, though, whether Catholic or Protestant or whatever, were molded by these values—especially at that time and in smaller communities. I doubt that your experience was unique. It matches mine pretty well.

ER: Does it? So there was only one thing to do and that was to go to Catholic school. They didn't have kindergarten then; kindergarten was in public schools. There were no particular religious delineations between people that I noticed. Catholics were, I guess, considered mackerel snappers.

PK: You didn't encounter any discrimination in the community?

ER: No, there was no discrimination. But the Church was so hypocritical. Then I learned more about the Church and it seemed even more hypocritical, to the point where I just had to say *adios*.

PK: But as you grew up, I imagine you were still required to attend mass.

ER: Oh yes. And all the holy days. Every Saturday morning I'd have to go to catechism. I remember the first thing in the catechism was a picture of the world. The first question was: "Who made the world? God made the world." I had to take catechism because I didn't go to Catholic school. I couldn't be an altar boy; I couldn't be in the Holy Name Society. My father was also a divorcé. This was one sin that he had on his mind when we were growing up. He was married in 1920, and he had a real bad marriage. He has a daughter also, who lives in Kansas, who is a scientist today at Kansas University. My father, in a sense, was excommunicated because he was divorced. This happened around 1922. According to the true ritual, a divorced person was no longer a Catholic. My father took that by rote and tradition. So he never went to Communion, but he would go to every holy day; he'd go to every mass and never miss a day. He lived a very Catholic life.

———

PK: This must have been a tremendous sadness for him.

ER: I think it was. He was deeply pulled back by it.

PK: Did this contribute to your view of the Church?

ER: Absolutely.

PK: You moved from Nebraska to Oklahoma. You said that your family bought a house in 1941.

ER: Yes, 1941–42.

PK: Your father was transferred, I suppose.

ER: Yes. He was in Danville, Illinois, and then he was in Omaha, and then he got transferred to Oklahoma by the company. I guess—just because of my background—I developed a certain hatred for insurance companies and all their policies. I developed a feeling that he worked for a company that was so large and powerful and inhuman in many ways. He was a figure, a number, like anybody who would work for a company like that.

PK: Do you think that this determined your attitude towards the business world in general?

ER: It could have.

PK: I don't know what your attitudes are . . .

ER: Pessimistic, pessimistic at best; especially about business and maybe the computer aspect of life. It doesn't frighten me because I know it's all to the better, but—

PK: Or inevitable, at least.

ER: Inevitable, yes.

PK: What interests me very much is your remark early on about how your mother somehow developed an interest in art and cultural things.

ER: I think my mother was a type of woman who would stand behind her man, no matter how her man is. So many women are like that. Not so much today, but back then they were. She was always secondary; she was the frail woman in the scene and my father always had the last word, of course. But my mother would be the one who would have the bust of Shakespeare on the mantelpiece. My dad would just forget it was there. He would be off reading the paper, doing his auditing and all that. My mother would be passive but responsible to her children. She always encouraged us; she had a good sense of humor. My father had somewhat of a sense of humor, maybe not as eccentric as my mother. If you'd met her for five minutes you'd see exactly what I meant. She's a real character, a real character. People like her. She did encourage us. I guess I was not really interested in art until I was about ten or twelve years old. But I definitely got approval from her, whereas I got a blank from my father.

PK: How did this interest in art come about?

ER: I got exposed to art by a friend of mine who lived about two doors down. His name was Bob Bonaparte—I think his father was a grandnephew of Napoleon Bonaparte. He was interested in baseball and football and also he was able to draw very well. He drew cartoons and he introduced me to the first factor in my life to do with art, which was Higgins India ink. I remember seeing Higgins spill out on a piece of paper, and you could watch it dry up and crack. It was really interesting. I had a real tactile sensation for that ink; it's one of the strongest things that have affected me as far as my interest in art. India ink and Speedball pens were real tools for beginning my interest in art.

PK: You didn't care about drawing.

ER: No, I liked to draw also. I was trying to emulate Bob Bonaparte, I guess. He did his drawings on two-ply kid finish paper which was real strong paper, a Strathmore paper, and I remember just that tactile sensation of the whole thing. It was almost beyond the whole cartoons that were drawn on them. He'd emulate styles of Dick Tracy. He'd use to save Dick Tracy cartoons: cut them out of the paper and put them in a little cheesebox. I remember he had a whole stack of them. Comics had a profound influence on me. I collected comics, but not to any great degree.

PK: Did you also cut them out from the Sunday paper?

ER: Yes, I did things like that. Then I'd throw them away and cut them out again, throw away. There was a constant shuffling of things which I found really interesting. I had no interest in painting whatsoever.

PK: Were you aware at that stage that it existed? Were there any articles in your house?

ER: Didn't even exist. Maybe a bust of Shakespeare? Hardly any books on art at all. Maybe a book on Rembrandt. There were, of course, some religious icons. There is a connection with my work and my experience with religious icons: the stations of the cross and the Church. Some of the flavors come over, like incense used in the Church, benediction. This was all that I felt was worthwhile in the Catholic Church—the trappings of the Catholic Church. Of course, they're now no longer—they've been streamlined, or disco-ized or something. I liked the ritual. I liked the priest's vestments—there was a deep mysterious thing that affected me.

PK: I don't suppose there were museums to visit.

ER: Oh no. There were no museums. The only thing that I saw was religious.

PK: Or popularized.

ER: Or popularized, like the *Mona Lisa, The Thinker.* I knew what *The Thinker* was but didn't have the idea of the levity of it, or the depth.

PK: You didn't distinguish between fine art and low art? Art was representation?

ER: No, there was no distinction. There was only the interest I had in things like comic books, because they were entertaining. Sometimes Dad would read us the cartoons. When I got the Sunday paper, that was the first thing—I'd pull that right off and I went right through the funny papers. Also, my Dad's job was downtown and I would go down every so often with him at night. It was fun to go downtown. I got a feeling of big city in this more or less country-ized environment. I remember going through the trash cans because I liked to look at the stamps on the mail. I got a real feeling for envelopes, stamps on envelopes, cancellations, postmarks, typewritten type. Anything that had to do with clerical,

---

typographical stationery items I got interested in. I got interested in twine—things that were in the trash cans in his office. I really liked those things.

Then I developed an interest in collecting stamps. I collected stamps a lot, and that was my geography lesson. I know a lot of countries. I'm sure those countries aren't British anymore. I remember a lot of countries, like Seychelles. King Edward's on that stamp. My connection with the outside world came through my stamp collection. Also, I guess it was the miniaturized aspect of the stamp—that it would have that much control over you. I became interested in the actual printing of the stamp. I have a cousin who is German, and his father was in the German army during the war. He was killed over in Russia. I remember writing back and forth with my younger cousin Herbert Buehler, and he'd send me Hitler stamps. And it was—"Gosh!" I'd get these Hitler stamps, and they were great. I was really interested in that. During the war I got this real sense of army. It didn't have that much effect on me because I didn't want to go off into the army to be a little soldier or anything, but through all this I developed this interest in stamp collecting. I think it still affected my art—the idea that American stamps were all engraved, and you could feel the top of them, feel the printing. In other countries, like some South American countries, they would have stamps that were just flat offset lithography.

PK: You were sensitive to the difference in quality.

ER: Yes.

PK: Were you aware of scale, the fact that these were small?

ER: Yes, they were small—these little scenes always from these foreign countries. They seemed to have a broadening effect on my outlook. For hours I'd study these stamps. Then I'd get off on some section, say of French stamps that maybe had a standing Liberty. There'd be, like, ten stamps, and they'd each be a slightly different color. It would be great.

PK: Serial imagery.

ER: Could be, could be. It is.

———

PK: Were there art classes available in your school? Certainly in grade school and junior high, you were interested in art.

ER: My close friend today, Mason Williams—I grew up with him and he was a neighbor of mine. We went to grade school together and ended up being the class artists, doing murals. I remember we spent practically the whole year doing a mural of the Oklahoma Land Run, with the horses and all. We'd take this butcher paper, stretch it out on the blackboard, and then he and I would work mostly on that mural for a whole year. We became known as the class artists at Hawthorne Grade School.

When I was in the sixth or seventh grade, I took a painting class. My mother thought it would be good for me to go to a painting class. My dad reluctantly agreed. So I went down to this guy's studio—Richard Getz, who I think is still operating in Oklahoma City. But he painted pictures of old people, funky old portraits. His was the most traditional approach to art. We'd look out the window and draw pictures of the houses across the street and all that. I did have a leaning towards that, but my mind was off somewhere else—it was actually in comics. That was where the real vitality was, in the comic drawings. I was constantly drawing cartoons. But I remember one thing, another tactile—no, olfactory—sensation that came to me the first day I walked into that painting class. I smelled turpentine and oil paint and linseed oil. Boy, that really struck me right there, and stayed with me ever since. It's a great smell.

PK: So even that introduction to the fine arts media—oil paint, turpentine and all that—was foreign to you?

ER: Yes, it was foreign to me.

PK: It didn't have an impact where you thought, "Ah, this is for me"—that there was something special or elevated about it?

ER: No, I didn't have a reverence for it. I wasn't in awe of the teacher necessarily; I sort of dumbly followed his instructions. So I lasted about three months.

PK: Back in school, though, I gather there really were no courses.

———

ER: Not courses as such, but there would be someone like Mrs. Laird, in the fourth grade. They called her "the art teacher." She was always developing kids who were interested in drawing and painting. But there were no real courses where you would come in and sit down and do that until later on.

PK: *You felt that she at least reinforced your interest.*

ER: Yes. She gave me the time and materials. But my involvement with finger painting and all that kind of stuff in grade school was sort of minimal. I was never really that interested in it. By the time I was in the fifth grade if you would say, "Who is your favorite artist?" I might say, "Norman Rockwell." My father would read the *Saturday Evening Post.* That was his favorite magazine. It would arrive every week. He'd start reading it and, of course, the cover had Norman Rockwell on it. So Norman played a part there.

PK: *Were you attracted to the great facility that one finds in Rockwell, the ability to reproduce so accurately?*

ER: I guess. But I didn't have a curiosity in that so much as I did in his statements about things. How he drew his figures and all that was not a mystery to me. I also didn't see any abstract qualities in his work that I liked. I think his color was just the color that it had to be. His stories were the thing. His facility as an artist, and his drawing ability and his delineating ability, were not even factors. I thought he was like a whimsical American storyteller.

PK: *So the anecdote appealed to you. Along with Munroe Leaf and comics, these were some things you appreciated.*

ER: Yes. There was another guy named Basil Wolverton, and he drew a cartoon strip called "Powerhouse Pepper" which I thought was real funny. He had a grotesqueness to his drawing style that I really appreciated; I loved his drawings. I think that Robert Crumb's style is very much like Wolverton's. I've forgiven Robert Crumb for that because I think he has a lot to say. I like Robert Crumb a lot, but I think he really was influenced by Wolverton.

PK: *He ripped off Wolverton.*

ER: Well, so to speak—in his drawing style. But he added the true meaning behind the thing. He gave it the statement. That's what Norman Rockwell had—the statement—the storytelling aspect that Basil Wolverton had. Sort of silly comics. But his drawings were good.

PK: *What were your most favorite comics?*

ER: I think Dick Tracy was one of my favorites. Blondie is another. I saw a little bit of Felix the Cat, and some of the older ones like that. Also the movies had a strong influence on me—Walt Disney movies. I remember seeing the *Three Musketeers,* or the *Three Caballeros, Tres Caballeros.*

PK: *Did you understand how they were made, and that commercial artists actually worked at Walt Disney Studio?*

ER: I guess I did. I left Oklahoma City and came to California to the Chouinard Art Institute. That was the one factor that my father agreed to, and was actually happy for me to do, because the school was supported by Walt Disney. A lot of the artists who went to that school eventually got jobs in the Disney studio. My dad really liked that idea. He could relate to that because Walt Disney was the great American, as Norman Rockwell was. Rockwell and Disney were two strong father influences, father approvals. Disney did influence me enough. I liked his movies, and the cartoons in the movies I really liked. That connected with the cartoons in the newspapers for me.

PK: *Did you ever create your own comic strips or illustrated stories?*

ER: Yes.

PK: *What kinds of things?*

ER: Like I'd hear a joke. Some guy would be on the street, running, and another guy would say, "What are you doing, training for a race?" And he'd say, "No, racing for a train." So I'd run home, break this down into three blocks, a little three-part cartoon strip, and make that cartoon. I'd have the guy running by there, and the little talk bubble. Also, wherever I worked or whenever I was at school, I tried to get my cartoons into the school paper or in the newspaper carriers' newspaper. I got to be known as somewhat of an artist, I guess.

PK: Were you a delivery boy then?

ER: Yes. I think that also had something to do with my feelings about surveying, my interest in diagrams, rigid street patterns. I even planned at one point to make—out of paper—a three-dimensional little town with all the little houses that were on my paper route. Never did it—started it, but never finished it.

PK: A little model—

ER: A little model. I always liked scale models. A friend of mine up the street in Oklahoma City made a scale model of Williamsburg, Virginia out of paper. I was impressed.

PK: Were you ever interested in being an architect?

ER: I sort of thought I might be, but then I just never was. My sister went to school in Mexico City and she started going out with this architect from the school. He was a student at the University of Mexico. I remember going to Mexico City in 1955, I guess, when I was in the eleventh grade. I went with my parents to see my sister, and she took us with her boyfriend to this place in Mexico City called the Pedrigal. It was like crazy modern buildings. I'd never seen anything like that in my life.

PK: You visited Mexico City when you were in high school.

ER: It was my first touch with a cosmopolitan city.

PK: Certainly your first time out of the country.

ER: First time out of the country, absolutely. I was just floored. Modern architecture affected me there. Not in the sense that I'd want to become an architect, but just the imagery of it—the bizarreness. They were doing all kinds of things, and the modern architecture was mixed with all the ancient things they had there. That really had an effect on me. It was like, "Modern, wow!" In high school I was thinking of modern things. I wore these crazy shirts.

PK: Were you ever into the pink and charcoal gray?

ER: Yes. Pegged pants. Well, those more or less came from California. I love that California style. That's why I came here.

PK: You actually moved here in 1956. That's an historical event, because of all the artists who come to my mind, you perhaps most identify with Hollywood and Los Angeles specifically. One of the few other artists that I can think of in the same position in America is David Hockney.

ER: I was going to say, David Hockney.

PK: Why did you move here, and what attracted you specifically to Los Angeles?

ER: Well, I visited here a few times before. I guess I went through a graduation trauma of some sort, not knowing where I was going to school. I wanted to go to an art school. I knew that by the time I was eighteen years old. I had become friends with Jerry McMillan who lives right upstairs here, an artist from Oklahoma City, and Joe Goode. They were in art classes with me in high school. I'd see Joe Goode and Jerry McMillan cutting up in art class, making these stupid sculptures and lighting them on fire. It all linked in with the idea of having madcap fun. We'd always make posters—I went from cartoons to posters. Then I became interested in printing and typography, more so than the traditional fine arts.

I knew I couldn't hack the Bible Belt. I wanted to get away from that, I wanted something more metropolitan. Do you want gum-popping girls for ever? You just can't do it anymore. So I knew I had to leave. I knew that there were only a few places to go, one was art school in New York, maybe Pratt or Cooper Union, and the other one was the Kansas City Art Institute, or the Chicago Art Institute, and then there was California! I'd been here before. And the East—that's just too old world for me. I had no interest in going to New York because all I could see were these oppressive buildings and concrete, and it just had sort of a feeling that I couldn't connect with. Oh, another aspect was hotrods and custom cars, which I began to tune in on in Oklahoma. That was another attraction of California, the idea of custom cars. I had a 1950 Ford that I had lowered and

———

105

put Smithy mufflers on. I knew I wanted to go to California, that was the only place. So I got my car and Mason Williams and I came out to California together.

PK: *Did you drive your Ford from Oklahoma City?*

ER: You bet. Burned thirteen quarts of oil. Kept it out here for a while, ended up selling it back in Oklahoma. Then I was sort of carless for a few years there, and it didn't bother me. I just didn't even think about cars.

PK: *Did you come to L.A. with a career objective in mind? Did you know you were go-ing to enroll in Chouinard?*

ER: Well, I didn't plan that much. When I came out to California, I knew that I had to have some of my artwork, so I packed up a portfolio and I tried to get into Art Center School. I wanted to be a commercial artist, and they were the strongest school in commercial art. Also, in the *Saturday Evening Post,* there was a story about Art Center School which my dad read, so he encouraged me to go to that school for that reason. I got out here and found out I couldn't get in, there was no opening. So I went to Chouinard. Now that was the Bohemian school.

PK: *How did you find out about Chouinard?*

ER: I wrote in advance. I got a little brochure from them and I also got one from Art Center. But as it turned out, I ended up at Chouinard, and that was beards and sandals and fine arts. They did have commercial art courses which I was in-terested in, but Art Center was no beards and no sandals, nothing like that. You wore clothes to school, and Chouinard was just the opposite. It was Bohemian-ism on the march. But still Walt Disney had a part in the whole thing, and they had animation. But that kind of courses I was just more or less cut off from—I didn't listen to Elvis Presley anymore. I became a serious person. I stopped going to church. The move to California was the big change.

PK: *Where did you live?*

ER: Mason and I found a place on Sunset Place, which is off of Lafayette Park, down near Westlake Park. I lived around that neighborhood for a few years.

Then I met somebody at Chouinard, a guy from Oklahoma, named Pat Black-well, who was a few years older than me, and he also was very much a Californian, sort of Oklahoma-Californian. With some other friends of mine—Jerry McMillan, Joe Goode, all these people—we lived all together. We rented this house up near Barnsdall Park.

PK: You were the first one to come, you were followed by Goode and McMillan? They probably came partly because you came.

ER: Well, it made it easier, anyway. But they were frustrated and wanted to get out. They wanted to be serious. So we're back here, living in California. I lived at 1818 North New Hampshire Avenue with the five of us, all from Oklahoma. We were all more or less seriously dedicated in school—with mostly commercial art. But we all did painting courses, fine arts courses, and all of us began to move over toward fine arts.

PK: Who were the instructors who were influential in this respect?

ER: Robert Irwin. Don Graham, who was a teacher of drawing there. Emerson Woelffer. Marvin Rubin, who taught commercial art courses—advertising—but he had an influence on me. There was another man named Bud Coleman who also influenced me. Woelffer and Irwin, I would say, had the strongest influence.

Herbert Jepson was there. I was on the periphery of Jepson's teaching, but I liked the idea that he would not even look at your drawings. It would be like, "How are you responding to the drawing?" rather than, "What does your drawing look like? How can you change that line and make it fatter?" It was like he was saying the real problem was not the drawing; it was in you, and you act out yourself in the drawing somehow. He taught life drawing, but he wouldn't come and say, "That leg's too fat." Nothing like that. He was more subliminal, more cerebral about it. Whereas someone like Don Graham would teach you to push and pull, put dark line over other shapes, so you would begin to get form. Then Irwin was really cerebral about it.

PK: What is Irwin like as a teacher?

ER: Well, he had a real presence. He was an extremely youthful person, and he embodied all the aspects of a Herculean Californian: sunshine, energy, surfing, football player. He had all these things about him that you identified with, and he made his point very clear. Plus he was a non-stop talker, just non-stop. It became like art was a frantic involvement with what you were doing. It was also a deep respect for materials that he taught us, and so we'd prepare all our canvases. I actually took a watercolor class from him—I didn't take painting classes.

Richards Ruben is another teacher there that I liked. I don't think he had as strong an effect as Irwin. He was a little more distant than Irwin. Irwin was the Californian, and so he would talk about things at hand, and not about ancient art. When he would work on a watercolor, or have a watercolor class, he would be furious. There was this kind of fury that went on—the fury of involvement with materials and subject matter that Irwin got across to us.

PK: *With these teachers, was it their work itself that influenced you or attracted you?*

ER: We'd see examples of their work, but I was surprised that there wasn't more of that. Because the work they did was not as important as what they said, with the exception of Irwin, because Irwin did have a painting style all to himself. He had a definite aura—probably the strongest aura of any teacher that I was around, and I wasn't even around him that much. He was closer to these other guys—Joe and Jerry, and all the other people.

PK: *What were the ideas specifically?*

ER: The ingredients were a collection of all the things that happened in going to an art school, and all the people that you'd meet. The instructors were almost not as important as the students were. Being surrounded by students who were really aggressive and inventive and full of life—this had more of an influence on me than the teachers themselves. On the other hand, the influence of the teachers was not through their work, but by the aura that they created about the whole thing. It was the group and the interaction of those people.

PK: *Was Billy Al Bengston there?*

ER: Bengston taught one class. I didn't study under Bengston, but he also had a strong aura about him. He was a friend of Irwin's. He came up there one time and taught a class that I missed. Joe told me about this: it was very funny, and I was extremely impressed by him because he came into a class and had these students stretch this paper all the way around the room and tack it up. Then every person would just get in there and start painting on this thing. Bengston would just go off and have lunch all day, or hang out all day. Then he'd come back at the end of the day, "Okay, I guess that's about it. Wrap it up. Tear it down and throw it away." It was the idea of, "Just get in and do the work, and don't think that you're doing a finished painting that you'll sign your name to and put on the wall." It's just the act of doing it. The biggest thing that I learned in art school was that I had to unlearn everything that I'd learned before—since my birth, literally. So I unlearned. I got out of Catholicism, I got out of all these old ideals that I had—without relinquishing my family, my family ties. I began to realize that I was living a hypocritical life, and was so glad that I had gotten away from the Bible Belt and all those people. Because there was just no room for poetry, no room for a poet there. An artist would starve to death there.

PK: *Art was perceived by you as a means to escape what you considered oppressive things in your background.*

ER: I wouldn't say it was an escape. It was just something I was doing at that time, a step to higher education which I knew I had to go through. Everything began to unfold for me. I began to be interested in other things like architecture and music. I got interested in symphonic music and then I became aware of Frank Lloyd Wright. It was a connection of all those things. Then I got interested in book printing and books, so it began to grow out of a general interest in all of this that going to school seemed to help out.

PK: *Who else stands out in your mind among the students?*

ER: A guy named Leo Monahan also had some good ideas. He's a cop now, he's an artist and a part-time cop. I just can't believe it. It seems like such a dichotomy.

PK: *It sounds like something that Ed Kienholz could have done.*

1818 North New Hampshire Avenue, Hollywood, 1958. Clockwise from top: Jerry McMillan, Pat Blackwell, Ed Ruscha (kneeling), Joe Goode. Photo: Don Moore. Courtesy Ed Ruscha.

ER: Yes. Monahan actually has a squad car and he operates out of a sheriff's station.

PK: *Do you ever see him driving around?*

ER: I saw him one time, yes. He's a real funny guy. He's got a great sense of humor. He does magazine covers for *West Ways* magazine, and he's got a commercial art business. He does really good work.

PK: *But he still is a cop.*

ER: He's a cop. Can you believe it? I just scratch my head. He's friends with the old guys who went to school with us. Aaron Cohen was another interesting Chouinard student. He was a friend of Larry Bell's. He was my first real introduction to a Bohemian. This guy had long hair, a beard, wore sandals and patchy jeans. He rode a bike to school. He actually took a bike across country, went from Los Angeles to New York and back. He'd do these paintings where he'd get down on the ground and scrub the paint into the canvas, and everybody's walking into class and looking at him aghast. Now I think he works for the Mattell Company, as an executive or something. I don't know where Aaron Cohen is now, but he was one of the true characters in art school. He also worked at this restaurant called "The Patio" with Joe and Jerry and I. We had jobs there. Then I got a job with a printer here at a place called the Plantin Press, which is a fine arts press. There was a man there named Saul Marks. He died a few years ago, but I think they still have the Plantin Press. It was a fine arts press. He handset type and I learned how to do that.

PK: *How long were you there?*

ER: Oh, about six months, I guess. I was back to the smell of ink. I really liked ink.

PK: *Were you an apprentice?*

ER: Yes, a printer's devil. I did that for a while. But it was mostly because I was curious about book printing. I was getting a respect for pages, and this tactile sensation. We all worked for a while, then we'd break our painting and wash up with paint thinner and go over there and work for a couple of hours and go back to

———

our class. It was a routine that I really liked. It was really casual and relaxed. There was no real vocation—it didn't have any goals. We were at a confused point in our education, but the main thing was that we had a real vital lifestyle in school. And that was all because of all these people—Bengston, Irwin. Then we began shifting and I saw that I couldn't handle commercial art anymore.

PK: Did you ever work as a commercial artist?

ER: Yes. I worked at a couple of places. I worked at an advertising agency here, and I did layouts and menial tasks, paste-up and things like that. I worked for about a year doing that.

PK: This is while you were still a student?

ER: Yes, partly a student and then a little bit after I got out of school.

PK: You were really trying it out to see if it was something you could take on?

ER: Yes, I was trying it out. I thought there might be some future for me there. But then I got highly supported by Jerry McMillan and Joe Goode. Joe was going to be nothing but an artist; he was a painter all the way through. In high school, I remember, he was rather lazy and directionless. You'd go over to his house at eleven o'clock in the morning and he'd be sleeping. Sleep, sleep, sleep. There was no way out for Joe except through the fine arts, whereas I thought there were alternatives. But any option except fine arts would have been a sacrifice.

PK: Was it a dramatic decision, or just quite natural?

ER: No, it was natural. It was slow and natural. I was in art school for four years—a good period of time.

PK: 1956 to 1960.

ER: Right. I had an opportunity to make a transition, and it just happened by the way. It was nothing planned. I just gradually began to lean over to the hot side of life, the stuff that really was happening, like the fine arts and the painters.

Being aware of galleries and the sort of things that were happening in galleries. That art could be made out of sort of flimsy fun, and that there was a lot of style involved in it, so it was very appealing. Then we heard about Kienholz and all these people, and there began to be a definite scene that we saw ourselves becoming a part of. I couldn't have been an ad man, I just couldn't have done that. There was no substance to it. It meant working with other people on an idea. That just became a falsehood after a while; I saw that it just couldn't last any longer. So I did a few other things off and on, like book design and showcard lettering jobs and things like that.

PK: You did that on a free-lance basis? Were you credited on any of the book designs? Are those some of the earliest Ruschas?

ER: Yes, I think I did get credit on them.

PK: Do you have any of these things left?

ER: Yes. I designed a catalog for Billy for the L.A. County Museum which probably is my best work along that line.

PK: What year was that?

ER: That was 1968, I believe. They did a show of Billy's, and I did a catalog that had sandpaper on the cover.

PK: By that time you had your own reputation; you weren't doing it out of necessity?

ER: Yes, it was more out of joy and also out of great freedom. They just said, "Do what you want." I just thought that was great.

PK: The Ferus Gallery had opened by that time?[14]

ER: Yes, it had opened by that time.

PK: Had you and your colleagues at school come in contact with developments elsewhere, the great world of contemporary art, American art, international art? At that time certainly New York was the center for the Abstract Expressionists and other developments.

ER: Oh yes, this was a strong influence on us.

———

PK: How aware were you and your colleagues and other younger Los Angeles artists of what was happening in New York, or for that matter, around the Art Institute in San Francisco? Was there any contact?

ER: Not necessarily that. In San Francisco at that time, Beatniks were in, and that lifestyle seemed appealing to us all. Jack Kerouac and so on had a strong effect on all of us. But I wouldn't say that much more than, say, Elvis Presley or some people in the other arts. San Francisco was just another town and we knew that there was a good art school up there, but that's about it. We knew that it was considered more of a fine arts town than Los Angeles. There was stuff that came back and forth. We knew that San Francisco was an option. There were artists making their name up there.

PK: Did you know about any of them? Were there any figures who were viewed as serious from this distance?

ER: Wally Berman and George Herms.

PK: But the connection was more with the poets, with the North Beach scene rather than the legacy of Abstract Expressionism?

ER: We had more of the legacy of Abstract Expressionism than we did from anything that happened in San Francisco. We got mainstream ideas from New York, from de Kooning and Franz Kline.

PK: [Clyfford] Still was teaching at the Institute, and a lot of students were emulating Abstract Expressionism after the war.

ER: Clyfford Still—didn't he live in New York?

PK: Yes, but he taught for five years in San Francisco, and Still, of course, is associated with the New York School.

ER: There were some interconnections there somewhere. Kenneth Price was also an artist who influenced a lot of us. But we really didn't know about Kenny until the last year of school, maybe. Billy Al went to school in San Francisco. He went to Berkeley, I believe, or one of those schools up there. Peter Voulkos was known

———

114

to a lot of us. John Altoon was another one of the most important people in the school scene, although I had never taken a class from him. He taught drawing classes. I think he was there at night, and I was going there during the day. I took a couple of night classes, but somehow missed John the whole time I was there.

PK: Did you know him then?

ER: No, I didn't know him then. Later I got to be good friends with him. I even did some art with him, I did lettering on his drawings.

PK: When was that?

ER: Oh, this was about 1964 or something like that, 1965.

PK: Wonderful artist, though.

ER: Oh, he's great. And a fantastic human being, larger than life, no doubt. Did you meet him? He just walks into a room and kids would laugh. Everybody just goes, "Hoo." He's just got this presence. He was real muscular, and had a big handlebar mustache and sort of this potential for violence. He had giant hands, but yet he was a deep, deep thinker and poet, and a red hot artist at the time. He was doing real good work, and of course he had a story that went along with it too. Everybody knew all about Altoon and all his capers.

PK: So he was a romantic figure.

ER: Oh yes, definitely. One of the most romantic of all the artists of that period.

PK: Was it again lifestyle he represented rather than the work?

ER: It was the romantic aspect rather than our study of his work. Like I went to a show at the Ferus to see a bunch of his drawings and I sort of skimmed through them. I think John was more important than his work. I saw two guys in there—would-be critics, I guess—who were verbally dissecting his work. I remember being repulsed by this for some reason. Maybe I didn't even give it an opportunity to sink in—I was over in the corner, listening to them talk about the John Altoon drawings and about this and that, push and pull. But John was a real force

---

in school. It was lifeblood, sort of an indefinable lifeblood. All you had to do was have a cup of coffee with him, and right away you'd get this—ohhh, boy. That was more than any artist could say or what any teacher could say to a student, how they related as a human being.

PK: Did you ever discuss specific art issues with teachers or your fellow students, over coffee or a beer?

ER: Oh yes. But you see, it became a visual thing rather than a verbal thing, because you'd see something and say, "He-he-he." That would mean much more than any number of words, you see. It would be like a notation of loving something, like there's something hot there, let's talk about it. Or let's not even talk about it, let's just say, "Yes, it's hot." That's the communication right there.

PK: You would know that you were probably on the right track.

ER: Yes. Oh, I'll say that one time something struck me. I became aware of Marcel Duchamp's work. It was something. It was like a mysterious sidetrack in my education. Its strength to me was because it was so visual.

PK: You got to know Duchamp's work through a book or magazine?

ER: It was through a book. But he had never had a one-man show when I was in school.

PK: Of course, there was the Pasadena show, but that was later.

ER: That was later; that was 1964 or something like that. But I began to see his work, and I liked the work of Man Ray. I think those two artists had a strong effect on me. Then I saw a reproduction in some obscure magazine of Jasper Johns's *Target with Four Faces* and Robert Rauschenberg's painting, the combine painting with the chicken.[15] That just sent me. I knew from then on that I was going to be a fine artist.

PK: What was it about their work that was so exciting to you?

ER: It was a voice from nowhere, it was a voice that I guess I needed; I needed to hear this and see this work. And it came to me, oddly enough, through the medium

———

of reproduction, and so it was a printed page I was responding to, and not the work itself. But the kind of odd vocabulary they used inspired me—it was like music that you've never heard before, so mysterious and sweet, and I just dreamed about it at night. It was so powerful that I was wondering, "What are these guys, who are these people, what are they doing?" I began looking more for their work. Each successive thing I saw by these men was a great work of art to me. It meant more to me than anything else. These new voices I was hearing transplanted the temporary excitement I had from Abstract Expressionism, which was the only thing at the time. We were all more or less piddling with paint in the same way.

PK: So, at one stage as a student, you actually were working in an Abstract Expressionist manner?

ER: Yes. It was the idea that you have the blank canvas, and you have all these paints in front of you. Then you attack it and see what you can do and how you can manipulate the colors, and then manipulate the shapes, and the paint-strokes. It was a solid way of thinking. It was great.

PK: Who were your heroes then, your role models?

ER: Well, I guess de Kooning was, and Franz Kline. Franz Kline had a lot to say at that particular time, and so they were more or less the passwords. You just emulated them, almost automatically. Then if you couldn't emulate them you weren't really on the right track. I still think that. But the work of Johns and Rauschenberg marked a departure in the sense that their work was premeditated, and Abstract Expressionism was not. You had to stand in front of the blank canvas, you couldn't know in advance that there was going to be a yellow shape over there. You couldn't know in advance that there were going to be two giant black brushstrokes over here. What you did had to happen out of your involvement with the painting at the moment.

PK: And you didn't feel comfortable with that method for yourself.

ER: I was able to swing a few paint strokes and all that, but was not really that way. I didn't really feel comfortable. I felt like something else had to come in there.

———

PK: Was that the message you received from these mysterious voices, that there had to be an alternative?

ER: Right, a definite alternative. It was like a new world for me to get into. I knew that within Abstract Expressionism there was no room for my ideas. So when I saw [Johns's] *Target,* I was especially taken with the fact that it was symmetrical, which was just absolutely taboo in art school—you didn't make anything symmetrical; symmetrical art was out to lunch. Art school was Modernism, it was asymmetry, it was giant brush strokes, it was colors splashing, it was all these other things that were gestural rather than cerebral. So I began to move towards things that had more of a premeditation. All of my art has been premeditated: having a notion of the end and not the means to the end. The means to the end has always been secondary in my art. It's the end product that I'm after.

PK: You're certainly not a process artist.

ER: No, I'm not a process artist.

PK: Did you view these artists as anti-artists?

ER: I saw them as rebels, in a way. Certainly they were rebels in the same sense as a lot of people who are rebelling against the standard of the way things are done. Johns and Rauschenberg certainly did that. I guess Johns even more so, because his things were just so quietly powerful. Oh boy, I just couldn't believe it. Even when I was in New York, I wondered where I could see his work. That was around my first trip to New York. Each thing that I saw of his was staggering. That American flag he painted with encaustic.

PK: When did you go to New York?

ER: 1961.

PK: What were the circumstances?

ER: I traveled to Europe for about ten months in 1961, after I got out of art school.

PK: It was your first visit to New York?

———

ER: Yes. And I also saw a Johns painting in Paris which they wanted seventy-five dollars for, I think. It was a painting of a little target. It was at a little bitty gallery. That was the only thing that I saw in Europe at all. Art in Europe was just out. I mean, there was no art in Europe except ancient art, and I had no interest in it.

PK: *Did you go to the museums, though?*

ER: Oh yes. But it was not there for me. I could get more involved with the graffiti on the walls, and a brick that might be over on the side of the road or something and other curiosities, rather than the established notions of what art is like and what art is, and the grandiose history of art and painting.

PK: *Where did you go in Europe?*

ER: I went to Paris, which I really liked.

PK: *Not the Louvre, but Paris.*

ER: Yes, Paris. I love that lifestyle. Then I went to Spain. I got a real good flavor of Spain. I saw people there and I took a lot of photographs.

PK: *Were you by yourself?*

ER: Yes. I was with my brother for part of the time, my mother even came there for part of the time, but I was by myself for most of the time. I went to Italy for a while. Then I went to Greece, all the way through Yugoslavia, to Austria, to Vienna, and then came back through Germany and met up with my cousin.

PK: *Right, the stamp guy.*

ER: Yes, I met up with Herbie.

PK: *Did you know people to visit along the way, or were you pretty much on your own?*

ER: No, I didn't. We just traveled along. I saw some high nightlife, went to the Cannes Film Festival, and just sort of made it along on very little money.

PK: *Did you do it as an art pilgrimage or a life experience?*

ER: It was a life experience that I definitely was ready for. I knew that I wanted to go to Europe. That was an important factor in my life. I had no interest in any sort of archival aspect, no scholarly interest in art whatsoever. As a matter of fact, I just turned away from that. I had some curiosities along the way—you can't escape it, it's just everywhere. I saw these wood carvings—I think the artist's name was Riemenschneider. He carved all the figures in this church in Germany. That was a "whew!" Boy, I walked out of there, and the only thing I could think was, "Carving wood . . . how can I use that? Can I carve some wood? No, I can't carve any wood—forget that!"

PK: *Was there anything that did really impress you among the great monuments of Europe, from an artistic standpoint?*

ER: Yes, only one thing. It was at the most unlikely place, and that was the British War Museum. I saw this sculpture by an artist named Bertelli. He's a modern sculptor and he did this head, a bust of Mussolini. It was about eighteen inches high and it was as if you would take a piece of black clay and put it on a potter's wheel, and just take your finger and go "zzzzzzzt" to make this man's profile. So you've got a totally round thing—his nose would go all around and his chin would go all around—and you saw perfect two profiles. From any point of view you've got a profile. It was black in color and shiny, about eighteen or twenty inches high. I was just stunned by that work of art, and it just happened by accident. I got a photograph of it and everything. That had more effect on me than almost anything.

At the museum they also had little miniatures of ambulances, and they had British airplanes there. You could go upstairs and go through a file of all these war pictures, a photographic library of war pictures.

PK: *What about the early Modernism you saw in Europe?*

ER: I read some Apollinaire poems, and saw some of the things Picasso did. I wasn't as interested in Picasso as I was in Apollinaire and maybe Francis Picabia, Duchamp, Man Ray. When I was in Paris I got this feeling of what it would be like to live there in the twenties. The total art production that came from this period was overwhelming. I'd run into some of that in galleries. I went to a lot of galleries in Paris, and I'd occasionally run into some new work that I liked, but mainly it was like dipping back into history. That was my history lesson—not back to the Renaissance, not back to ages of old. It was more like recent history, the twentieth century. I was more curious about that. Every so often I'd run across a Jasper Johns painting there, which was stunning. Also I saw a Rauschenberg show.

PK: In Paris?

ER: "Combines" at a gallery in Paris. I guess in 1961 he was already on his way, making shows. That was the only art to me. The Europeans weren't doing anything, there was no art in Germany, no art in Italy. There was no art anywhere except in America. It was all happening in New York and Los Angeles.

PK: What about in England? By that time British Pop Art had emerged.

ER: Richard Hamilton?

PK: Exactly. Did you have the opportunity to see any of their work in England?

ER: I didn't know their work at all. When I was in England it was such a cold place. I was disappointed because it was not like Charles Dickens.

PK: That's what you were looking for?

ER: That's what I was looking for. I went all over England, Scotland and Ireland. Ireland was funny. I got to see the little town where my mother's folks came from.

PK: No contact with the British Pop Art scene?

ER: None whatsoever. When I was in England I was cold, and I was really low on money and all I could think about was getting back to France. I was going back to France, and I was going to stay there for a couple of weeks and then go back to America. The second I hit French soil I just felt like I was at home. I didn't speak French, didn't speak any language except English. I found out right away that you don't have to. It's helpful to know a few words like numbers. The food was so good. There was something there that just made life easy. They took life

---

121

Bicycle sign, Switzerland, 1961. Photo: Ed Ruscha.

Ed Ruscha, *Bicycle Sign*. 1961. Oil on paper, 12⅞ × 9¾″. Photograph shows work before signature. Courtesy Ed Ruscha.

easy. In England it was all cold, gray and all that. Now it's totally different. I feel just the opposite; I got to like England better. Now I know a lot of people in England and most of the artists in England are friends, so I began to see how American they are. They're more American than we are.

PK: Let me ask you about one more artist you probably saw in France, Fernand Léger. Was there any interest there at all?

ER: No. Well, historically now I can go back and look at his work and I see that there's a real trademark; there is a mark of history in his work. I appreciate it more than I am excited about it. I would be more excited maybe about Stuart Davis, who has some of the same blendings, I guess, as Léger does. I liked what he looked like better than his paintings, with these round glasses, dark glasses.

PK: Did you make art in Europe?

ER: Not very much. I painted some little pictures, sort of impasto oil painting on paper that I soaked in linseed oil, so that they looked semi-translucent, except where the paint is. They were paintings of words.

PK: Those would be some of the earliest paintings of words?

ER: Yes, some of the earliest of what I consider my work after I got to be a serious artist.

PK: Had you been doing any of that before you left?

ER: I'd done some things like that before I left. And in school I'd done some things. I did a few homages to Jasper Johns. I did a map on a canvas, where I stretched a map across the canvas and then painted the bottom half blue. I did some things like that which shocked me. I wanted to do some art that shocked me. It developed into a little personal travel kit which I took along with me.

PK: Not related to your experience in Europe, I expect.

ER: No, I wouldn't say that completely, because some of the things in Europe became part of my work. Some of the street iconography, like a round sign with the motif of a bicycle on it, meaning bicycle path. That was, "Whew!" So I painted a picture of that. I would combine some photographs that I had taken and do a collage. I was into the syntax of doing collage and oil paint and ink. I did little things that were about 11 × 14 or 8 × 10, something like that. I guess in Paris was when I did most of those things. I did about ten of those.

PK: You just set up in a hotel.

ER: Yes, and was quite into what I was doing. I'd wander around during the day, and walk, walk, walk. Boy, I did more walking than I ever did in my life.

PK: Did you get lonesome?

ER: No, never got lonesome.

PK: Did you meet people at all?

ER: Yes, I met people who are still friends of mine. A guy in San Francisco named Ed Zak. He's got a studio up there. I met him and a few other people, but he's the only one I still stay in contact with. It was a real rich time in my life. I was in Paris for about two months. Then, coming back [to New York], I went to see Leo Castelli and I made a point of going to all the galleries. I was really intrigued by the whole thing.

PK: What about New York? We can't ignore that.

ER: Oh boy, my first visit to New York was a total shock. I was thrown back by the coldness of it. I didn't know anybody there. I remember I was just overwhelmed because of the number of people there and the impersonality of the whole place. I didn't like it very much.

PK: How long did you stay?

ER: Oh, a couple of weeks.

PK: Did you spend time coming and going, on your way to Europe, and then back again?

ER: Yes. Coming back I was there for just a short while, but I stayed with some people I knew from Oklahoma. That was, like, nine months later. I got a better feeling for it then. Actually, I met Leo Castelli then and showed him some work

———

that I had done in Europe—this was in 1961. He was really interested. Then I met Ivan Karp, Castelli's assistant at the time.

PK: You just went and introduced yourself?

ER: Yes. I took my things in. I had some little things on paper that I did in Europe.

PK: Did Castelli promise to take anything?

ER: No, he just said, "I really like your work." From then on he knew my work. We didn't actually do anything until about ten years later, in 1970. But Ivan was a real funny character, a real joker. He said, "Hey, come on back in the back room. Let me show you this stuff I've got back here." I went back and there was a Roy Lichtenstein painting of a tennis shoe, and it just floored me. That was my first knowledge of what was the beginning of Pop Art.

PK: You were impressed.

ER: I was very impressed with his things. It was something that he was like holding back in the closet, and didn't want to show too many people this work. But he thought I'd get a kick out of it, which I did. It was completely aggravating and inspirational.

PK: Did you go to the Museum of Modern Art or the Metropolitan?

ER: Yes, that's exactly what I did. Filling in.

PK: What about the Museum of Modern Art?

ER: I guess I was in awe of that because it had more of a direct relation to me and my feelings about things than, say, the Whitney did. I was not as connected to the Whitney, because they were more interested in traditional painters like John Sloan and maybe Wyeth and Winslow Homer. They showed those kind of artists. Charles Sheeler—I didn't find him interesting at all. I found Walker Evans interesting. Walker Evans was great. People say, "Well, Hopper, he didn't influence you?" and I say, "No, Hopper had no influence on me whatsoever." I've almost always stood back and asked myself, well, why didn't they have an influence on me? But they didn't. I was not repulsed. I was left flat by their work, actually. If I'm really repulsed by someone I might be influenced by him.

PK: Do you still feel that way, or over the years have you developed a new way of looking at, let's say, Hopper?

ER: Yes, I went to Hopper's opening. I was still a bit flat with him, but I could see that there was some connection there. I could see his whole lifestyle, and then I compared that to the Picasso show. I found him very serious and very straight and very firm in his way of being an artist, and almost unwavering all the way down the line. There's nothing crazy about him at all, nothing eccentric.

PK: He had a strong position.

ER: Oh yes, he had a strong position. It's just that I never spoke his language. But some of his paintings are really nice. I remember one thing, another artist who influenced me considerably with one work of art. His name is Johannes Baargeld. He operated back in the '20s, and I don't know whether he was European or American. I don't know his history, except that the Museum of Modern Art owned a drawing of his which I saw once in reproduction, in a book. It was called *Beetles,* I think. It was a pen and ink drawing. It looked like a diagram from the air—an aerial view, almost like a parking diagram. It had five or six beetles, walking along a line, almost like a racecourse. One of them was veering off to the side, and there were some little ink splotches. I just went and inquired about it at the desk. They took me down in the basement, where they had it stored, and showed me that drawing. I was impressed. That was another thing that I was after when I went to New York: I wanted to see that particular work. I think the work was done around 1920 or so. I think he was associated with the Dadaists. That's one of the reasons I went to the Modern.

PK: Were you let down when you saw the work?

ER: No, no, I loved seeing it in the raw. There was something about the personal aspect of seeing something, actually holding it in your hands, so to speak.

———

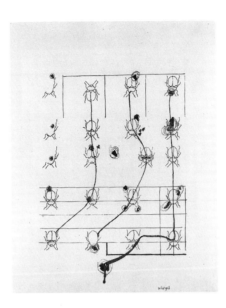

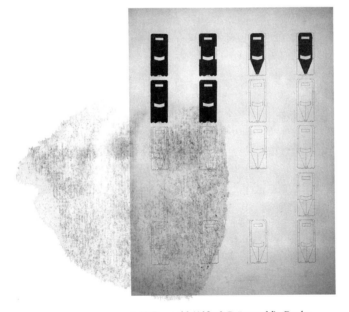

J. T. Baargeld (Alfred Grünewald), *Beetles*.
1920. Pen and ink on tissue paper, 11½ × 9⅛″
(29.2 × 23.2 cm). The Museum of Modern
Art, New York. Purchase. Photograph © 2001
The Museum of Modern Art, New York.

Ed Ruscha, *Parking Lines*. 1961. Oil, ink, and
pencil on canvas. 65¾ × 48½″. Photo courtesy
Ed Ruscha.

PK: Apparently your experience in New York wasn't such that you felt it necessary to relocate there which, of course, has happened increasingly with California artists.

ER: Yes, it's like a standard move.

PK: Why was that then, do you suppose? It seems that you felt you could very successfully and satisfactorily carry on your career right here in L.A.

ER: I thought so. I didn't look at it on a vocational level, as to whether I could, say, get a gallery and make a better living there. Well, I'm sure that I could have, but also I would have been chewed up by the whole machine.

PK: It worked out all right.

ER: Yes, I'd say so, in the sense that I was able to see New York as an onlooker. I consequently made a lot of friends among artists back there. I've been lucky enough to maintain myself out here. That's what I'm after, a long shelf life.

PK: What was the attraction for you to come back to Los Angeles from New York? You apparently then viewed L.A. as your working place.

ER: Yes, I did. I developed a real closeness to the place. It has to do with the movies, it has to do with palm trees, it has to do with a collage in your mind of what this place is all about. I had developed roots here that I couldn't resist coming back to. There was a definite art community here that I was becoming a part of, and so I was just drawn back here. It was not like I was a destitute person and had to find some new roots; I had roots here. Maybe a couple of times I was tempted to move off and go back to New York because of the big apple side of it, but I have a suspicion that my work would have been chewed up and spit out. You see, the paintings I was doing at the time were being overlooked by the people in power who are all centered in New York; they were being overlooked by those people in favor of other artists who were being included. So I wasn't really even a Pop artist; I wasn't really even a Conceptual artist. I was nothing until gradually; later, later, later. I'm real surprised that I've been able to keep this thing up this long, I'll tell you.

PK: So you did come back to L.A. then, in 1961.

ER: Yes, I came back in 1961.

PK: Did you then find new digs?

ER: Yes, I came here and I found a place over in Highland Park. I kept in close contact with Joe Goode and Jerry McMillan, Pat Blackwell, and my other friends that I had here. We were all painting, we were all in a limbo land between school and "what are we going to do." When I was traveling in Europe, Henry Hopkins was having the *War Babies* show,[16] and that consisted of Ronny Miyashiro who was a student at Chouinard at the time, Larry Bell, and Eddie Bereal and Joe Goode. Do you remember the *War Babies* poster?

PK: I've seen it, I think.

ER: There were four guys sitting around a table. Ronny Miyashiro, Oriental, was eating rice with chopsticks. Joe was Catholic—he was eating fish. Larry Bell was Jewish—he was eating a bagel. Eddie Bereal was black—he was eating watermelon. It's a great picture, and it was a milestone in what was going on at that time.

PK: Was that show on when you came back?

ER: They just took it down when I came back. But I saw a lot of the work. I knew what they had put in it.

PK: Was that at Ferus?

ER: No, it was at a place called the Huysman Gallery. It was right across the street from Ferus on La Cienega. I think they were paying $100 a month rent, and they were almost going out of business, it was so expensive.

PK: This was at a time when Henry Hopkins and Walter Hopps were so actively trying to generate interest in new art and educate the community. Did you know Walter and Henry at that time?

ER: Yes. Actually I knew Henry before. I met Henry through Joe because Joe was right on the scene, really involved with it. Henry ended up buying some work from Joe, and buying some work from me one time, and we used to go down to the L.A. County Museum in Exposition Park. Henry would buy us lunch and give us a check for ten dollars and then we'd come back a month later and do the same thing, another lunch, another ten dollars. So we had a good time and Henry was deeply involved with everything that was going on. At the same time he was not a part of it—the same way with Walter Hopps. Well, Walter was maybe more buddies with the artists. Henry was a scholar, but he knew exactly what was happening and gave due respect to everybody who was operating at that time.

PK: Well, here you were, back again, and you settled in Highland Park.

ER: So I lived in Highland Park. Before I left, I was kind of known in this new generation of artists that was springing up—Larry Bell, Ronnie Miyashiro was another one, Eddie Bereal—who's still right here, he teaches at Irvine—and myself and Joe. So then Joe brought Walter—we called him "Chico" at that time—over to my studio one time, and then Chico brought Irving Blum over and Irving brought Henry Geldzahler over and I sold him a painting for fifty dollars. Henry [Hopkins] bought this painting that I did in school. It was called *Sweetwater* [1959]. It was a real ambitious Abstract Expressionist painting on the top half, and on the bottom half it said "Sweetwater" in old traditional letters.

PK: That's an historical piece. Is that going to be in the San Francisco Museum of Modern Art show?[17]

ER: No, unfortunately, that painting met its demise.

PK: How?

ER: Well, Henry taught art history at UCLA. He took the painting and stuffed it back in the racks there somewhere, and one of the teachers there—I think it was Jan Stussy—gave that painting to a student and said, "Go ahead and use that for a canvas, paint on it." Henry didn't tell me about this painting until a few years later. I said, "Well, God, are you sure you can't get somebody to clean it off?" He said, "No."

PK: Henry must have been just devastated.

ER: Well, yes. He was upset. I've got a black and white photo of it someplace.

———

PK: Wasn't that vicious on Jan's part?

ER: Oh God, I don't know. I don't really know the details on that. I wanted to get to the bottom of it, just like I want to get to the bottom of this attack on my painting. A couple of other things happened like that. A lot of those people who've taught at UCLA were down on my art, down on Joe's art, but now they've learned to respect us and even imitate us in a lot of instances.

PK: You taught at UCLA for one session.

ER: Yes, 1969–70.

PK: So obviously whatever antagonism existed earlier was softening.

ER: Oh yes. But during my teaching up there, I just kept wishing I was back in my studio working. I felt like I didn't have enough to say to students.

PK: You don't think of yourself, then, as a teacher?

ER: No, I don't. I do believe some people have good teaching inclinations, but not me. I really don't know what to tell people. I think there's too much of a gap between what they think you are, as you're telling them, and what the actual message is that you're to get over to them.

PK: This is probably 1962?

ER: This is 1961–62, 1962 probably.

PK: This was a very important time right then. The Ferus Gallery was in full swing, and you were familiar with it and were beginning to meet some of the Ferus people. What about Edward Kienholz?

ER: I never really knew Kienholz. He seemed to be like a peripheral figure, but he was the father of the whole thing.

PK: You didn't go to Barney's Beanery and hang out with him?

ER: Yes, but I mainly met Billy Al Bengston and Bob Irwin and Kenny Price and John Altoon. Those were the people that I really knew. I didn't know Kienholz until eight or ten years later. I never saw Kienholz. He was always gone somewhere—down in Idaho. My main connections were Billy Al, Larry Bell, Bob Irwin. Craig Kauffman was there, peripherally. Ed Moses came in there, John Altoon and people who I knew mostly from openings, and then we'd all hang out at Barney's. That got to be a regular scene.

PK: It sounds like fun. I'm sorry I missed that.

ER: Oh it was, it definitely was. It was like lifeblood. It was great.

PK: So all the talk about Los Angeles having no sense of community and no meeting place, at least at that time—

ER: That's false. No, there was definitely that. Barney's was the only place we really met, a beer-drinking place. We'd have parties and Irving was right in there too, he was part of it.

PK: You mentioned before that that Joe Goode was a good friend and had a much more focused career objective than you did. You were, perhaps, more feeling your way, but it was Joe and your other friends who pointed a direction for you.

ER: I think so. Joe, in the beginning, had more troubles than I did. He was married and had a kid and a lot of miserable stuff.

PK: When was this?

ER: This was like 1962–63. Joe developed a lot of disgust for a certain faction of the art world whom he felt was not on his side. I was always inspired by this for some crazy reason. I watched him just be vindictive in many instances. So Joe adopted a very salty attitude towards the art world. I began to admire him for this.

PK: It doesn't exactly sound in character from what I know of you.

ER: Yes, but I did see Joe's side of things. He would, because of his nature, either hate someone or love someone.

PK: Would these be dealers or other artists?

———

133

ER: It could be dealers, artists, museum curators. A few shall go unnamed. But I watched Joe have certain troubles with the art world which I suppose I got inspired by. Maybe I didn't have as many problems as Joe did in coming along in the art world. He was an example to me all the way through. I've known Joe for a long time. I knew him in Catholic school, in first grade. Joe has always been the perennial altar boy with the black eye. It's gotten into all of his work, and the way he does things. It was a renegade stance that Joe took which inspired me. Not in the colors he used, not in the way he put things on the canvas, although his own personal vision and the way he makes his art are almost separate from him as a character. As a character he really inspired me to deal with the art world. For instance, if he's wronged by someone, I'd know about it right away because we'd have this chat. We'd always have chit chat together. We were always very candid with one another about what's going on in the art world, and injustices here and injustices there, and good things that happened. His stance on things made me stronger. He was always indignant about the way things happened. If he was wronged, he let the person know it. He was a fairly vocal person. I guess lifestyle is what it comes down to. He conducted himself as an artist.

PK: *In other words, he provided an example to you of how to relate to the art world?*

ER: The establishment and the art world, yes.

PK: *In practice, how did this affect your behavior, your relationships?*

ER: Well, it gave me more sense of responsibility—not so much responsibility, but a sense of pride. And it was Joe, along with a lot of other people—Billy Al Bengston and Larry Bell and Ken Price and Ed Moses—all the people that I grew up with—who helped me see that we're almost in a minority, as artists. We're, in a sense, a lower class of people, and looked upon as a lower class of people.

PK: *Did you guys perceive it that way at the time?*

ER: It seemed like we had our opposition. It wasn't only just from the general public, who we didn't care that much about, but it was in the art world itself. It was in gallery dealers, it was in museum people—not that we had hard knocks, because we had a lot of advantages, too.

PK: But you felt that, in this community at least, the artist was treated like a second-class citizen.

ER: In many senses; such as when it comes to issues surrounding the protection of our work, people using our work and compensating us for it. Artists have always been forced to represent themselves in cases like this. We don't have ASCAP, we don't have a union—we're really not protected. So if we do get into some contractual sort of thing, luckily we have a few attorneys around town who are eager to help artists in their curious positions.

PK: There's one attorney who has worked so closely with artists.

ER: Well, Jack Quinn might be one, but Monroe Price has taken it on as a cause. The artists' compensation for their work, and royalty payments.

PK: Did you have access to this kind of legal advice and so forth in those years?

ER: I did, but it was so sketchy. We were all interested in making our art, and not how we could possibly get ripped off by it.

PK: What about the dealers in town? There wasn't a great commercial establishment here as one would find in New York.

ER: No, but it was definitely the beginning. There were certain people around who made touch between the artists and the people who buy work, and they did it in good style. Walter Hopps and Henry Hopkins, and you have to name several people who began the galleries, like Ed Kienholz and Irving Blum and Nick Wilder and Rolf Nelson. People with the museum staff that really helped us out.

PK: When did Riko Mizuno[18] come on the scene?

ER: Later, I think.

PK: I've always understood that she was enormously supportive of other artists.

———

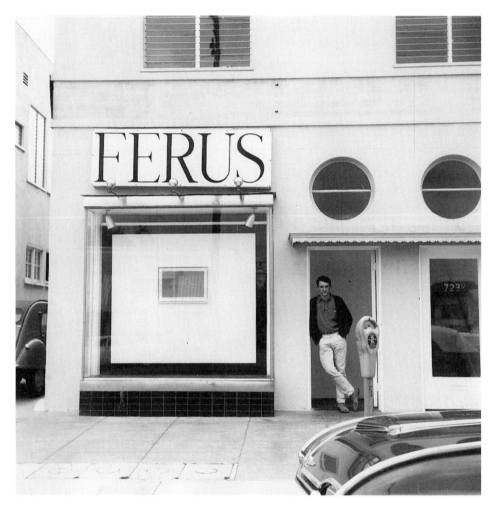

The artist in front of the Ferus Gallery, May 1963. Photo: Unknown. Courtesy Ed Ruscha.

ER: Oh yes.

PK: Basically you don't have strong complaints about the way you and your friends and other artists were handled by these several dealers in town.

ER: Oh, we had rows.

PK: But you felt that you were fighting the same good fight. Where is the great problem? Was it more with the museums?

ER: One of the problems with me was that I was never a businessman. But then, in a second sense, I was always very careful about the work that I sent out of my studio. Some artists were not, and for that reason they created their own trouble. In other words, a dealer would come by and the artist would say, "Take twenty works," various sizes. Then a year later the artist is running to punch the guy in the face because there's no money for it and the works are gone. Well, you have to sit down and sign a piece of paper.

PK: Did Ferus operate that way? That was pretty hang loose.

ER: Oh, it was very loose.

PK: I'm not suggesting that any of them were trying to rip off the artist, but it appears that perhaps the records weren't kept very well.

ER: Oh, there were some mild or minor misunderstandings. Occasionally there would be an outburst of indignancy between artists. Joe got into several things with dealers. I think Joe probably had a basic distrust for the support system. I have some of that myself.

PK: Still?

ER: Yes, absolutely. There's some basic idea about museums that makes me wonder what they're doing with my work. I'm trying to understand the real purpose for a museum from time to time. So I adopt a wait-and-see attitude about institutions who are going to talk about art. I'm not saying that I know the answer about where art should end up. But Joe might chew the head off some collector

137

who had just bought a painting of his because he didn't think that the person put his work in the right spot.

PK: So, your first contact with the Ferus group was after you returned from Europe. What happened during that time? Pop Art had been introduced out here, earlier in 1962, at the Ferus Gallery. I guess Irving Blum gets the credit for the Warhol show.

ER: Yes, Irving had the first Warhol show in 1962. He was selling these paintings for fifty dollars apiece. I remember definitely liking him. I felt a great kinship with Andy and Roy Lichtenstein because it was like a logical departure from the kind of painting that was happening at the time. This is outside of the characters themselves and the personalities themselves. But the work was a real departure, a logical departure from Abstract Expressionism, if there is such a thing as a style cycle, and I believe there is. Walter had this show at the Pasadena Museum called *New Painting of Common Objects*.

PK: That was in September 1962.

ER: That was the first show of Pop Art. Walter had my painting in the show, and Irving came along and sold one of the paintings in it. That was my first painting that I sold. That was a great feeling.

PK: Except for the one that you sold to Henry. Would you mark the Pasadena show, along with the Warhol show, as an introduction of what became known as Pop Art?

ER: Well, yes, historically it is. Walter's was the first of any organized show of that kind of work. Walter just chose to call it *New Painting of Common Objects*. I thought that was really good, the way he defined it as the "New Painting of Common Objects." I even liked the way he said it, just his words coming out of his mouth. He had a way of nailing a subject down. So, the Pasadena Art Museum is where I really had my first exposure. It meant a lot to me, and I could see that that was a real jewel of a place. It had its own private interest. Even artists as far away as Europe, artists from New York—everybody knew that the Pasadena Art Museum was a hot thing. It really was. It's only as good as its directors; they're the people behind it. They always made the best decisions and

---

consequently had the most vital shows there. I began to perceive that. Then the L.A. County Museum was down in Exposition Park, and they seemed to show some interest in contemporary art. Mainly I just worked. I had a studio that was about 500 square feet that I lived and worked in.

PK: Where was that?

ER: Glassell Park, between Glendale and Silver Lake.

PK: You were living alone at that time?

ER: Yes.

PK: It was your own studio, you weren't sharing a studio?

ER: Joe was living in Pasadena at that time in Walter Hopps's house. He had his studio there. There was one period when I moved to Pasadena. I had a studio at 60 West Colorado Boulevard that was about 20,000 square feet.

PK: When was that?

ER: 1962–63. I was there for one month. I couldn't take it, the room was too big for me. My paintings looked like postage stamps. They were so tiny. I couldn't believe it; it just disoriented me completely.

PK: You must have been doing fairly well at that point to afford that space.

ER: No, it was fifty dollars a month. For 20,000 square feet that's not bad. But I had to move out. The idea was that I had to move out immediately. Also, from Christmas to the sixth of January I had to give up the studio because people would use it as a viewing point for the Rose Parade.

PK: No wonder the rent was so cheap. Where did you go from there?

ER: From there I went to Echo Park. I had a studio there for probably a year or two. Then I went back to Eagle Rock. There was a little community out there. I had a studio out there for about two years.

PK: Were there other artists in the area? There must have been reasons for transferring.

———

The artist's studio, 3327 Division Street, Los Angeles, 1961. Against wall, beginning of *Ace* (1961. Oil on canvas, 72 × 67″) painting. Photo: Ed Ruscha.

The artist's studio, 2215 Echo Park Avenue, Los Angeles, 1963. On wall, *Smash* (1963. Oil on canvas, 72 × 67″).
Photo: Ed Ruscha.

ER: Jerry McMillan had a studio not too far from me in Eagle Rock. But no artist lived around me in Echo Park. Mason Williams, my friend, came and lived over there for a while in Echo Park. Then, in 1965, I moved into this place here.

PK When were you married?

ER: I got married in 1967. I had a son in 1968, and lived in Echo Park and Laurel Canyon. Mostly Laurel Canyon.

PK: Keeping this space as your studio.

ER: Oh, yes, I always had this place as my studio. I did all my work here, and didn't really work at home. Only on a few occasions was I able to. I couldn't mix the domestic life and the free-form life, I just couldn't. They're sort of difficult to mix. I just couldn't work, I can't work with a kid over me. Sometimes I think I can. I like to have my boy come over here, and he sits down and draws and I encourage him to do that. But it seems like, no matter what, you just owe your attention to a child if he's going to be around. If you think you're not giving him attention, you still are, your mind is preoccupied with it. So when he's around me, I can't really get that much work done.

PK: Going back to the '60s, the next year [1963], there was a show that Lawrence Alloway put together, called Six Painters and the Object, *that was in London. When the show came here to the Los Angeles County Museum, he had a section called* Six More, *and you were included in that. So by that time you were considered part of the Pop phenomenon.*

ER: Yes, I guess, at that time. As maybe a second wave or something. I remember having four or five good-sized paintings in there. I was really happy with that show.

PK: I think Wayne Thiebaud was in that show.

ER: Mel Ramos might have been in there, and maybe Phillip Hefferton.

PK: So, at least in the eyes of one or two critics, there was already then a Pop school out on the West Coast, and you were part of it?

ER: Yes. Billy was marginally considered a Pop artist. Billy did some great paintings earlier, these motorcycle paintings. I remember seeing an exhibit of that, and people were coming out of there saying, "God, I just think they're bad illustrations." Of course, that ended up being their strength. He was doing that imagery literally before the Pop artists, or at the same time, but oblivious and quite separate from the other Pop artists. But they gave him the label of Pop Art too, just like they did Joe. Joe had milk bottles in his work, so he was a Pop artist. It was an easy term to fling around.

PK: I would like to read a brief statement that Lawrence Alloway made in connection with the activities of the independent group[19] in England—part of the Institute of Contemporary Art—which is credited for first focusing on attitudes that then became defined as Pop. Alloway writes in Lucy Lippard's book on Pop Art:

> *We discovered that we had in common a vernacular culture that persisted beyond any special interest or skills in art, architecture, design or art criticism that any of us might possess. The area of contact was mass produced urban culture: movies, advertising, science fiction, Pop music. We felt none of the dislike of commercial culture standard among most intellectuals, but accepted it as a fact, discussed it in detail and consumed it enthusiastically. One result of our discussions was to take Pop culture out of the realm of "escapism," "sheer entertainment," "relaxation" and to treat it with the seriousness of art. These interests put us in opposition both to the supporters of indigenous folk art and to anti-American opinion in Britain.*
>
> *Hollywood, Detroit, and Madison Avenue were, in terms of our interests, producing the best popular culture. Thus, expendable art was proposed as no less serious than permanent art. . . .[20]*

Do you feel what Alloway said there reflects your own view?

ER: I've always felt that there have always been Pop artists in all ages. The term Pop Art made me nervous and ambivalent. I did not understand my position in this new so-called movement which was defined by—was it Richard Hamilton?

PK: I think Alloway gets credit for the term.

ER: It could be. I originally did not know about this term "Pop Art" in the "art phenomenon" sense of it until later. For me, it was Walter Hopps who first made a definition of the kind of art that was being produced at that time. He used the term "New Painting of Common Objects," which actually goes beyond painting. It was culture. It was so many other modes of making art. "Pop Art" was only a popularized, public catchword which was used and misunderstood by many people. If you speak of "Pop Art"—meaning the artists who are producing paintings, drawings that had to do with common objects—that's one thing. But on a public level, I think that "Pop Art" was never truly understood. It was meant to encompass movies; it was meant to encompass the car culture; it was meant to include all these things that had nothing to do with the museum-type of art. So there was a broad usage of it; and there was a defined, more refined usage of it, too.

I never truly understood whether I was a member of this movement or not. On the surface I was, because I used popular imagery. I used imagery from commercial sources that was not usually meant to be cloudy and poetic and sensitive. I used subjects that came from a less thoughtful side of life, a more decadent side of life, something that was not born out of a true poetic background.

PK: Would you say then that your notion of "Pop" is really an openness to life experience, to the environment in all of its manifestations?

ER: Well, you're saying that I'm using "Pop Art" as a general term. I think that the so-called Concept artists are also Pop artists, in a way. A Pop artist can be anyone who has thrown over a recent set of values. I speak of artists who make paintings, drawings, sculpture—that mode of thinking. I wouldn't call filmmakers "Pop" artists, no matter what kind of films they make—with the exception of some artists who have also made films, like Warhol. You could say that this sort of film could come under this category, but commercial films don't. Pop is a throwing over of anything that is considered establishment, I guess. So I see new Pop artists emerge every so often. When this term "Pop Art" first came around,

I was not really included, only because I was tucked away in a different part of the country, I think.

PK: But very early on, strangely enough, artists like Billy Al Bengston, Wayne Thiebaud, Mel Ramos, were all considered Pop artists. It seems to me that the term is a confusing one. One could debate whether Wayne Thiebaud was ever a Pop artist, and I don't know that he would describe himself as such.

ER: He responded to the call within it to explore subjects which were not commonly explored. That made him a Pop artist.

PK: Then it's subject matter that distinguishes Pop artists?

ER: It's simple subject matter.

PK: Do you feel that style is an aspect of Pop Art?

ER: It's a superficial, first-contact reaction, yes. If something looks like the grill of a 1958 Buick, then you could say, yes, that's Pop Art. That would be the simple way of approaching the subject. But there have been Pop artists throughout history. Picasso, all along his career, picked subjects that were known to be taboo, and so might be considered Pop. There are certain established ways to do things. Artists get in a swirl of feeling about their work, and they get trapped into ways of seeing, and then someone else will come along and explore a subject that is unheard of. I think the Pop artists have been probably labeled for that reason— that they picked taboo subject matter.

PK: So within your definition of Pop Art as something that has existed throughout history in different forms and with different artists, could we then include, say, the so-called Ashcan painters in New York in the beginning of this century who turned to the city streets for subject matter?

ER: Yes, absolutely, they're Pop artists. It's about popular culture. All the trash in the streets was part of the popular culture. I don't think we're stretching the meaning of the word, do you? I felt there were artists who would never be considered Pop artists, but who approached their imagery like Pop artists. They worked in series, which I found to be a foreign confrontation as I first approached it, but then I began to envy artists who could work in series. It seemed like the original Pop artists were able to do that. Also, a lot of abstract painters did the same thing. The paintings may have no physical or visual relation to anything in the popular culture; they may be total abstract paintings. But their method of production had to do with the method of production that we use in our popular culture, like manufacturing cars. The notion of mass production was used by more people than just Pop artists.

PK: Under that definition of serial imagery, you would have to include Claude Monet with the series of haystacks, and the series of Rouen Cathedral façade. Would you agree with that?

ER: Yes.

PK: Does serial imagery then come closer to reflecting in art the way we actually live and experience life? When Monet observed the haystacks under different light conditions, he was interested in producing a record of the way we actually see these things over a period of time.

ER: Maybe you mean that Monet gave each of his pictures within this serial imagery tender loving care, whereas you might say Pop artists do not do that; there is a colder, more artificial, mechanical approach to the way the work is done. The Pop artists are more mechanical. Monet may be more individually caring about each one of those things he painted, even though they all use serial imagery.

PK: Do you feel that this capturing of attention to the realities of the way we live is a "Pop" attitude?

ER: I don't know what the "Pop" attitude is. I don't know whether it's meant to be mechanical about things, or whether it's meant to be thoughtful about things. Probably Abstract Expressionism gave reason to the birth of Pop Art, and then later Pop Art maybe began to fizzle, which gave forth to God knows what: Minimalism, Conceptualism, and a number of other isms. Looking at it historically, you can understand why Pop emerged, because there was so much that happened

———

at the turn of the century—the revolution of the camera, for example—which gave birth to a need of this kind of thing.

PK: I gather you feel that indeed Pop Art is in part a response to an earlier revolution, which was Abstract Expressionism. I gather you feel that, in part, the Pop artists were responding to what was then being held up as the correct way to do something.

ER: Yes. I think the tendency is to look at it as though these soldiers—later to be called Pop artists—suddenly marched in and laid waste these old ideas done by the men who now have gray hair. The style cycle continues and continues; there will be other forms of art which keep coming along and the style cycle will keep moving on. But if you think about the paintings that were done in the 1950s, I find them overwhelming, nothing but quality. I think the Abstract Expressionists were great painters. When you go back and look at some of the things that happened in the late '40s and early '50s, it was a very powerful time in art.

PK: Do you see Los Angeles as a peculiarly—or even uniquely—Pop environment, Pop city? Do you feel that your imagery and your work were conditioned by your environment, by Los Angeles?

ER: Without any question. I felt like Los Angeles always will offer things to people—through just the multitude of industries that happens here—that another city could never offer. Just the fact of physically being in this place, traveling around on the streets, and living in this community right here, makes the difference. I could almost have lived anywhere to produce art—but the inspiration came right from this city. I don't think I could have drawn inspiration from another town and had it reflect in my work as directly.

PK: But Pop Art emerged first in England and then in New York. It certainly became very prominent with its manifestations out here in L.A. In these other places that are less dominated by Pop culture, Pop Art had perhaps more of a fine art artificiality than here in California.

ER: I can't argue with that. But even if the English artists were the first to push forth this idea, their ideas nevertheless came directly from Hollywood and Vine and other spots of interest in this city of Los Angeles. The products of Los Angeles have greatly influenced all of those people, the movies and music primarily. Not art—there was no history of art out here. There might be a handful of people who have pushed themselves along as artists, but they have never become identified with the city. Or the city has never become identified with them, at any rate. But the efforts and culture that came out of this Los Angeles, California is what has basically affected the first people who did Pop Art—even, as you say, the English artists. If not Los Angeles, then the culture of New York City and all the ramifications of Madison Avenue have shown to the people of the world what this culture is about.

PK: In the passage I read from Lawrence Alloway, he pointed directly towards Hollywood, Detroit—meaning the automobiles, certainly, but maybe Motown music—and then Madison Avenue—not so much the life of New York City, but advertising. So apparently at a very early stage, these American elements attracted this group in England.

ER: They knew more about the culture than we did. It's a fact. The artists there are more aware of the happenings in America, I think, than we are. Probably because they view it as strangers, and they see the kind of life that they don't have, and see maybe the potential of that life. So I think that those artists seized the potential they saw, and consequently were affected by the things that went on over here, not necessarily from a cultural standpoint. The English painters were not particularly influenced by American painters and paintings, as much as they were by the overall cultural push. I found all of those artists to be engaged by anything American: soap, TV, autos, any subject that was screamed about over here. Those people seemed to know more about it than we did.

PK: There seems to be a fundamental—and I think profound—difference between British interest in American Pop culture, whether it comes from the export form— movies, cars, or whatever—or from the experience of living here; and New York's actual life experience.

ER: We may just be blasé about it. I think that there is one fundamental thing, and that is that artists are attracted to glamour. The American way of life possesses a certain siren voice of some kind, which is glamorous to almost any society. Maybe it's because the English happen to be English-speaking, and they could see our culture much better. They saw it as an ideo-social revolution beyond their style of life. God knows, they're so socially conscious in England anyway, no matter what strata of life they're from. They're so socially conscious—to the point of being boring. They're naturally going to feel the appeal of our glamorous American culture, because it offers an absolute form of escape from those social values that they suffer from and keep telling us about.

PK: I've been told that Los Angeles is something of a Mecca for the British, perhaps more than any other foreign group. Obviously, we can think of one well-known English artist who is very much in residence now, and that's David Hockney. I'm wondering whether it isn't an element of the exotic, a romantic notion that attracts these people; a longing for something else.

ER: The English are so refined—despite all their class troubles and maybe because of all their class troubles—that they have a particularly refined take on the sleazy side of life they find here in California, the decadent side of life. It takes a particular mentality for those people to come here, and another kind of mentality and talent to reflect on it. David Hockney has said some very poignant things about the style of life here in Los Angeles. His work becomes non-national; it becomes a statement from an artist rather than an artist who happens to come from England to live in Los Angeles. When people talk to me about David Hockney's work, I don't necessarily see David's style coming from the fact that he's English and transposed to Los Angeles. I see him as someone who just sees the life here. I don't see him as an Englishman; I see him as an artist. But it is true about English artists, that they see that particular, curious sort of destruction of life. They see the almost biblical frustrations that exist here in Los Angeles, more so than a lot of American artists.

PK: What separates you and your work, in its Pop manifestation, from somebody like David Hockney? Do you feel it's possible that your work—and that of other artists who grew up within this type of culture—was more authentic than that of an expatriate living in L.A.?

ER: No, because my statements about this place called Los Angeles are never self-consciously attendant on the idea of making it specifically a commentary upon Los Angeles. My imagery can come from almost anywhere in America; it's American. The pictorial goings-on in my work are almost always from American sources, and American in subject matter, American in feeling. My work has less to say specifically about this city of Los Angeles, but it's the city that gave all my inspiration to me.

PK: *If, as you say, you don't feel that your work is necessarily tied specifically to place, what is the work about—beyond the specificity of a Hollywood sign, something that is physically located here?*

ER: First of all, I find it curious that people have so quickly identified me with the city of Los Angeles, saying that I have so much to say about this city. There are many other artists who do that. There are many other artists that take their pads and pencils and draw pictures of buildings here in Los Angeles, and in a sense are more local than I am. I think maybe that people feel like I'm local because I've operated as an artist here for so long and survived.

PK: *But I think there's more to it than that. I know it's always difficult to be forced to finally say what your concerns really are in your work. We've agreed that it's not to record or immortalize or illustrate elements you run into in Los Angeles. But these are the images that you use, perhaps randomly. You use them to do what?*

ER: Well, the subject will always go back to things so incredibly, stupidly simple, like the idea of sunset—not only just the sunset, but the word "sunset." I find that the pictorial look of something almost always stays close to the word that represents it, such as "sunset," "desert," "beach," and then you can keep moving on and on. Pretty soon you've pretty well described Los Angeles.

PK: *How do you see words as images?*

ER: I guess I'm a child of communications, and I have always felt attracted to anything that had to do with that phenomenon of people speaking to each other. Maybe that itself becomes synonymous with popular culture in that newspapers, magazines—printing, specifically—have had the most dramatic effect on me.

Printing was it, to me. When I first became attracted to the idea of being an artist, painting was the last method; it was almost an obsolete, archaic form of communication. I found painting to be the least interesting of all those forms of communication. I felt newspapers, magazines, books—words—to be more meaningful than what some damn oil painter was doing. So I suppose it developed itself from that—into the idea of questioning the printed word. Then in questioning, I began to see the printed word, and it took off from there.

PK: But you really do feel that there is an equivalency, in some way, between a word and what the word denotes? You mentioned "sunset." Not everybody would agree that "sunset"—in sound or in appearance—connotes anything other than what our language teaches us that it connotes; e.g., an actual sunset.

ER: Well, isn't it curious that those little squiggles—the way they come about, and the way they form and follow one another and precede one another—go to make up that funny word? If you isolate a word for just a moment and repeat it ten, fifteen times, you can easily drive the meaning from the word and from the sound of the word. I do that a lot with the printed word. I find it curious that I've never wanted to misspell a word.

PK: You've never wanted to misspell one?

ER: I've never wanted to misspell one.

PK: Haven't you ever?

ER: I haven't misspelled one word.

PK: On purpose or accidentally?

ER: Accidentally. I did a drawing called *Chilly Draft* [1974], and I spelled "Chilly" c-h-i-l-i.

PK: But that's an out-and-out pun. Are you interested in the device of punning? In this case, one might say you were creating visual puns.

ER: Puns are, I think, a form of humor which is limiting.

———

151

The artist's studio, 1024 N. Western Avenue, Hollywood, June 1974. Photo: Ed Ruscha.

PK: You're not seeking that.

ER: No, if I was, then I would be restricted by a set of rules that, as an artist, I couldn't possibly answer to for more than two days' time. Say, if I did the word "sunset," then logically I would have a set of rules to make sunset-like colors and sunset-like shapes in spelling this word out. But my concentration is not there; it's in the word itself. I'm not trying to divorce what the word means from what I use it as visually. I'd rather the word be, say, off by itself; and yet at the same time, know that it means that thing out at the beach that you see, the beautiful colors. But as a little warrior, or a little thing to use, it becomes a subject unto itself, and doesn't necessarily have to represent that thing at the beach.

PK: But this hasn't always been the case with you. I seem to remember at one time you used the word "frijoles" made out of beans.

ER: No, the word "adios," in the painting [*Adios,* 1967]. The implication is easy to see but—believe me—unintentional. I've seen other words come back to me like this. People will say, "Oh, you do that because of this," but it's not always that absolute. I'm recalling this statement that Dave Hickey made about a Standard Station painting [*Standard Station, Amarillo, Texas,* 1963] that I made, and then another painting that I did of a restaurant on La Cienega, called *Norm's La Cienega on Fire* [1964; destroyed]. He saw those two paintings as making the same sort of statement, like standard is also a "Norm"—normal. The strain of that is totally unintentional to me but, nevertheless, it makes me wonder about my intentions at the time. Maybe there was some inexplicable, invisible strain which goes through me which makes me put things down as I do. Obviously I had little or no intention of, say, glorifying the Standard Oil Company when I painted a picture of a gas station. I had nothing further from my mind.

To go back to that question, I think that the artist doesn't always know what he intends to be saying. I know myself that I work on a system of rough impressions of things and incomplete sputterings. Some of my work—whether it's considered finished or not—might be actually sputterings and incomplete, although maybe coherent. It might be incomplete thoughts about a particular thing. The artist has to open his work to the interpretation of the public, and the public's reaction is part of the work of art. Although I don't feel as though I'm trying to use the word "standard" in my Standard Station painting to describe something that is ordinary and standard, the implication is still there, and I didn't see it until the painting was completed. It could have been "Mobil," could have been "Shell"; but no, it was "Standard." I guess that there's some deep-rooted reason for my choice of that, a reason I don't even care to investigate. It's just immediate subject usage for me, it's like snipping and being able to use subject matter as a way of making art.

PK: What about food for thought, food for art? The series of drawings, like some that are reproduced in Guacamole Airlines *[Harry N. Abrams, 1980], where you use these peculiar materials in the drawings?*

ER: The first work that I did involving vegetable matter and organic materials came out of a frustration with materials. I wanted to expand my ideas about materials and the value they have. I was concerned with the concept of staining something, rather than applying a film or coat or skin of paint on a canvas. I started looking at ideas as though they were stains, rather than skin. I had to open my eyes to all kinds of stains. It falls into categories of vegetable things, vegetable matter, liquids that come from them and get put onto paper. So *Stains*—it was the first book I did. It was a folio of various kinds of stains, one on each sheet, and then from there it spun off into a series of silkscreen prints, called *News, Mews, Pews, Brews, Stews & Dues.* Then I did a series of paintings using fragments of thoughts, incomplete sentences. Like I did a painting called *Various Cruelties* [1974]. Where it came from, who knows? It was just a spark that came to me in one way or another. I used backgrounds of taffeta and silk, rayon, and those kinds of materials and just painted these materials on with a brush.

PK: How do you get the medium?

ER: Oh, just by crushing them up with a mortar and pestle.

PK: Like you're making pesto or something.

ER: Yes, the very same thing. There was no scholarly concern with it about lasta-bility or preservation. Of course, I want it to last, but if they don't it will be a product of my ignorance. They'll throw me in jail for vice, inherent vice.

PK: *You ought to do something called* Inherent Vice. *Probably you already have. So that's the origin of the works done with food?*

ER: I was not mystically directed by any great spirit from up above to move in that direction. Except that I felt it was a short-term playground for me to investigate.

PK: *What did you learn?*

ER: Well, I learned a lot just working with the materials. I learned that cer-tain things wouldn't work. I didn't want things to chip and fall off, or bleed and do other things. I had a loose set of rules for myself when I used those ma-terials. They also made rather beautiful pictures sometimes. I liked the way all of the stuff would sweep together, and the lettuce would end up drying out, and leave little flies behind it. Each material had its own peculiarities that I began to like. I gradually just grew away from it, so there's no more room out there for me to do it.

PK: *What years were you working on these?*

ER: It started in 1969 and went on all the way up through last year. But not ex-clusively; I had to break my time to do other things.

PK: *What about the gunpowder thing? It sounds to me like it's part of the same interest.*

ER: Yes. But I had misgivings about that afterwards because people expected a performance stunt or something: that these works on the wall would catch on fire or deteriorate or something. That was not the gist behind it at all. I soaked some gunpowder in water once, and I saw it separated all the salt out of it. I just did it as an experiment. The gunpowder itself is in granules. I could see it would make a good choice of materials; it could actually impregnate on paper. You could use it almost like charcoal—which it is, it's part charcoal—so then what I do is I'm removing the salt from it. It became a material that I could correct; mistakes could be corrected. The imagery is pretty much the same as with charcoal. I can't look at charcoal and tell the difference between it and gunpowder.

PK: How do you apply it, with a brush?

ER: No, just with a sponge. Rub-a-dub style with a piece of cotton. It was a more fluid and a faster medium than charcoal or graphite. Graphite was much more laborious, but it has a different feel altogether, a different appearance. It has a smoother appearance than either gunpowder or charcoal. It's much more difficult and time-consuming to produce things with graphite, because it's so slimy and so apt to make mistakes and streaks and things that I didn't want in the drawings. So gunpowder was simple, it was easy to get going. It became a fluid medium for that reason.

PK: Have you ever heard of anybody else doing that?

ER: I'm sure someone has done it somewhere, somehow. Natural dyes have been used for centuries for various tintings and dyeings. Any material that will make a mark on paper has probably been thought of or used in some form or another throughout history. The nature of my interest wasn't in broadening horizons of artists' materials; that was secondary. I was more interested in the curiosity of all of those things coming together. I painted a number of pictures with egg yolk and egg white—they've been traditional artist materials. And yet I kind of like the impossibility of a selection of words I might use, applied with egg yolk. It just sort of completed a whole cycle of my work.

PK: In some cases, actual words appear in the drawing identifying the materials you used. I'm thinking of Pepto Bismol, for example.[21] What are the words there?

ER: "Pepto Bismol, Made in U.S.A." But there's no pun or suggestion that Pepto Bismol has anything to do with the United States. If there is an amusing side issue that people would want to create, then that's in the viewer's eyes; it's not in mine, really. Because as I was doing those drawings in a series, it just seemed like the material would go with any idea I had. So I was working this way

---

and pouring the stuff into this general soup that I was mixing and stirring. The materials were not in any way selected to represent the words that were there. They were not embellishing the words, and there was no pun intended.

PK: You've told me before that this is invariably the case with your works. Going back to the painting Adios, *I've managed to carry that around in my mind as the word saying "frijoles"— beans. But as we talk, I see that this kind of play seems never consciously to be your intention.*

ER: Yes, although some of these things are actually done by me unconsciously. Other people have come along and pointed out various things that have surprised me, so then I think that they maybe are really a part of my whole working habit. I also did a painting called *Eye* [1969], e-y-e, using kidney beans. The same thing I did with *Adios*. Now, "eye"? The connection's not there in the same sense. It might be in another case, like *Adios*.

PK: That interests me a great deal because so often the conjunction is just perfect—in ways that perhaps you hadn't even anticipated—but which nonetheless become part of the work of art and the way it's perceived.

ER: Part of what I call my romance with liquids.

PK: Romance with liquids?

ER: Yes. I painted illusionistic liquids, like in *Adios* and *Rancho* [1968] and *Western* [*with Two Marbles*, 1969]. *Mint* [1968], *Eye, Steel* [1969]. There were a lot of paintings I did like that. But some of them were more or less anonymous liquids. They were just liquids, and they didn't mean anything.

PK: Aren't these the very works that led you to prominence?

ER: I would say that the *Standard Station* painting was the most popularly known. Or maybe the *Hollywood* [1968] painting is most known.

PK: Now these came, of course, before the romance with liquids.

ER: Yes, they did. *Hollywood* came about the same time. But the *Standard Station* was the most popularly known, and a few of the earlier works, like *Spam* [*Actual*

Size, 1962] or *Smash* [1963]. Some of those earlier word paintings are the ones that are most known.

PK: Meaning most reproduced.

ER: Most reproduced and most identified with my work.

PK: That's interesting because although, of course, I know those well, I came to associate you with the liquid letters. What about the one called Steel? *It's dripping, molten steel. You don't normally associate steel with liquid.*

ER: No, and there's no intention on my part to take a word from its context and, say, pull a switch on you so that I'm making something hard seem soft. It's just free form and that's the way it came out.

PK: It doesn't mean that it's always perceived that way. That's where it goes beyond the artist's control, really.

ER: The viewer definitely has a say in the whole matter.

PK: On the subject of the Standard Station, *I took the liberty of mentioning it in this article that I wrote for the* Archives of American Art Journal *on cars. I say, "Ruscha's variations on the Standard Station rank as a definitive statement of America's automobile culture. More so, in my opinion, than any representations of actual cars by the Photorealists. In form and content,* Standard Station, Amarillo, Texas *is truly an American icon." What I've done here, as an art historian, is to cast that work as an "icon." How do you feel about that?*

ER: It has to be called an icon; that's the main thing about that painting. It sort of aggrandizes itself before your eyes. That was the intention of it, although the origins were comic. I had quite a bit of fun doing the painting, and then making two or three variations on that painting. Those more or less completed the cycle I went through with that image, rest in peace as it is. I felt there was absolutely nothing more that I could do with that image, and so I saw it through as a gargantuan approach to a big canvas, the biggest canvas I've done. It became a motif for me to explore in other ways, too. I saw it as a loaf of bread; I saw it as several other things.

———

PK: How do you mean?

ER: I saw it as a trademark. I did a painting, *Large Trademark with Eight Spotlights* [1962], depicting the 20th Century Fox logo. I saw it as a *Standard Station*, a comic comment on the idea of speed and motion in a picture. Also, just the physical doing of the thing was important. If I was only interested in the image that it created, I could have made it simpler by working on a smaller scale. But I wanted to work on a large scale. I wanted it to be a large painting.

PK: Most of your work up to that point, if I'm not mistaken, was generally on a smaller scale.

ER: On a smaller and a different scale, yes. I arrived at a formula for making paintings, and it seemed to me that the canvases came out seventy-two inches high by sixty-seven inches wide. In the sixty-seven, it was a matter of buying six-foot lumber and cutting it to the shape. Sixty-seven inches wide was a canvas that I could handle by myself, by extending my arms and moving physically across the room. I painted maybe fifteen or twenty pictures that size that I kept around my studio for two or three years. I was continually moving them, walking straight up to them and grabbing the sides and physically moving them from one place to another. They seemed like friendly characters to me. The *Standard Station* was the only painting that went beyond this. It was almost like a diptych, without it being in two canvases.

PK: That's 121″ wide. That may be the first, but that's not the only large scale painting you've done.

ER: No, I've done a lot of large scale paintings since, but it seemed to be a perfect format for the kind of idea I had.

PK: What about [Large Trademark with Eight Spotlights]?

ER: Well, that was the first painting like that that I did. It had the same format, about 120″, and it maybe was a little bigger than the *Standard Station*. But it contained that horizontal thrust.

PK: So Standard Station *in part is a refinement, or further investigation, of your ideas in* [Large Trademark with Eight Spotlights]?

159

ER: Yes. I needed a simple answer to delineating a canvas, I suppose. I used a lower right-hand to upper left-hand corner diagonal across the canvas, and sliced it in half. Then it was a matter of filling one half of that canvas with some sort of idea that I had. I could see that a lot of subjects could work their way into this format. It was like broadcasting something from a tiny point, then expanding beyond the limits of things. That was the basis behind it.

PK: How did you decide that that larger scale was needed?

ER: I was being a painter, I think.

PK: You used it as a challenge, I gather. You really needed to attack, or try, a larger scale.

ER: Oh yes. Otherwise it would be parlor games. If I had set up a little drawing table, I obviously could have made the same image, but it was the overwhelming size that I had to have.

PK: Very Abstract Expressionist.

ER: Yes, but even by Abstract Expressionist standards, by Pop Art standards, they're small paintings, or medium-sized paintings. To me they were big. See, I live slow; I keep living slowly, slowly, slowly. How many artists have done paintings over fifteen feet wide? Lots.

PK: It seems that the really large scale paintings, whether it's Abstract Expressionist or Pop we're thinking of, grew up in a New York situation.

ER: I think the size of Pop Art came out of Abstract Expressionism.

PK: But nobody in L.A., it seems to me, has ever felt the need to work on a very large scale—at least the Pop people.

ER: Oh, yes. It's one of the oldest dance steps in the history of art, this idea of doing something that will either hang on a wall or sit in the middle of a courtyard and cosmically overwhelm you just by its size. The imagery is almost secondary to that physical fact of hugeness. That's always been there.

PK: You said earlier that, within the last few years, you seemed committed to this very wide format. I don't know how wide they are, but they're certainly not very high, so you have these long, skinny things. How come?

ER: Oh, just a natural progression of extensions of syntax.

PK: What does that mean? Is it related to Standard Station, [Large Trademark with Eight Spotlights]*?*

ER: Yes, it is. It's the idea of things running horizontally and trying to take off. It's almost like an airstrip in a way. My newer paintings have all smaller words, very small in some cases, a quarter of an inch high.

PK: Yes, you can hardly see it. One hardly knows that it's a Ruscha.

ER: Yes, and consequently, they make terrible reproductions. It's impossible to make posters out of them. But I suppose that I'm working through this period of paintings now because I feel like there's some kind of a mechanical motion behind it, some robot motion behind it that asks you to walk from one side of the canvas to the other, to read what was on it. I suppose that's what is really attracting me to those things now. I feel like I haven't actually rounded out my statement with them yet. But they do relate to that motion which is implied in the *Standard Station* painting, and some of those other paintings like that. Possibly it all goes back to abstract art, just the—

PK: —scale and the motion and energy—

ER: The scale and the motion both take part in it. You see, it's not so much subject matter I'm painting. I'm a combination of so many things. I feel like abstract art has really affected me, and I think it's affected anybody who even paints in a realistic manner.

PK: What about the idea of mobility in your work as a possible reflection of one aspect of American culture: gas stations, the automobile and car culture, the importance of mobility in our life? I suspect that not very much of this is conscious, but are you willing to acknowledge that it plays a role at all?

———

ER: Yes, it sure does. I used to have a 1939 Ford. I'm more interested in the function of getting around than I am in the stylistic happenings of cars. I don't think today, in 1981, there's as much of an emphasis on style as there was in the old days. The styles of car don't represent the kind of people who drive them around, and they don't represent the frustrations that those people have. There's no particular style of car that represents teenagers today; there's no style of car that represents anybody. You can find a banker who drives the same kind of car a bank robber might drive. The only thing that people *do* use is possibly the success symbolism of an automobile. People who have more money drive Mercedes-Benzes, Cadillacs and all that. That seems to be the only strain of truth behind cars anymore. The stylistic visuals of cars have been more or less reduced over the past fifteen or twenty years, and have less effect on us than they did before.

PK: A more fundamental issue that they also represent is mobility. You mentioned the word "mobility" in connection with these paintings, whether it's the diagonal, the composition, the perspective, and so forth. You're talking about creating movement like a broadcast. Is this a concern in your work?

ER: It's not a concern of mine, but there is an underlying fact of the way the pieces fall together in the story, how the imagery gets to be like it is. In a sense, the manifestation might be like the beauty of the speeding automobile. But it's something that I'm not trying to make paramount in my statement. It just goes without saying that I like a car as a cultural symbol, a cultural implement; and yet I'm not glorifying the idea of the car. The car's probably soon to be a dinosaur. Motion is certainly always going to be around. We'd all fizzle up if we had to face life and not move around.

PK: Mobility is particularly important—and in the form of the automobile—in your town, in this community. Ed Ruscha, to do anything, has to get in a car and move around.

ER: Isn't it funny how the word "streaking" has to do with the whole subject. Taking your clothes off and running down the street is connected with the chrome strips on cars; and to the motion in my painting, possibly, and also to sex. It's there in streaking in that you're exposing your body before people, and it's

Installation view of *The Back of Hollywood (Hollywood Rear-View Mirror),* Wilshire Boulevard near Spaulding Drive, Los Angeles, 1976–77. Acrylic-vinyl on canvas, 16 × 50′. Photo: Paul Ruscha.

there in automobiles because of motion. Motion is always a metaphor for, or a fact of, sex. The interconnection of the two is just so blatantly obvious that I always felt like it was discourse for subject material.

PK: There's another element that comes into play here and that is the notion of freedom. Taking off one's clothes is a very definite pronounced statement of freedom. Does that fit in with your thinking at all?

ER: Oh, I guess it does. The idea of throwing off the old is almost a matter of throwing off your old clothes and running out in the street.

PK: God, there's a book, or at least an article, on this subject, don't you think?

ER: Oh yes. I think that some psychologists have worked that over pretty well. Also streaking a girl's hair, putting a blonde streak in your hair.

PK: It sounds to me like you've got another painting.

ER: I've got a definite fixation.

PK: L.A. is blessed—it depends upon your point of view whether blessed or cursed—with a great deal of public commercial art. I'm thinking of the billboards, for instance, which spring up almost everywhere. In addition to that, there are many examples of the really eccentric architecture, Pop architecture. Then, more recently, there are the wall paintings which have sprung up—not just in the barrio, the Mexican mural movement—but the mural movement itself, with Terry Schoonhoven and Vic Henderson, the L.A. Fine Arts Squad and Twitchell. Do you feel personally, in your own work, a special relationship to this aspect of mural art?

ER: No, I don't.

PK: Does it interest you?

ER: Well, I see stylistic tendencies. There's something animal and organic about graffiti-ing on walls. I'm sure there's some basic human thrust and frustration, convulsive outpouring of human spirit that comes out of throwing yourself into graffiti-izing some wall. I see that as a viable means of expression for human beings. But my work is not that affected by it. It only happens to be that there are some similarities, even though graffiti is not considered art—billboards are, but graffiti is not. Billboards go back to communication, and communication is what I've always been interested in. Images on the billboard become functional images in that they sell products. Mine don't, but it's still paint on a lifted-up surface. People see it and it's on a grand scale. I'm interested in billboards from that standpoint, but it has nothing to offer me beyond that. I don't want to go out and paint billboards. Occasionally I'll see a billboard that I think is better than another. There are some ingenious billboards, even billboards with three-dimensional objects, and the ones done up on Sunset Strip have this sort of gilt-edged, rock world touch to them. But as far as them having any direct relation—they only make a collage for us to respond on a general level, and that general level has touched me, but not in a specific way. I would never want to paint a billboard.

PK: What about the quite natural connection here to Hollywood: the relationship between the visual artists—by that I mean painters and so forth—and the film community, the celebrities, movie stars?

ER: It's really a minority of visual artists who are involved with Hollywood, I think. Artists are not really considered that important. There's a token artist now and then, a concession to the conception of an artist representing something that is . . . oh, chic. Actors and people in the entertainment business I find to be narcissistically flamboyant. Artists are just not. Artists may be a little more uncertain of their position in things. But actors tend to have more neuroses than artists do because of their appearance, because of their need to have direct communication with the public. They might have insecurities, but they do tend to be flashier than artists are. That's the main difference between artists and people in the entertainment world.

PK: Don't you feel that to an unusual extent here, our fine artists have this contact with entertainment people, and that there is some sort of an effect from that contact?

ER: If you do compare the two worlds of thought—the entertainment industry and the artists—there's less understanding on the part of the entertainment

———

165

industry towards artists then there is vice versa. Artists have more respect for their craft than, I believe, they have for ours.

PK: How do you guys get invited to their parties then?

ER: God knows. But there's less of an understanding. Witness all the movie stars who buy clown paintings, and go off to make their own clown paintings. They have less tolerance for us and for the limits of our craft. Yet we share similar problems. The artists in the industry—the actors and the directors and the people who are directly concerned with the creative side of the business—are less in touch with us than we are with them. It's just a cold fact. I think it's easier for us to understand entertainment industry people because we're naturally drawn into, say, a story in a movie about some man who's gone off and had his own struggles. We sympathize with this, but how, on the other hand, can they sympathize with us when we go off and paint a picture of a square and say, "This is my art"? They don't see our side of things. We see their side of things because what they produce is something that the world can enjoy. We don't do things that the world can enjoy. We only do things that a certain very minor group of people respond to. Ours is very eclectic and very elitist in a sense—small scale—but every bit as honest as what they do. But I don't feel that there's a general sharing.

PK: Isn't it strange, though, that there isn't an opportunity for greater appreciation on the part of the entertainment industry, a greater understanding of the fine arts than apparently is the case. Have you ever found this sort of peculiar?

ER: Yes, I do, because on one hand, they're artists, but on the other, they're doing an entirely different kind of art. They're doing stories that are intended to appeal to the intelligence of people, but the stories don't deal with the deep innuendoes that we might be involved in. We might be involved in something that we truly believe, in the notion that we don't know what it is we're trying to set up by putting one color next to the other. We're presenting things as problems to people and not explaining them as stories, which is what they do.

PK: They're experimenting, basically.

ER: Yes. Now, I think musicians are the same way. We can listen to their tunes and see their tunes and yet they can't necessarily come back and see our art.

PK: That's strange.

ER: It is strange, it is strange. See, we don't have a tune to keep, we don't have a rhythm to keep up. A tune has got to sound right or the tune is off. We deal in combinations of things that don't have to do with the tunes being right, and we might work deliberately out of rhythm. That might be our subject, to work out of rhythm. But the musician is definitely locked in by rules of rhythm and rules of making sounds and tones working right. Or, for moviemakers, making stories work right, making motion across the movie screen, so that the action properly works together. They're interested in the logical side of things, and we're interested in the things that clash, or are inexplicable.

PK: On the other hand, there's a whole branch of music which addresses some of these very issues and goals you're describing in painting. As a matter of fact, some of these composers—a great example is John Cage—are extremely close to some of the painters in New York, like Johns and Rauschenberg. It's almost as if these composers are dealing with exactly the same problems in different media. I'll bet you there's a community like that around here. What about your friend Mason Williams, who I believe is involved in music?

ER: He is. He's interested in symphonic music at this time. He's gone through many changes, and has always loved being a comedian. We share a certain black humor in our reaction to things, and found our spirit to be much in common. Consequently, we've produced a lot of things together. We've made some books together. We made Royal Road Test together.

PK: But do you feel that he has an understanding of what you're doing?

ER: I think he does.

PK: Or is he supportive just as a friend?

ER: He's both. But I think he has been seeing some of the things that I've been doing long enough that he understands what I'm doing. That's another thing I've discovered along the way. If you do something enough times, the message begins to change direction and take on a more serious note. If you do one silly thing a hundred times, a hundred different variations, people begin to see the perseverance in it and it makes a stronger statement.

PK: What about your books? I'm certainly familiar with some of them, Various Small Fires, *and then* Some Los Angeles Apartments, Every Building on the Sunset Strip, Twentysix Gasoline Stations, A Few Palm Trees. Crackers—*when was that?*

ER: 1969, I believe.

PK: That was a collaboration with Larry Bell?

ER: See, it was a movie best of all, but first it was a book. It was a book that was a movie fallen short. I didn't realize I was going to make a movie, but I wanted to make one and had no funds to. So I made the book first, and then came the movie. The book was from the short story by Mason Williams, called "How to Derive the Maximum Enjoyment from Crackers." The story follows his story, and it possessed some of the shaggy dog techniques that he and I responded to in everyday living situations. He got the story down. I saw it as a potential story for me to use, and I wanted to investigate this telling of the story in some way. I couldn't do it with a painting; it wouldn't work. I couldn't make a drawing of it. I couldn't write a song because I'm not a songwriter. So it came to pass as a book. But as a book, I could see that this was my least favorite. The book *Crackers* had less to do with me as an artist. I felt it was possibly, for that reason, one of the weakest things I've ever done.

PK: It was fun, though.

ER: It was fun, but the important thing about it was that I stopped for a moment and saw a story, the telling of a story. It was being a sort of visual raconteur. But even so, I felt like the book was not the proper way to do it, even though, unfortunately, I saw that only after it was finished. But the thing that was good for me about it was that I was able to make a film out of it.

PK: Was that your first film?

ER: Yes, it was the first film I did. I subsequently called it *Premium,* because of Premium crackers. The idea of making a movie was like a whirlwind project. I had gotten a Guggenheim grant for $13,000 and literally spent the money in five days making the movie. I couldn't write checks fast enough, and I immediately saw immense problems in putting together a movie project. I taught myself an expensive lesson.

PK: Luckily it was at the Guggenheim's expense.

ER: Yes, luckily it was at their expense and not mine. But I had gotten the Guggenheim grant because of the work I had done with books, which I've always felt to be one of the private sides of me that is particularly strong. I felt like my books had been in a sense . . . oh, unique. They have not had to endure criticism. They don't ask to be criticized because in doing the types of books I was involved with, I wanted something that was on a non-critical platform. They were things that were just curiosities unto themselves. I didn't want people to look at them and say, "Oh, well." A painting has a direct function; you can hang it on a wall. It has several thousands of years of history and weight behind it, but the books didn't. The books represented an excursion off onto some side issue that was even puzzling to me, and yet offered me a platform for speaking, in a sense.

Crackers was a narrative. It was lighthearted and not as stoic or as severe as the other books. For that reason, it's my least favorite. If I could go back and restructure and replan, redo, it would be first a movie and I would never make a book. It was like a little flip picture book, in a sense. You remember those old books that were made years ago that you just flip through? It's almost like that.

PK: It's interesting that you mention the little flip books. They worked as manual animation, if I remember correctly. What about your other books that incorporated serial imagery or series? You would show not the same image, but related images throughout, sometimes page after page, whether they're apartments or palm trees, or fires; Sunset Boulevard or gas stations. It seems they share this interest in repeating similar images. Do you see any connection between these and your other books?

———

169

ER: You're speaking of the technique where, up in the corner of each book, the thumb flips the pages, and you actually see the motion going across? No, I've never used that, and I don't think that could apply to my books at all.

PK: What I'm interested in is not so much the flip book, but the use of repetition. Especially in Sunset Strip*, where you have a foldout and you have photographs of all these buildings as one would drive by them on Sunset Strip. What you have is if not animation in the flip technique, but the implication of movement.*

ER: It's implied anyway. It's implied in a lot of the books. Many of the books are architectural in nature, like the gas stations, and the apartments, and a few of the other books. They all possess a ground line, a landscape line that is actually horizontal, all the way through the book.

PK: Were you at all conscious of, or interested in the idea of passing time as you leaf through a book or survey the Sunset Strip?

ER: Yes, time is one of the things that interested me, but in none of the books did I explicitly explore the element of time. But I had worked on a book that was never produced called *Standard Station at Various Times of Day*. It was a book that was never that interesting to me because the concept was too simple, I guess. In other words, I experienced the study of time with this thing. The expression of it, or the book that would have resulted was almost unnecessary, so I just never made the book. I photographed this gas station as the sun rose and fell throughout the day, and I was going to repeat that. I just felt it was a subject that had been maybe explored by other artists, a question that had already been answered. So I shelved the project. It was unnecessary.

PK: You're right: the theme has been explored. The great example that comes to mind is Monet himself, with his haystacks or Rouen Cathedral, showing the same view, but at different times of day, exploring the effect of light on the haystacks or on a façade.

ER: His study was light, and mine was being behind a camera and letting the light fall as it did. I was more involved with the inhuman aspect of it, the mechanical aspect of it: of simply recording time as it was, and not so much the study of light on a particular subject. I was more interested in the process. I didn't care how it came out; I didn't care how it changed. It would have been as good at night as it was during the day. There was no qualitative judgment. I was recording something.

PK: Does that relate in any way to some of Warhol's films?

ER: Probably. It could easily.

PK: Where the camera is set up and allowed to run, whether it's the Empire State Building for God knows how many hours.

ER: He turns the camera on and walks away. Yes.

PK: That would be closer to what you were interested in with the Standard Station at different times of the day and night?

ER: Yes, right. Rather than studying the aesthetics of light falling on a particular subject.

PK: After all, Mr. Monet already did explore that subject.

ER: Yes, he did pretty well, didn't he.

PK: I was looking at the very long horizontal painting that's hanging here in your studio, which is called Ancient Dogs Barking—Modern Dogs Barking *[1980]. As is the case with much of your recent work, it's a fairly long horizontal format, rather narrow. What are the dimensions?*

ER: Thirteen feet by twenty inches. One hundred and fifty-nine inches by twenty inches.

PK: It's a very atmospheric landscape, again with a ground line in little tiny white lettering, on the left side of the picture, it says "Ancient Dogs Barking"; then you have to travel along the canvas in order to see it all. Of course, we read in Western society from left to right. As your eyes go over this long canvas and get to the right corner, it says, "Modern Dogs Barking"—

ER: —suggesting maybe that there's centuries in between. The reason I'm happy with these pictures is because, even with the width of the canvas, I'm able to

---

171

miniaturize things so that there's almost thousands of miles between the left side of the canvas and the right side of the canvas. When that happens in one of those pictures, I feel it succeeds. The lettering also brings you down to the miniature aspect of it. That's why the letters are not larger than they are.

PK: What interests me here is again these two elements I suggested in connection with the books: the element of motion—traveling, covering space, a journey—and then the time that it takes to move.

ER: Well, horizontal movement. Maybe it has to do with the fact that our eyes run in a horizontal line. There is a big difference between vertical movement and horizontal movement. I seem to be on horizontal movement, and I've been there for a few years. Since I've started painting, actually. Most of my work has been affected by that.

PK: Do you have any vertical format paintings?

ER: I have a few, but they're odd-shaped, not exactly vertical. They're not dramatically vertical. This painting has to be dramatically horizontal, I guess, in order to work. There's something mildly amusing about it in that it reminds me of ancient civilization, or winds blowing. The color of it has to do with sand blowing in the air. It has something to do with time, for me.

PK: I see a remarkable consistency in your work, from the earlier days right up to now, which has to do again with the emphasis on the horizontal; plus, most of your work incorporates letters. You've carved out this specific area of concern and interest.

ER: Well, it's not only in paintings. The movie I did, *Miracle,* was in a sense, a shaggy dog story about a guy who works on a 1965 Mustang, repairing the carburetor. In the beginning, he's a crude mechanic; but he undergoes a transformation from being this crude mechanic to being a lab technician. His overalls get lighter and lighter and lighter throughout the movie. In a sense, that was like a blending to me, and even the ideas were a blending. It had crude language in the beginning, and in the end he spoke like a lab technician or scientist. The movie itself is like a horizontal blending that I begin to see in a lot of my works. One

(Left to right) Joe Goode, Jerry McMillan, and Ed Ruscha in front of their studios at 1024 N. Western Avenue, Hollywood, June 1970. Photo: Jerry McMillan.

aspect is through the painting. I don't know why they connect, but they do. I see that tendency in other forms of my work, too, and not just in these paintings.

PK: Let's talk about the current exhibition at the L.A. County Museum [Seventeen Artists from the Sixties], a core exhibition in the bicentennial project at the L.A. County Museum.²² Do you think that this exhibition represents those years in a fair way?

ER: Basically, the exhibit has a flavor of the '60s because the works selected were created then. There are some glaring omissions—John Altoon, to name one. I can't pretend to have a better idea for what an exhibit like this would be. It's up to the director or the curator to select the works. I could have seen a show with maybe forty or sixty artists from the '60s: one that was not necessarily as in-depth, but a larger show with more works by more artists. There are lots of ways to look at it. I don't think the exhibit can be taken to fully represent the '60s. It's a very selective and yet encompassing show. But if the intention of the exhibit was to refine the selection to the most important artists, then John Altoon is definitely missing. A lot of people feel that David Hockney doesn't belong in the group be-cause he's English. I don't feel that way. Even though he came to Los Angeles in the late '60s, he probably brought as much—or said as much—as any of the artists in the show.

PK: You have run into comments to the effect of, "Why is David Hockney in the show? He had nothing to do with L.A. artists"?

ER: Yes, but I don't feel that way. First of all, he's a good artist, and secondly, he did make a contribution in the '60s.

PK: Almost everybody would agree with you—no matter how they feel about this some-what controversial exhibition—that Altoon is a glaring omission which basically compro-mises the integrity of the exhibition.

ER: Yes, it's like having a Robin Hood film festival and leaving Errol Flynn out of it. It's that glaring.

PK: What was Altoon's importance? Is it simply the special vision, the quality of the work that he produced?

ER: And particularly his style of life, which touched everyone he was around. He had a way of living, simple and direct and from the gut. He was constantly making mistakes and constantly putting his foot in his mouth, so that people actually learned from him. He was a dynamic character, as well as a great artist. That makes me wonder why he's omitted.

PK: *You feel that he really was influential, a role model.*

ER: If you could take one artist who was a swashbuckler of that period, I would say it was John Altoon, without a doubt. Just for that alone, he deserved to be reckoned with as a character and as an artist; or as an artist and a character.

PK: *Do you imagine that most of the other artists who are included in the exhibition would have that same feeling?*

ER: I think so. I think every artist in that exhibit wonders what happened to John.

PK: *Are there any other omissions that might come close to that?*

ER: I think George Herms was an artist who was definitely working with a great deal of momentum in Los Angeles at that time. He's also missing. But then the line becomes sketchier as you try to determine what the focus of the exhibit is.

PK: *What about DeWain Valentine?*

ER: DeWain is missing. Possibly Vija Celmins is missing. But she was a marginal character during that period, as I'm sure she'd agree.

PK: *What do you suppose were Maurice Tuchman's goal and guidelines in putting that show together?*

ER: I'm a little unsettled about the subject just because of the fact that I'm included in it, and so I must introspect on whether I think I belong in it. I do think I belong in it, within the guidelines they've drawn up. But I'm a little in awe of the whole thing because I don't feel like that period was so long ago—until I see an exhibit like this.

PK: In other words, it's clear now that we're looking at art history, not contemporary art anymore.

ER: Yes. It's drawn up as a piece of history, and so we're forced to look at it that way.

PK: Of course, you and I are getting a little older.

ER: It could be. It takes an exhibit like this to prove it.

PK: One of the points of the exhibition—at least as I understand it from my conversations early on with Maurice and Rusty [Earl A. Powell III, then director of LACMA]—was to try to give a fresh look at that period, starting from the premise that it was a vital time in the history of art in this area. The exhibition recognizes that a mythology built up around the Ferus group that perhaps didn't represent all of what was going on. It was my understanding that this particular exhibition, by bringing in some younger writers—not the same ones who have been writing about the subject for years—was intended to poke some holes in the myth. Do you feel that this has been accomplished? Frankly, to me, it seems that almost every inclusion there is safely predictable.

ER: The exhibit itself forces us to see this group of artists as a very close-knit group, which I can't believe is true. I don't think I've ever met John McLaughlin. I had very little to do with Richard Diebenkorn, having met him once or twice. It's not a seafaring group of artists who are all under the same banner. These artists lived in different places in Southern California, and while we'd all come together at certain points, we were not close-knit. The exhibit says that the artists are of a particular club, which we weren't, unless you view it as being, say, the history of the Ferus Gallery, which all the artists were a part of.

PK: It is an interesting grouping of pictures from the '60s. I think the earliest of your works in the show is Boss *[1961]. What struck me was the impasto, the painterly buildup of paint of that particular painting, which I don't normally associate with your work.*

ER: That's because it's early. It represented an escape from painting a flat surface, which I was terrified of doing. So what do you do when you can't paint a flat surface? You paint impasto. That's an old artistic trick.

PK: It's interesting because there's a painterly quality in the texture, the pigment, that brings to mind a number of Bay Area artists of that time—Wayne Thiebaud, Mel Ramos.

ER: Yes, there are some of the same characteristics—pushing a glob of paint up and making its own realistic dividing line, making the edge of the subject with three-dimensional paint. Paint by number, so to speak.

PK: It's almost like sculpture.

ER: Well, it is.

PK: The first thing you see is the Standard Station *as you walk into your section of the show, and then you turn the corner and you see* Boss. *I think that this is one of the exciting things about this show, to see your work developing.*

ER: I didn't argue that much about the selection of my work, although I vetoed one or two things. My inclusion in it encompasses several different facets of my work. One is faithful rendering of an object unto its own size, like the comic book and the pencils. The other is a kind of altruistic or visionary approach, rendering something that is as realistic, but not unto its same size. For example, the *Standard Station* is not the same size as a gas station. Another facet is the impasto effect, which becomes a game in itself. So I've got several things going in that show, as you can see.

PK: That's for sure. One does learn a little bit more about you, though not as much as one will, I presume, learn from the big retrospective exhibition.[23]

ER: Well, I learned from it myself by looking back at that *Boss* painting. I think even when I painted that picture, I knew that this impasto business was not going to be used much longer by me.

PK: Do you feel that your use of impasto was a natural reflection of things which had to do with Abstract Expressionism, action painting?

ER: I had two ideologies coming together when I first started painting. I had Abstract Expressionist modes, and also I was beginning to see the possibility of using non-subjects for subject matter, like words and certain objects.

PK: There's been a tremendous amount of controversy about that show rising from matters of omissions primarily, and perhaps historical misrepresentation. Do you feel that certain minority or women artists have cause for complaint? You mentioned Celmins as someone who could have legitimately gone in the core exhibition. But do you feel that there were important omissions of artists who were neglected because they were black?

ER: No, I don't think there were any minority omissions there. First of all, the exhibition was not established as being a particularly democratic choice. You can't really have the exhibit and try to be democratic towards everyone. Otherwise you would find yourself taking a map of Los Angeles and quartering sections up and picking one artist from each section of town to make an exhibit. The point is that the curator decided that the show should be about people committed to a particular art scene at the time, and there were really no minorities. There were no black artists in that particular scene in the '60s. I mean, I can think of one, Eddie Bereal, whose work I really like. He was active all the time, but he was a hermit of his own choosing, and so really not part of that scene. But he was the same age as me; I went through school with him.

PK: If you were organizing the show then, despite the fact that you know Bereal, you think then you would not necessarily include him.

ER: I would probably include him if I had made a show about the '60s, but then my thing would be entirely different than Maurice Tuchman's. If I had made a show of the '60s, I would have picked different artists. I might have picked some artists who were more obscure. I would include artists that you may never have heard of, but who may have been peripherally connected to the art scene. We would have seen an entirely different kind of exhibit had Walter Hopps been the curator of an exhibit like this. You can't attack Maurice Tuchman because of the style of his show. He did it, he picked it.

PK: Who would be some of the Ruscha additions?

ER: Well, I would say Eddie Bereal, for one. I would say that Jerry McMillan would be another, and even some of the younger artists, like Chuck Arnoldi,

Laddie John Dill and people like that. They were definitely there in the '60s, but their thrust was not heard until later on.

PK: They're associated more with the '70s.

ER: Yes, but I may have picked some artists, like Martial Raysse from France, who did work in Los Angeles during the '60s. He showed his work at the Dwan Gallery. He didn't contribute that much, but he was definitely here. I would pick artists like George Herms. The omission of DeWain Valentine was a mistake.

PK: What about Peter Alexander?

ER: Sure, Peter Alexander. I would certainly have Peter in there. DeWain and Peter were working on the same kind of course in the '60s. It's just a matter of rethinking the whole show. I would have done an entirely different show.

PK: Susan Larsen, who was one of the contributors to the catalogue of the exhibition, makes an interesting observation. She writes that the '60s L.A. look was cool, aesthetic, well-crafted, and is represented by artists such as Bell, Irwin, McCracken, Kauffman, and then—for our special interest—Ruscha. But then she goes on to say that there were really more differences than similarities between these artists, even though all of you—mostly Ferus people—were viewed as participating in the same sensibility. Do you agree with her statement and her perception? [24]

ER: More differences than similarities—I always felt that. I thought it was all so amazing that artists could be friends with one another. Visually, their ideas don't look alike, but the similarities are definitely there. There's no one school of thought amongst the friends themselves. There was a camaraderie between all the artists, and yet the ideas, the look of their work didn't really go from one to another. It was more like a spirit that went from one to another, rather than the visual look of the work. You don't see a lot of close relationships of influence from one artist to another.

PK: Everybody's been writing about L.A. art of that period, and using certain descriptive terms that they apply to the art of the area: a high polish, finish fetish. That term is used

---

over and over again, as if that explains the look of the art of the time. Do you feel that that's accurate?

ER: Well, I know what they mean when they say "finish fetish." I really wasn't included in that because my work didn't have that extra-machine-craftedness to it, that extra final polish to it that made it fly free.

PK: The custom car look?

ER: The custom car look, yes. That's not so far off. The custom car look was part of the fiber of the whole business of being an artist out here.

PK: So you do agree with the idea of "finish fetish"?

ER: Yes, but I don't think it's necessarily geographically correct. These artists happened to live in L.A., and do consider this so-called final appearance of their work as being rather mechanical or finely finished and polished. But you can find artists in New York who do work in the same way.

PK: How would you place yourself and your work in relationship to this finished L.A. look?

ER: I was definitely affected by it. To see that people made art which was not brush-strokey made an impression on me. But I was less influenced than other artists. I suddenly came out of art school and I found artists that were working this way. One artist was building a dust-free chamber, and I thought that was strange, but real curious at the same time. It had a new in-road into the manufacture of art that impressed me.

PK: Who was that, Bell?

ER: Well, Larry Bell, I think, and then there's another artist named Norman Zammitt. I'm not that in favor of his work, but his approach to the work could be definitely considered part of this finish fetish. He made a dust-free chamber to spray paint in. He took over a studio of mine at one time. Craig Kauffman's work—those big bubbles, those hotdog bubbles that he was making—that had a workshop-created feeling to them. It was a complete reverse from the easel-

———

Leo Castelli (left) and Ed Ruscha (right) outside 4 East 77th Street, New York, 1973.
Photo: Samantha Eggar.

painting concept which I grew to feel conservatively connected to somehow. So I was jolted by these other people. Ron Davis was making cast polyester works then. I began to see that this work was also part of this "manufacturing" of art. I thought this was a new direction that could open up possibilities. But personally, I never got into it myself. I still remain a conservative easel-painter. My contribution to the whole thing would be in the manufacture of my books. The word "manufacture" comes into this concept of the finish fetish. It's a negating of the easel painting concept.

PK: Most of the L.A. artists seemed to have moved into relief, or into three-dimensional sculpture, and ditched the painting and the easels. Your interest in easel painting really does seem to separate you from the others.

ER: There were quite a few artists out here who were working independently in those directions. I can't see that Ron Davis's work influenced Craig Kauffman, or vice versa. But they were working with the same sort of manufacturing procedures, in that direction of a more mechanical way to make art.

PK: Do you feel that particular preoccupation or direction is being maintained as you look around now in this area?

ER: The original thrust of that kind of art seemed to crest, and now I don't find it to be that way. Most of those artists are going back to traditional ways of making pictures—Kauffman, Davis. Billy Al Bengston is back to painting with brushes. There's less of an emphasis on glass, there's less of an emphasis on plastic in the work you see produced today. You would see more kinetic works back then. They were getting into mechanics, which was a departure from easel painting. In my '60s show, if we shall imagine such a show, I might include some kinetic artists in there. H. C. Westerman was actually working in Los Angeles at the time, and he made a real impression on people.

PK: Christopher Knight's essay in the L.A. County Museum exhibition catalog has a section which deals with you and those who were supposedly closest to you in the '60s. Knight's main point seems to be that L.A. Pop comes out of an American realist tradition, specifically the nineteenth-century landscape school which has been dubbed "Luminism."

Luminism involved a preoccupation with things—sometimes humble objects, more often landscape elements—things in nature, carefully controlled and constructed and assembled in a way that might suggest "manufacturing."[25] Can you see any legitimacy in this particular effort to place L.A. Pop—and therefore your work—within a realist tradition?

ER: I'm not sure. One point he makes in there is that there was no cultural tradition in L.A., so far as painting goes. In this period, we gradually found artists selecting subject matter that could only be dealt with through the rendering of these things realistically. I can only speak for myself. When I choose an object, generally a small object, I can't render this object unless it is somehow faithful. I even go to the extent of measuring the object, and measuring the canvas. I give myself to a set of restrictions that I call it my duty to express, and so most of the objects that I make are actual size, even to the point of my using that in a title of the picture. Like the Spam picture is actually called *Actual Size* [1962]. I was using a vast plane, a vast open area that was the limits of my canvas. And this subject I selected was even more dramatized by the fact that it was made actual size, rather than if it had been made four times that size. That's one of the differences between me and most of the other Pop artists: they were able to expand the sizes of their images, of the objects, and I didn't really do that. I wasn't able to do that. The only time I would be able to change something like that is if I were to go off into a fantasy world and make something smaller than what it is, like a gas station, or the L.A. County Museum on fire. Then there are certain subjects that have no size—which is the area I really moved into—and that was words. I mean, what size is a word, after all? Is it six-point, is it twelve-point, or is it as big as the wall?

PK: I think what you've said actually ties in with some of the concerns of certain nineteenth-century American realists, including the Luminists. It has to do with this emphasis on being able to measure within the picture. It has to do with control; it has to do with honesty.

ER: Yes, but my intentions were not to expand the faithfulness of the subject of, say, a Spam can. There are all kinds of ways of looking at the picture, but I think it's the selection of the object which is more important than anything. It's almost

———

like the idea is more important than the actual physical presence of it. Once you pick the object and reproduce it faithfully, you want the thing to glimmer. You want it to have inner power. You want to instill a thing with some earth-shaking religious feeling. You want to hear this organ music.

PK: That sounds very much like some of the interests of the nineteenth-century Luminists.

ER: It could be. In another sense like those artists would paint a still life, and they may not measure the objects, but they would be people-size in their paintings. But then when they'd go out and paint the Grand Tetons in 36 × 40. So I probably share some of the same problems in my work as some of those artists did.

PK: Because fundamental to Luminism was a reverence for matter, for objects—not necessarily for their own sakes. In other words, the things themselves—as physical objects—weren't the subject matter, weren't the content that they were really after. Finally, for you, the result of painting an object is something more than can be apprehended from, say, looking at that tape recorder—if you should paint the tape recorder sitting there—or even its appearance on canvas, its representation. But within this process of making that particular object part of a work of art, something is revealed that becomes more important. Do you agree with that?

ER: Well, yes. If I did choose to paint a picture of a tape recorder, then I would be, in a sense, endorsing its value as a possibly obsolete item, because it's topical only to today. Whereas if I painted a picture of an orange, that would be universal. And an apple would be universal. But the minute you paint something that is stylized unto itself, then it's open to becoming obsolete.

PK: It dates the work.

ER: It dates the work. I mean, people a hundred years from now will say, "What is this little thing that says 'Spam' on it? What's Spam?"

PK: Do you like that? Is that part of your artistic intention?

ER: No, it's the immediacy that's really important. I'm not going to go around painting things that are universal just for that. Like an apple's timeless. But it's the immediacy that takes over and makes you not even think about whether something could be ever out of date.

PK: Do you have a special attachment, as Christopher Knight suggests, to such things? Do you feel you're interested in accumulating things and incorporating them into books and paintings?

ER: Well, I carry with me an imaginary scrapbook of ideas. I'm constantly seeing shapes and things. My mind doesn't work like, say, Claes Oldenburg, who is constantly looking at objects and making distortions, idea distortions on those objects and using objects in that sense. I'm not like that. When I do pick an object, I want to pick it with a certain amount of reverence. It's got to be sort of a clean contact between me and the object and what I intend to make out of that. Sometimes an object would never be good subject matter for a painting, but I may just want to look at it in some other way. Maybe it would kick off an idea. Gas stations might be an example: I made a book out of gas stations, and I also made a picture of gas stations. I look at all my influences as being material, more like a songwriter or a filmmaker or a poet. That's why I have a scrapbook of potential ideas, of properties that can be used in one way or another. There's no logical order to it. There's no logical reason why I might make a painting of, say, a Spam can, or whether I might want to take a photograph of it and put it in a book. It's a constant shifting of material: taking it out of context and putting it back in context; glorifying it in one way, and putting it in the background in another way.

PK: Does this scrapbook actually exist?

ER: I do have notebooks that I write ideas down in. The words "gas station" may actually appear there, but I've never actually done a painting that says "gas station." I've done a word that says "gas."

PK: But do you refer to these things?

ER: I refer to them, and they're food for the entire business.

PK: It's like a novelist, a writer of fiction. Generally they carry notebooks and as ideas come or situations appear they will take notes—they might even be at a party, sitting down taking notes. Then one would presume that an author goes back and reviews this, and actually lifts things that seem appropriate into a novel. I gather you work somewhat that way yourself.

ER: Yes, in that I am not uniformly directed to make oil paintings on canvas. Throughout my work, these ideas have come out of different media. It may appear in a movie in one respect, and then it may come back and appear in a lithograph in another. Then it may be a drawing in another, and a painting in another.

PK: You just said that you wanted to approach the objects that you used with a certain reverence. What do you mean by that?

ER: It means something very simple. When I say reverence I mean that I have to bring something to it, and so I have to treat it right. I want to, in a sense, put some breathing life into it. Whatever subject I choose to make a picture of, I've got to singularize this object, breathe life into it, realize that it has a certain amount of potential in itself. Once it's selected as a subject matter, then it's my job to bring the thing alive.

PK: How would you describe specifically that which you sense is trapped inside this object, and through the act of selection and incorporation into your work is released? Or is it too nebulous to describe, this life inside the object? How does it manifest itself, if it is indeed released?

ER: Sometimes it has no meaning. If I paint a picture of a pencil, it may not have as much meaning as a utilitarian object as it does take on a particular shape in space that might attract me. The idea of a pencil being an object to make marks with, or to write with, to draw with, may be the secondary strength. The primary strength at the time I paint it might just be that it's a flat thing. That it's a long, skinny object in the painting. It becomes almost abstract.

PK: From what you're saying, the value of the pencil is really formal, certainly not iconographic in the sense that there's some meaning or symbolism of a pencil itself. Are you more interested in abstract formalist art theory than symbolic?

ER: Neither necessarily, or maybe both at the same time. It's a kind of drama that I'm after. Maybe long, skinny things interest me, like every building on the

---

Sunset Strip or a painting that's 20 inches high and 159 inches long. Or maybe even a pencil. It's almost an abstract drama I'm after, rather than any kind of story-telling device.

PK: That sounds to me as if it's largely a formalist, compositional consideration rather than anything else.

ER: That puts me back on square one, doesn't it?

PK: I'm not sure. But assuming that there are basically two ways to go: on the one hand, there is an emphasis on abstract formalist qualities; and then on the other hand, there is an emphasis on anecdote, narrative, storytelling—a preoccupation with formal, abstract qualities within a realist framework. Which do you feel is more important to your own work? Are you leaning towards one way or the other?

ER: I'll lean either way. My work is loaded with all kinds of prejudices. I do find myself, ultimately, kind of summing myself up by saying I'm conservative. You mentioned Photorealism. I think Photorealists are more dedicated to the camera and photographs than they are to faithfully rendering subjects, because their work is described by the photograph. You can look at Photorealist paintings and almost tell what kind of lens the camera took.

PK: Which obviously doesn't interest you at all.

ER: It doesn't interest me at all.

PK: Do you think of yourself as a realist painter in light of the fact that last month's Art in America *announces that realism is okay again, realism is back, it's all right?* [26]

ER: I would never describe myself as a realist. Do they mean "realism" to mean faithful rendering of subjects? Because I don't believe in that. I'm only a realist in the sense that I might measure the ashtray and if it's five inches I might tend to want to make it five inches on the canvas.

PK: Of course, realism is being redefined in its broadest application; it has to do with recognizable subject matter. You would agree that in much of your work there is some recognizable subject matter?

Richard Eurich, *Withdrawal from Dunkirk*. June 1940. Oil on canvas, 30 × 40″ (76 × 101.5 cm). National Maritime Museum, Greenwich, London SE10 9NF.

Pablo Picasso, *Guernica*. 1937. Oil on canvas, 349.3 × 776.6 cm. Museo Reina Sofía, Madrid. N. de Registro: DE00050. © 2001 Estate of Pablo Picasso / Artists Rights Society (ARS), New York.

ER: Well, let me tell you about just sort of a quick lesson that I taught myself at one point. I saw a painting of the Battle of Dunkirk, painted by I don't know who—English, back in the '30s.[27] When was the Battle of Dunkirk?

PK: Who was the artist, do you remember?

ER: I'm not sure. It was the most bucolic, restful image I could imagine. It was a large aerial view of the harbor of Dunkirk, with the ships in flames and the battle actually going on at the time. I couldn't imagine any picture being more sedate and more charming and tranquil—and here a war is going on. That picture, say, compared with Picasso's *Guernica:* the jagged lines and explosions and people's arms cut off, gestures toward the sky of life-giving—the drama behind that. Yet it was less literal, but more emotional—more abstract yet more realistic—than the picture of the Battle of Dunkirk. I mean, what says "war" more: the *Guernica* or this other painting? I don't have particularly one choice over the other; but it is a primer, or lesson, about what a picture can evoke.

PK: Are you yourself interested in the philosophical questions concerning the nature of reality, in notions of things reflecting basic principles pertaining to space, the real and the ideal, the specific and the general?

ER: We're talking beyond pictures; we're talking beyond painting; we're talking beyond art, in a sense; and we're talking about space. The notion certainly occurs to me, and I like any kind of attention given to something that doesn't require attention. Because of that, I may be philosophical in a sense. I like to embellish a subject that doesn't need embellishment. Maybe that's what you're thinking of. The reason for, and what about the hereafter: questions like that I am curious about. I don't study philosophy as such, but I like attention and time given to a subject that doesn't need attention and time.

PK: Why do you like that?

ER: I guess maybe it's a little bit of the showman in me or something. Maybe I like to say that there is really more to a subject than anyone else tends to acknowledge. Because, after all, it's an artist's job to do that despite the fact that you

---

189

have to use tricks and devices in order to put that idea across. I like to give attention to the lonely paintbrush, or make a tribute to something that is humble, or something that does not require explanation. So some objects to me are stupid for that reason: tools and fastening devices. There are things that I'm constantly looking at that I feel should be elevated to greater status, almost to philosophical status or to a religious status. That's why taking things out of context is a useful tool to an artist. It's the concept of taking something that's not subject matter and making it subject matter.

PK: Especially if they're trivial objects.

ER: Trivial objects usually have that, but sometimes even objects that are important can also have the same effect. It might be in the way of dealing with it, or in the context in which it's placed.

PK: This, of course, is one of the qualities attributed to Pop Art: to take routine, everyday objects and elevate them to fine-art status. This, I gather, is close to your interest.

ER: Well, it's not necessarily elevating it to fine art status, but elevating it to a see-able status, calling attention to something. The idea of making it fine art is a euphemistic way of elevating it from its low status to something of recognizable status. In other words, showing that it deserves to be recognized.

PK: Do you suppose this has something to do with your own basic attitude toward reality? The ordinary hierarchy of what's important or unimportant in the things that surround us is unacceptable to you?

ER: I guess it is. It means that there's a certain frustration that I'm suffering and that most artists suffer just by being artists. They have some strange way of looking at the world: jumbling it and coming up with their own statement.

PK: But do you feel that there is implicit here a commentary on your part on the nature of reality?

ER: One thing I don't have is a need to tell things like they are. Now, that's implicit in realism in a way. But my ideas have never been crystallized to the point where things are rolling along, and I'm telling things exactly like they should be told. Because my realism is only part realism. If I choose to make a subject, the context in which I make that possible distorts the realism of the subject itself. Back to the Spam can falling through space. What's the space? What does it mean? It's only space on a canvas, but the faithfulness of it—the realism facet of it—is all by itself; frozen, in a sense. I like the ideas to be frozen in their environment, in that respect. It's not total realism: it's not total explanation. Total realism is like telling it like it is, and I'm not that kind of artist.

PK: You're very much associated with words as subject matter. Do you view your words in terms of realism or abstraction? Are words perhaps formal elements that go into the arrangement of the picture, help to determine the structure and formal quality of a painting?

ER: Well, first of all, the English language is the hottest language to hit the U.S.A. I use the English language and each word I use has its own definition; I am leading the viewer of my work into what the definition of the word I've used is. A lot of times the words are unimportant, their definitions are unimportant. They become almost abstract objects. When I first started painting it became an exercise in using, oh, guttural utterings, monosyllabic explorations of words, like "smash," "boss," "won't." I've noticed when I look back on my work that most of my early works had less of a fascination with the English language than they did with just trying to imitate monosyllabic words like "smash," "oof." They all were power words like that, rather than words which represented the lighter side of life. They were words that represented things being broken or smashed, damaged. I wonder what my fascination with that was, except that they seemed to be words with less subject matter than, say, if I had painted the word "patience," or words that were of a lighter nature. I think that I could have been involved in painting an environment for what the word sounded like and looked like at the same time.

PK: It seems to me that the words in your paintings could be viewed on three possible levels, or in three possible ways. First of all is the formal level, the abstract level. These are simply compositional elements in a painting that help determine the structure of the work of art; nothing beyond that. A second way would be that the words are there, but without specific signification or meaning other than perhaps a general reference to language, to sound and noise. Which is what you seem to be suggesting in terms of these harsh words. A third possibility is that, indeed, the words connote specific things or sensations. Even "Annie"— that's a girl's name. Immediately it's loaded—that's immediately part of the work whether you like it or not.

ER: I'm not really a purist and don't think my work is about any one particular facet of these ideas you have here. Because sometimes I don't care about the definition of the word. Sometimes they are just a simple excursion, start-stop unto itself, and not meant for any dictionary definition interpretation. Then other times, like you say, I can't escape the fact that, say, the word "Annie" would mean many things to many people. It's a name of a woman, and possibly it goes beyond and suggests something else. So I'm a victim of whatever that happens to be.

PK: Let's take Annie *as an example. It's painted in that cartoon lettering: Little Orphan Annie. So that immediately is brought to mind for only those people who are familiar with that strip. Another possibility—my wife's name is Ann. I don't call her "Annie," but then just think of the enormous personal connotations that could arise from that. And you, without knowing who's going to be looking at the work, have then sparked that. That's what words are all about. I know you have no control over any given viewer's personal associations, but does that aspect interest you?*

ER: Not really, not beyond its factual connotation. It's parlor talk. I've never been able to look at my work as though the words I use can be used for anything more than what I've done with them. In other words, I'm not combining words to make word gestures. Each word is an excursion unto itself.

PK: Do you hope that people pronounce the words, to themselves or even aloud?

ER: No.

PK: What about the harsh words?

ER: Well, pronounced in their minds maybe. Maybe "smash," for instance. I want them to be simple, monosyllabic—I don't think you even have to pronounce

---

them in the back of your throat. They've made a test with instruments in people's throats and in their mouths with their tongues, testing the pronunciation of words when they read. I guess everyone tends to move their tongue slightly towards the back of their head when they're reading softly to themselves, when they're not reading aloud. There's a tendency for people to do that. I would like to think that people looking at the painting will not pronounce it out loud, but will get this kind of throat motion. It's almost like a non-movement in the back of your throat that pronounces the word and gets it out.

PK: *Looking at where your work has come from, what direction do you see it taking now?*

ER: I think the unknown is one facet of being an artist that has the most to offer for me. Not knowing what's in the future. I've always felt that way. I've always wondered what direction I will take at some point in the future, or how will my future unfold itself. That's one thing that I'm baffled by, but I'm also committed to. So I have really no direction; I have no plans. I can't write my future. I can't write my own history. I'm most fascinated by that one idea of the things that are undone now, will be done in five years' time.

PK: *In other words, you're interested in seeing what will happen.*

ER: Yes. I'm interested in what is interesting, and less about what I happen to be involved in right now, which is always maybe really mundane by comparison to maybe other people's lives. Making art is a kind of curious individual enterprise. It all depends on me and not somebody else. I can't get fired from the job. I've felt like firing myself, but I know I'm helpless.

PK: *So what you mean is you want to fire yourself as the executor of your own ideas. That it would be nice to have like a robot that would have the same facility as Ed Ruscha and the same skills in making something.*

ER: Yes. As quaint as that sounds, it's still a possibility, literally. I'm not one who subscribes to the idea that the artist has to actually with his own hand produce his own works. I'm not so enthusiastic about that subject as to go off and look for someone to do my own work, find the robot. But I'm just saying there are no real answers to the way of getting art work done. I don't have a lot of helpers around here, you can see.

PK: How do you find time for this execution? Because the way you work now, you still are tied to that.

ER: I do find time for it. While I don't produce a prodigious amount of work like some artists do, I still find time for it. I guess I spend less time running around the city than a lot of people do. I spend a lot of time in the studio.

PK: You mentioned before that you found it difficult to mix domestic life and the responsibilities that go along with professional life: the free-form life of an artist, which means you work irregular hours and all this. Did you find significant difficulty in maintaining that balance?

ER: I didn't find much disorder in my family life, as opposed to my working in the studio. I always did like the idea of being single. I am single now, really; legally, I'm single. But I'm not the kind of artist who can have a family setup, and then a little shop in the back room. The domestic is almost like practical life. Studio life is almost like the impossible fantasy. So you want to keep the impossible fantasy going and have less of the practical side of things. I've always tried to minimize the practical side of life, and the practical has been the domestic.

PK: Do you find that attitude puts a strain on your relationship? You did get separated or divorced.

ER: Oh, gosh, yes. It does, it sure does. My domestic life has been real sweet at times. It's been through periods of upheaval, deep problems and all that. But I still maintain it. I keep my studio open, and it remains mostly untouched by the problems of my domestic life. It gets back to the old question of art is life is art is life. They all feed off one or another. Some artists are very four-square responsible; they hold their family in high esteem and hold their art in high esteem. Somehow they are able to manage and juggle this set of circumstances together and do it very well.

PK: Show up for dinner on time and all that.

ER: Yes, show up for dinner on time and do all that. Some of those artists, unfortunately, run scared. The real backbone to them is the family life, so they have to use this, which is the creative life, to go off and feed this, which is family life. I never, never like to hear an artist say, "Well, I've got mouths to feed." I know what that means, that they have to do that, but if it affects the free spirit of the mind, then it's taxing their creative side. And then the domestic becomes primary.

PK: Do you find your personal life has any direct effect on your ability to work? Let's say a crisis.

ER: God, yes. Without being psychoanalytical about it, it's true. All my personal life does have a great effect on what I do. Something will happen in my personal life which will make me useless over here. I can't function; I'm strictly at the mercy of this other thing that's happened. It's happened before many times. It's like I'm made of very sensitive chemistry or something. The things that happen on the personal side of life actually do affect me.

PK: Under some cases, have life experiences determined a certain direction in your work?

ER: Oh, yes. I would say those movies I did were examples of me taking from life and realizing how people act. I lived with a girl for a couple of years, Candy Clark. Her birthday was rolling around, and I felt like, "God, I wish I could give you the world." So I painted a picture of the world for her, a painting called *It's a Small World* [1980].

PK: Like in Disneyland. They've got that rhyme.

ER: I've never been to Disneyland. Well, speaking of that, I did a drawing called *Bengstonland* [1976], like Disneyland. Just the word "Bengstonland." I did a painting for Joe called *Joe* [1961]. It had a spark plug in it like a collage out of the newspaper, because in high school Joe once painted a picture of a spark plug. There are a lot of examples of things that I have done where I've gone directly from my experiences and put that into my work.

PK: These sound like things that have very much to do with close personal relationships, and trying to express something very personal that has meaning on a one-to-one basis.

———

I know that you did some published photographs of Lauren Hutton. Was the photography the result of a friendship with her?

ER: Yes.

PK: I don't know what magazine published the series that you did.

ER: *Esquire.*[28] But it was not part of my artwork; it was a lark, and I was not on an assignment. It was just having fun with a camera. I wouldn't consider those a work of mine at all. I'm actually exercising the right of an artist to just experiment, or just to knock off something, or just to have fun with the camera.

PK: That's true. There's no reason why everything you do has to be an exhibition piece.

ER: Right. It's not made for exhibition. It was not meant to be in any way art, or I would have changed the entire concept, which I wasn't up to doing. It was not that serious a thing. It was fun and games.

PK: At least you didn't think you were doing fashion photography.

ER: No, I'd need my seamless paper here, wouldn't I?

PK: It reminds me of Blowup. *Did you ever see that movie?*

ER: Yes. That was very good. I liked that movie. All of Antonioni's movies were. That's funny, because Antonioni came to my studio one time about 1967, and I remember him really responding to *Standard Station.*

PK: Have you been or are you attracted to the high fashion world as represented in Blowup*, as an example?*

ER: Well, not specifically as an artist. The character from *Blowup* definitely was in his own world, wasn't he? But as far as the fashion aspect of it . . . I don't know, maybe. I liked the character in that movie. He was sort of a free agent, wasn't he?

PK: Basically amoral, and somewhat confused.

ER: Yes. But the life of a fashion photographer, I think, would be a morbid life to live. They're cousins to painters in some strange way. They're making images

---

too, but they're more bound by the commercial world than we are—depending on the photographer. There are some good fashion photographers, aren't there?

PK: Oh yes. Some of them are viewed as artists; they make exhibitions of their work. Richard Avedon . . .

ER: But they become instantly obsolete in the sense that they have to show the world clothes that have been already made. They're almost behind the times in a sense. It's just constantly changing, and they're part of the style cycle. We are too, but our cycle goes around much slower than theirs.

PK: It seems to me that the fine artist is working to affect our perceptions of the world. The fashion photographer is trying to affect our idea of what we must have. It seems to me there's that similarity. In the case of fashion photography, it's almost brainwashing, telling people what they should be, and what they're not.

ER: You make it sound like a conspiracy, though.

PK: No, I don't mean that. But in effect, it works that way. It's insidious. It's advertising. It doesn't mean that it's necessarily bad, but it seems to me there's a fundamental, shared quality between making art and fashion photography, and it has to do with directing a viewer. But then there's a fundamental, very important difference which you suggested.

ER: Yes, because our work is more or less purposeless, isolated and purposeless. It doesn't have the function that advertising does.

PK: Don't you think that your work can fundamentally change perception?

ER: It only sort of aggravates the theme of the style changing constantly. Everyone who works as an artist eventually contributes to that whole thing. It's like a bandwagon that continually moves. So every artist that does it, even mediocre artists; even bad artists affect it.

PK: That's true. And maybe commercial artists and photographers are participating in the same phenomenon in a less important way.

ER: Yes. You can broaden the concept and include musicians and writers and anybody who is involved in communications at all. Painters are on the outside of

---

communication because the word "to communicate" is a little sketchier for an artist than it is for a fashion photographer, or a writer, or a musician. Or a film-maker, because those people are called on to actually reach the public. Artists are exempt of that. By and large, artists stand behind their own fifth amendment, which is artistic license.

PK: You don't have to meet a client's requirements for the layout of a magazine or some-thing like that.

ER: In some funny way, it's a cop-out. But I like the idea that an artist should never be questioned about what he does, because he deserves this right of artis-tic license.

PK: So part of what originally attracted you to this strange activity of making art—and what still attracts you—is the ideal of complete freedom to do what you want in terms of making things. You're not beholden to anybody.

ER: I'm not an artist for that reason, though. But it is real important to have the freedom, because otherwise there are rules to follow. I've always felt like the number one rule is that there are no rules.

PK: It's simply that you feel that this freedom is an essential ingredient to making art. It's not a goal in itself for you.

ER: Yes. It's such a strange activity, once you think about it.

PK: You've been talking about, from the very beginning, an attraction to a Bohemian no-tion, a Bohemian ideal, which probably, in the beginning, was a fairly romantic idea.

ER: Well, it involved a gut passion, I suppose, that everything is secondary to the goal of making things.

PK: Do you feel it's more possible now to pursue a satisfactory career as an artist on the West Coast than it was, say, ten or twelve years ago?

ER: Yes, probably because there seems to be more public support for art than there was when I was first here. But where's a Walter Hopps? I don't see him anywhere. There are some people that are operating along those lines, but I don't really see any new upheavals as far as possibilities for artists to show their work. There's more public support, but it seems like it was more vital when I started out. It was on a much smaller scale then, but certain figures are missing from the scenario now. We're a metropolis now and we weren't then.

PK: It's the biggest city in the country now. What about the new plans for a museum of contemporary art, the Museum of Contemporary Art [MOCA]? What about Pontus Hulten?[29]

ER: Pontus Hulten is a "cosmo" character in the whole picture. I think that his appearance and involvement might even be monumental; it's going to open up a different frontier. It's just so hard to say—I don't know what those people have in mind. But by the looks of things, I think that Pontus's arrival here is going to multiply things—or double things, at least. What's going to happen there [at MOCA], probably, will be twice as much as what's happening everywhere else in Los Angeles. The new museum is dedicated to modern art, to contemporary art, and to areas that are lacking in other institutions. So I think it's a real growth step.

PK: Is this something that causes a certain amount of excitement among artists, among your friends?

ER: Well, DeWain Valentine was spearheading the thing, almost. Actually, he spearheaded a complaint against the L.A. County Museum about two years ago, which a lot of artists got fairly indignant about. He was complaining about the fact that the L.A. County Museum was really not representative of contemporary, local artists on any level.

PK: That, conceivably, could have a positive influence on the programs at MOCA: number one, to take some of the pressure off the L.A. County Museum, which has a broader area of responsibility; and also, then, to serve as the competition.

ER: It could be the reincarnation of the original Pasadena Art Museum.

PK: I gather your response to the new leadership at MOCA is: some changes could happen, yes, but not as many as some people [think] who are very excited about it now.

———

ER: Oh no, I'm as excited as anybody. I think that the new museum has got everything going for it. I just think that Los Angeles may not be the best place to begin an art career. I don't know where the best place is. I think it's all a struggle, myself.

PK: *If they really do create what they are now billing as the most important museum of contemporary art in the world, do you think it's possible that a whole support system might spring up and some galleries that might want to be in the shadow that's cast by this institution? Perhaps then more artists will be attracted to the area. Is it something you look forward to?*

ER: Oh yes, I look forward to it. It makes my growing up scene seem medieval.

PK: *You have mentioned before some of your concerns about having your work in museums and participating in the machinations of the art world. Is the concern as far as museums go about whether or not your work is hanging all the time, or if there are proper conservation measures, or how is it interpreted, like in a special exhibition?*

ER: For instance, in the case of the exhibit down at the L.A. County Museum, I was given priority. I really selected my own work, discussing this show with the director. They gave me that respect. But as an artist who lives by himself and produces by himself. I'm sort of quizzed by the institution that finally sanctions that work of art for the public and makes it okay to the public. I can't really believe in the whole system unless I understand what the whole system is about, and sometimes I don't. So I have reservations about institutions showing art, you see.

PK: *Do you suspect they have ulterior motives?*

ER: There couldn't be any. All they want to do is put the show on. They want to have a circus and everybody to come to it, which in a sense should be my part, too. But I never really understood where the work of art should finally end up. I want my work to be handled properly. The museums attempt to have an archival, preservation aspect to everything they do with works of art. I think they do, even though there is damage here and there. The primary concern is that I want my work to be kept in primary condition.

PK: The major responsibility of the museum really always has been, first of all, the care and preservation of the work of art, whether it's an old master or contemporary. That's number one, and then number two is to show important examples of important art. That's where a curatorial process comes into play, because somebody has to make that decision about which are the important artists worthy of showing in a particular museum. It seems to me that's an area where we all can call them to task, or question the performance of a museum.

ER: Well, yes. The L.A. County Museum of Art seemed to fall asleep about art that was being done right under its own nose for several years. Now it appears as though they've worked themselves out of that, and they're back in the community spirit thing. No matter what the institution is—the museum, the gallery, what have you—they're always faced with those problems.

PK: There's one aspect of all of that which is extremely relevant to what we're discussing now, and that is the issue of an institution that solicits gifts from artists. Artists make a contribution to an institution because they believe that the institution is solid, will last, and has a commitment to showing this type of art. As we all know, things unfortunately didn't quite pan out that way at the Pasadena Art Museum.[30]

ER: The agreement was broken.

PK: Yes, and Norton Simon didn't appear to be sensitive to the spirit—maybe to more than the spirit—to the contractual agreement between artists and some collectors in that institution. Does that make you wary? I don't know if you gave a piece to the Pasadena Art Museum.

ER: One of my works ended up there, yes. It was subsequently put up for sale. But I didn't donate that work. They acquired that work through the Men's Committee of the Pasadena Art Museum.

PK: In that case, there's not much the artist can do about their work being deaccessioned, at least under the present arrangements. I was thinking of a few cases where artists actually donated works, believing in the purpose of the institution.

ER: Those artists may have more of a cause for concern and repulsion than I do, because my work was actually purchased and given to the museum. But

The artist in his Western Avenue studio, 1976. In background, *Hope* (1972. Oil on canvas, 54 × 60″).
Photo: © Sam Shaw.

nonetheless, my painting is also a part of that collection and should be treated with the same respect as all the other work.

PK: In other words, you are very concerned about what happens with the work as it takes its journey from hand to hand, institution to individual.

ER: Exactly. This man Simon, who is treating his works as commodities, is treating them just like he would a bottle of his catsup: supply and demand. On the one hand, he's probably surprised that the works can get that much money from the market. On the other hand, he's saying that they're not art, or it's degenerate. There's some of that spirit behind him, I think. The work of the twentieth century—he just doesn't like it.

That work of mine that was embraced by this institution of higher learning, this museum, which now changed hands, and that work of mine now has put back on the marketplace. It hurt me that the work is gone from a museum back onto an open market. DeWain Valentine has a perfectly good reason for bringing suit against those people. And Bob Irwin, and a few other artists who donated those works because we knew that was a great museum. But we've learned from those little scratches. Next time something happens along those lines, the artists are going to have to have representation. The artist had no representation there. I think that if artists are going to donate works to a collection, they should be properly represented by some form of contract which says that if anything ever happens to the museum, the work reverts back to the artist. Why should it go out on the open market somewhere, and be sold through an auction house?

I think the people at the new museum [MOCA] are not going to want anything like that to ever happen, and have learned through this Pasadena Art Museum escapade. They are not going to make the same mistake. There'll be larger areas for mistakes, I'm sure, since it's starting off so big.

PK: Right now, you're spending a lot of time working on the retrospective exhibition being organized by the San Francisco Museum of Modern Art which is opening in—

ER: March 1982.

———

PK: *How do you feel about that? There are a lot of implications that arise from having a retrospective.*

ER: I'm forced to be academic about it. We get into a lot of questions like: Was this 7⅛ inch or was it 7³⁄₁₆ inch?—questions I'm really not interested in. It's such a self-involved project. It becomes too much reflection back upon myself and I can't look forward. I can only look back with a situation like that. So I'm at battle with myself, wondering whether this should all happen or not. I'd rather have it quiet in another sense. Working on the show has been so time-consuming that it really affected the work I'm doing now.

PK: *In what way?*

ER: Just the pure consumption of time it takes to do something like that. I want to keep the future open to myself. I find myself doing less and less projects on the outside and more and more time spent in my studio.

PK: *You said working on this retrospective affected your current work. But I'm wondering if having to deal with that particular subject, taking stock of your career with the retrospective, affects the direction of your work.*

ER: No.

PK: *Does this sense of your own art history then impinge upon your current work?*

ER: No. While it has to do so much with the self, I'm responsible to myself for representing myself and being faithful to what has happened in the past. I still don't find that it's going to have that much affect upon what I do in the future. It just hasn't. Because I don't know what the future has to offer.

PK: *Maybe you will find that this exercise of working on a retrospective—maybe even without your knowing it—pushes you in a certain direction.*

ER: It could easily.

PK: *You've designed the exhibition catalog.*

ER: Yes, I oversaw the making of the catalog. I felt I was lucky to be able to control that. I could show the pictures I wanted to show. The one hope I have

———

is that when all this work is assembled, the condition of the work is better than what I think it's going to be. Because paintings get damaged. I'm hoping there's going to be some standard of excellence that comes out in it. There are some artists and some curators and some directors that would rather see a good catalog made than a good exhibit made. I feel less that way than I used to. I used to think a catalog meant quite a bit to an exhibit. I feel differently now that it's my own work, and I'm really concerned that those pictures are in good condition.

PK: On the other hand, a catalog is a document. It will live on. An exhibition offers the experience of seeing the actual works, and then it's gone. Doesn't the staying-power of a catalog interest you?

ER: Oh, I suppose so. In my history, I'm fairly committed to the book form. In a sense, the catalog is one of my books, although it's about my work rather than actually my work. I'd like to see the whole thing behind me. It's so self-indulgent. There's got to be some more air coming in from someplace.

PK: Does the whole concept of a retrospective at this stage bother you in any way?

ER: It's a semantic discussion as to what "retrospective" really means. I think that I, Ed Ruscha, forty-three years old today, living in Los Angeles, working here, have a few more things to say that will not be covered in that so-called retrospective. A real retrospective is for someone who has gone through all the periods of his creative endeavor. This is a retrospective up to a point. It has not really encompassed all of the moves I know I'm going to go through. It's like a view, a survey, of my work. So I've denied calling it a retrospective. But then I've given in to the semantic aspect of it, and not been so critical of it, sensitive towards it.

PK: But does it make you feel as if you've become an institution?

ER: No, because I'm not. It represents everything that I've done and everything I represent in the last twenty years. There's enough discord and enough dissatisfaction in things as they are, and I've got the proper negative environment to live and keep producing. I'm just never really satisfied. It's not writing, it's not putting the cap on the whole situation.

———

PK: Do you think the exhibition will reveal that the whole thing is still in process?

ER: I think so. I know the show will.

PK: What's the latest work that's going to be shown?

ER: The latest work will be the bamboo pole I painted. 20″ × 159″ [*Bamboo Pole, 1980*].

PK: Like Ancient Dogs Barking?

ER: Very much like that. Almost the same background. Actually it's more like the upper background. Then there's a bamboo pole. I had this dream that I could work right up to the time the exhibit went up, and then maybe put some very brand new things in there. But I could see you couldn't make a catalog and be correct with the archives if a work was left out of the catalog.

PK: Why not?

ER: I don't know why.

PK: It sounds to me like you've been convinced.

ER: I'll have another art show on the street in front of the museum. I actually may have a show at the Weinberg Gallery. There are going to be some works that are back in New York and maybe a few new things.

PK: That would be good because that could accomplish what I think you'd like to show: that your art is a continued process. It isn't stopped.

ER: I think most people will know that. It's implied in the whole process.

PK: How are the recent works being received? You had a show in New York not too long ago.

ER: Yes. It was a mild reception. I didn't sell them all. But I never sell any of my work until it's about three or four years old. Very seldom do I sell something. Most of my shows go unsold.

PK: Why do you suppose that's so?

ER: I don't know. Every artist I know has always said, "Hey, I had an opening last night and sold everything." It's never happened to me.

PK: But you don't worry about it.

ER: No.

PK: I'm surprised, because you certainly are known internationally, and you're collected internationally, as far as I know. Are there certain periods of your work that are in demand now for historical reasons?

ER: The only response I get from that is usually from auction houses. It seems like my work does go for fairly high prices at auctions. But mostly the older works. For one reason or another, the newer things don't show up at auction, because they're bought by people who have not owned them long enough to resell them. I guess older work generally gets sold at auctions.

PK: Well sure, and many of them have gone into museums, they're less available. Historical L.A. art of the '60s has become more desirable.

ER: Right. Well, I think my best painting is in that show Seventeen Artists from the Sixties, which is Noise, Pencil, Broken Pencil, Cheap Western [1963]. I still feel like that's my best painting.

PK: Let me ask you just one more question. I was looking at your record collection, which is a pretty good one: pretty interesting, pretty eclectic. You have obviously an interest in popular music. You even have some Disneyland records—I don't know if they're for you or your son. There's a whole catalog of Frank Zappa, and you've got some Captain Beefheart, rock-n-roll, jazz, some new wave things.

ER: Country and western songs. I like country and western.

PK: Do you see any connection between that interest and music?

ER: Absolutely, absolutely, yes. Because there are thought patterns that people put into their music. It's music and it's also words, and I'm involved in words, too. I guess they're artists on the same plane as I am, but in some funny way they're very distant from me. But close enough to me that I'm intrigued by it, and I'm also influenced by it. I find that some of the musicians are making a more cohesive statement to me than many artists do, even artists whom I admire. I think that some of the musicians are bridging many gaps that I'd like to see myself bridge. For that reason that music interests me.

PK: It's interesting that you are drawn to Zappa, and especially to Captain Beefheart, a somewhat esoteric figure and self-proclaimed artist who lives out in the Mohave Desert, not too far from where your place is in Joshua. Beefheart really is a cult figure. His music—for anybody who has listened to it—is difficult, unusual. They're usually very short pieces with a lot of talking and strange images. Words are extremely important; it's almost a free-form poetry. As a matter of fact, Zappa has produced some of Beefheart's music.

ER: They've even sung on each other's albums.

PK: Picking up on one thing you said about the importance of words in popular music—this seems to fit perhaps with your own interests, in particular with Captain Beefheart.

ER: As artists, they're less fearful of parts of history and making contemporary thoughts out of it. Frank Zappa will use some Tin Pan Alley music for seven seconds to make a certain statement, whereas I don't go back and borrow things from the past like that. I'm more involved in my own style. Yet musicians—especially these musicians we've just talked about—are constantly using music as their whole power. They go back and use all kinds of things through history to make their statement cohesive. They borrow from one another more easily than I, say, borrow from other artists.

PK: Are you interested at all in Gertrude Stein's poetry, and the use of language or of words that evolve into concrete poetry? They're poems but they're set up in ways that have a visual effect that's finally almost divorced from the significance of the words themselves.

ER: Apollinaire . . .

PK: Yes, well, some of the Surrealists, the Dadaists. Does that attract you?

ER: Yes, it really does.

PK: Sometimes it's nonsense, or seems to be.

ER: I would be attracted to it because it was nonsense. I like the idea of some-one making a statement about something that you don't make statements about. That really attracts me. When musicians do that, I see that their statement is not far off from what mine might be.

PK: *What about Punk rock? I was thinking of one aspect of some Punk groups, where noise and volume seem to be the goal as much as their lyrics. It's almost impossible at a performance to understand what they are saying.*

ER: Yes, which is unimportant. Punk's basic statements are alienation and the frustration theme. They use that in almost everything they do, so you don't even have to listen to their words. They're just talking about how they hate mommy and would like to slit her throat. Words to me have never been that; if they were, I'd be more under fire than a musician. Musicians get away with murder. They've got the widest extended set of artistic licenses than anybody. That's what I like about it.

PK: *All I need is that back beat, the sound . . .*

ER: Yes, and so it's a drone that they're able to do. I really like that about mu-sic—you don't have to understand the lyrics.

PK: *It's moved to the point where the words themselves don't even have to be understood in a performance. If you listen to X,*[31] *for instance, some of the L.A. groups. They're singing English, but you can't understand what they're singing. You've got to read the sub-titles. There are words, and they tell stories.*

ER: That's why I like to get a libretto on lead sheets, along with the dust jack-ets. It really makes a curious connection when you can listen to them sing and then you can read their words.

———

"ED RUSCHA: AN INTERVIEW"

Henri Man Barendse

HMB: With regard to the decision-making process in your books, the implications are quite clear: a random number of random subjects. But why did you, Ed Ruscha, choose gas stations?

ER: Because they were there. I saw them when I traveled.

HMB: There was no personal interest in gas stations?

ER: Well, it's a matter of subject matter. As an artist, I had to pick a subject that I considered art, so that was my choice. I could have picked flowers, or graveyards, or headstones. There's an endless number of possibilities [. . .]. I don't know why I picked gas stations, except that they had been unreported.

HMB: But it seems like a fairly logical choice of subject matter. You did travel often and the gas stations punctuate, measure that. There's something to be said for the poignancy of those things on a trip through the desolate southwest.

ER: Well, I didn't necessarily stop at those gas stations to get gas. I ran into some peculiar situations while working on that project. I had to go across the street

———

Originally published in *Afterimage*, v. 8, n. 7, February 1981, pp. 8–10.

sometimes to take the pictures and it seemed like everyone would stare. A couple of the workers tracked me down, followed me, and asked me what I was doing. So I ran into a little opposition, but nobody really minded that much. The project was a smooth, flowing kind of thing. You see, the strange thing about it was that I knew in advance what the whole concept was going to be, and that made the work itself much easier. That's true with everything I do. [. . .]

HMB: Do you regard [Some Los Angeles] Apartments, [Nine Swimming] Pools, [Some Real Estate] Opportunities, [Twentysix] Gas[oline] Stations, *and* [Thirty-four] Parking Lots *as having something in common, as being linked thematically, and do you regard* Babycakes, [Royal] Road Test, Records, *and* Dutch Details *as outside of that group? Would you categorize your books?*

ER: I suppose you could, if you wanted to say they were culturally connected because they're all architectural or landscape. Personally, I've never categorized them. But if you looked at them from a common-sense standpoint, put them all out on the table, it would be easy to. You could say these have buildings and these have people and so forth.

HMB: With regard to the former group, the "landscape" books, do you see the gas stations, pools, parking lots and so forth as symbolic? They are archetypically American things. On the other hand, of course, you've talked about the specific quality of your titles and the "fact" of each photograph, which suggests that they're not at all transcendental things: metaphors, symbols, or anything like that. Yet when you think of the books together, it's almost as if there's some kind of message there, for they seem so related. Does Ed Ruscha have a "vision" of America?

ER: My intention in doing the books was to create something that was black humor, in a sense. I didn't want anybody to know the answers. But if people came up to me and asked me, well, I'll give them an answer. I'd try. The books have their strength when they're encountered by strangers.

HMB: You mean it's that "huh?" business that Willoughby Sharp discussed,[32] *that element of surprise?*

———

ER: Well, it could be.

HMB: So you don't see yourself as having a statement to make about what the books may mean in a social/historical context?

ER: I don't have an artistic, verbal statement to make about the books. I could say certain things, things that I really feel, and you may be able to draw conclusions. But then it may not add up, you see.

HMB: What I was trying to get at was that in the whole set of books there are these Los Angeles/American things. But you'd rather not commit yourself to that.

ER: It's that that's the way it happens to be. But then, every once in a while I do one that's not particularly L.A. and someone will come up to me and say, "You sure do L.A. things," or, "That's sure L.A."

HMB: But it's like Andy Warhol pointing out that there were no people in your pictures, ever! There are certain consistencies that suggest you had something in mind. As you said to Willoughby Sharp, "After you see all the books together, they begin to make some sense. It shows more about the attitude behind them than any single book does." *What I want to know is whether you can say anything about that attitude.*

ER: The attitude is just following through, following through with a feeling of blind faith that I had from the very beginning. That's what made the whole thing so fluid for me. The books were easy to do; once I established a format—the first one was agony—it was fluid because I had a format and I could almost fit these ideas. Each one could be plugged into the system I had. It's like a system of expression, if you want to look at it that way. [. . .]

   Probably my least favorite [book], the most foreign book, is *Crackers*—the most unlike me. *Records* was another. I did books piggy-back, two at the same time. *Records* was . . . I felt like while it was clean, it was sorted through at the same time another one was. I felt like I was overdoing it.

HMB: I don't mean to be fishing for things, putting words in your mouth, but if the books didn't have any social implications. . . .

ER: Oh, they do, they do, by the nature of what they do. But my intentions are not there. I'm not broadcasting anything with those books. I like the idea of doing the books and sort of slipping them here and there. I've encountered some strange people and strange reactions from the books—some intellectual friends were disgusted, which surprised me. It really did. People who I admired, people involved in the intellectual world, were not so much stumped as they were insulted. "What's he trying to put over on the public?"—that old idea.

HMB: I don't mean to beat a dead horse, but I wanted to ask if you feel your books are at all autobiographical, because they do have a peculiar existentialist thread running through them. Part of that has to do with the fact that there are no people in the pictures, I suppose. The whole thing is somewhat desolate.

ER: There's a dryness which I went for, actually. I liked that, having it dry and simple and, in a way, unartistic. I came here from Oklahoma when I was 18 and it was like romping around Los Angeles, seeing all these things, meeting all these people. The whole thing was a lasting experience for me. I still have it; I always will. That's why I'll never leave Los Angeles. I go to the desert maybe once a week for two or three days. I spend almost half my time out there but I can't stay away from this town. I love it. I still get lifeblood from this place. So the books are autobiographical, sure. Sometimes I say, "What if?"—what if I'd gone to Chicago or what if I'd stayed in Oklahoma City? And I think that whatever I might have done in art would have come out of those sources. I may have done oil wells.

HMB: You've said, half-seriously, I suspect, that you came to California because you liked palm trees and hot rods. You've done the book of palm trees but never one of cars. It seems like cars are a missing link in the books, quite literally, since they would tie them together, be the conduit between the pools, apartments, and of course, the parking lots and gas stations. Perhaps I'm taking things too literally again.

ER: No, cars are too much like people. It would be hard to make a statement about cars without flavoring it too heavily. I picked more or less neutral subjects

213

that would not ordinarily be chosen as subjects for art. I think cars would have been . . . I just couldn't do anything with them. It may have to do with the people aspect. It's not an idea I rejected; it's just an idea that never got off the ground.

But now that I think of it all these subjects lead you back to people. Gas stations have obvious implications—industrial culture. I was going to do a book on industrial buildings. I took a lot of pictures of industrial buildings, and finally *Real Estate Opportunities* came out of that. In a way it's the crash of all that immediate culture that I was interested in. I don't know why cars weren't in there.

HMB: Were you familiar with the photographs of Walker Evans when you made Twentysix Gasoline Stations *in 1962?*

ER: Sure, but they didn't have anything to do with that book.

HMB: Since then, your style, or rather, your "non-style" of photography has been compared to that of Evans. This is partly, I suspect, because he photographed gas stations on several occasions and partly because he also sought a kind of objective photography.

ER: I've always found that surprising, because I don't see that. Evans takes pictures with people in them.

HMB: I don't see it either and though, as I've mentioned, you've been compared to Evans by several critics, it strikes me as a comparison of the most general and superficial kind. But in trying to come up with an answer to the question, "What do Ruscha's pictures look like?" I keep thinking of real estate pictures themselves, the kind you see in the office window in a small town. And that's curious, because they are all about real estate in one way or another. The terrific irony about Real Estate Opportunities *is that they look right. They don't look out of place at all; they look like exactly what you see in the real estate office if you're looking for an opportunity.*

ER: There was no conscious effort to imitate that style, but at the same time it is really functioning in the same way as a real estate photographer who just goes out to shoot a picture to show somebody what the land looks like. That's all I was doing, showing the land.

———

HMB: The idea of the readymade begins to suggest itself. How has Duchamp been an influence for you in these books?

ER: The readymade was more or less a guiding light to me, the idea of calling something a work of art. It's not necessarily that the artist has the freedom to call anything he wants art; it was another side that intrigued me—I suppose it's an extension of a readymade in photographic form. Instead of going out and calling a gas station "art," I'm calling its photograph art. But the photograph isn't the art—the gas station might be. The photograph is just a surrogate gas station. The photograph by itself doesn't mean anything to me; it's the gas station that's the important thing.

HMB: I'd like to go back to your statement that you just yawned when you got Colored People *back from the printer. You haven't made a book in six years. Duchamp wrote: "Anything can become very beautiful if the gesture is repeated often enough; this is why the number of my readymades is limited." Does this suggest the reasons you stopped making books?*

ER: First, let me say that I never meant that I would never make a book again. I simply meant that the thrill of doing it was no longer there, as I said before. In fact, I'm working on another book right now. I'm doing it with Lawrence Weiner.[33] We went out and got a few girls and shot some pictures on the street and down at the marina and on the Santa Monica pier. We're going to make some kind of story out of it. I'm not sure what direction it will take. There'll be dialogue.

Anyway, the Duchamp statement makes perfect sense to me. But I don't feel restricted like that—I could see a thousand books, a thousand titles. I thought that way from the very beginning. The format was part of that; that's what I meant by plugging anything I thought of into that system. But along the way I found I had to make changes, like with *Parking Lots*. I got the photographs back from the photographer and he'd made beautiful 8 × 10 glossy blowups. It was amazing that I'd gotten this guy to go up there and shoot the whole thing and give me the negatives for $250. He'd hired the helicopter and everything. I got the photographs back and was floored by them. I couldn't bring myself to reduce those photographs to fit the original format, so I just said, "No."

But to get back to Duchamp, yes, the sheer number of the things waters it down, weakens it. When it's an established thing, and everyone understands it, it's lost its original function. If everyone knew what the books were about, the whole thing would be totally different. That's why I was interested in the book form. Duchamp had already killed the idea of the object on display. After what he did, it would be hard to surprise anyone. So books, conventional books, were a way for me to catch my audience off-guard. But every year I have at least two shows of my books in galleries and they put them on the walls, because that's what they want. Though it's okay by me, it's not the same thing. They're easy to see, easy to accept because of the context they're in—you know what to think, everything's spelled out for you. It's on a gallery wall so it must be art. The way they're supposed to be seen, of course, is when someone hands someone else just one book at a time and place where they don't expect it.

HMB: Jasper Johns has said that he got the idea for his alphabet from a children's book illustration. The format, shape, and size of your books looks like one of the books Johns might have been referring to. You've talked about your interest in "unusual publications" and that you consider your books as "manuals." Where did you get the idea for the format?

ER: The printer helped me settle on the size. I went to one printer and he seemed to be real sympathetic with what I was doing. We sat down and went over several papers, figured out size and spoilage and things like that. Then, with a half inch here and there to play with, I came up with that size. So the format came out of personal design, taste, aesthetics, but only within the confines of the economics and the practical factors involved. It was a matter of completely happy compromises to get something that was satisfactory. My decisions have never been nerve-racking decisions; they're mostly practical, simple, and easy. All my books have been free-flowing things; there's no tortured artist in these books. And that's what I like about it; I like waking up in the morning and saying, "Well, I guess it's swimming pools today."

As far as unusual publications go, I don't know. [. . .] But I was always interested in small books and I traveled to Europe and saw books over there very unlike the ones here. I just like the feel of them. It's basically aesthetic. I just like books—not to collect them but to look at them, feel the pages.

HMB: But you've said you have "little sympathy for the hand-made book." You've said: "One of the purposes of my books has to do with making a mass-produced object." You've also said: "I am not trying to create a precious limited edition book but a mass-produced product of high order."

ER: Well, do you know Wally Berman's books?[34] He's done about six or seven books called *Semina*. They were abstract cloudy thoughts and images montaged, naked women and all. They were all done on a hand press; pasted in the covers and everything. When I first met him, we exchanged a few books. We hit it off immediately, but we had nothing in common as far as our approaches to making a book. Mine was industrial, his was personal—making it on his own press, binding it himself, carefully handing it to somebody. He had a different aesthetic, but there are still a lot of similarities.

HMB: Getting back to the subjects of your books, you've talked about your sequencing of the images within a given book so that "a mood doesn't take over," which is in itself a non-sequencing that complements your non-style of photography. But I'm thinking of the whole series. It's a kind of list, isn't it? You are interested in lists, things that rhyme: banks, tanks, thanks; and keeping lists of words for your prints. Do you see the whole series of books as a kind of list?

ER: No. Here again, for me they are what they appear to be. But if that's what you want to think, then that's fine, too. It's not a conscious list, though.

HMB: How do you describe the way you photograph?

ER: There are a few people who have thought that I was simply after the raunchiest things to photograph, but actually what I was after was no-style or a non-statement with a no-style. It became a mixture of those things. I wanted to eliminate any self-consciousness about style. I'd rather have no style than any style. Some people have thought that certain pictures in *Apartment Buildings* and other books were interesting as photographs, but that was never my intention. Again, that's only me; the viewer has to make up his own mind.

———

217

HMB: So when you took those photographs of the apartments you didn't have it in mind that you would draw them later?

ER: No, I think that was just nervous energy. I could have made drawings from any of the photographs at any time.

HMB: Do you look at much contemporary photography, and if so what do you like?

ER: I get a lot of catalogs and announcements in the mail and that's mainly how I get exposed to it. I know Lewis Baltz's work, though I've never met him. I know Stephen Shore, and I like William Eggleston's work. He does such varied stuff; he's like a filmmaker who can make a film on a religious subject and then turn around and do one on baby raping. He does a lot of nature things— his trees are just dynamite. And then he'll have something like a '63 Chevy that's equally good. I can't think of any photographers that are real standouts, but then I'm not very involved with it.

HMB: John Baldessari?

ER: Yes. But then some artists use photography as a medium, which is almost not photography. I mean, they're not speaking to photographers.

HMB: At the end of Twentysix Gasoline Stations *is the photograph of the FINA station. It's the one picture in the book that looks self-conscious, composed. Did you. . . .*

ER: You mean more so than the others?

HMB: Well, it stands out. . . .

ER: I think it was empty. Isn't that in Albuquerque?

HMB: I think so. No, it's in Texas.

ER: It's either in Texas or it's in Albuquerque. I have a feeling it's in Albuquerque.

HMB: It's not in Groom?

ER: Groom, Texas! Yeah, Groom, Texas, which is no longer on the highway.

———

HMB: Did you put that in on purpose, so that it said FINA at the end?

ER: Oh, I see. You mean about it being the last picture the book? No. Eleanor Antin also wrote about the sequence of it [*Art in America,* November–December, 1973] and she said something about having expected a travelogue or something like that. There it goes again—the bubble being shattered! To me it was just a collection of pictures and I more or less kept them in pace. That's where it gets into no-man's land.

L.A. SUGGESTED BY THE ART OF EDWARD RUSCHA

[. . .] The idea of Hollywood has lots of meanings and one—to me—is this image of something fake up here being held up with sticks. That to me had more in meaning with the term "Hollywood" than the other usual associations. I looked outside my window here and I saw the sign "Hollywood" and it became the subject matter for me. It only lasted for a while so the actual remnants of the sign are not even important to me. I don't even think it should stay; it doesn't even mean "landmark" to me. It might as well fall down. That's more Hollywood—to have it fall down or be removed. But in the end, it's more Hollywood to put it back up, see? *[Laughter.]*

[Ruscha descending the stairs in his studio]

[Ruscha mechanically raising a large unfinished canvas]

[Shot of the "Hollywood" sign]

[Montage of Los Angeles night-life scenes]

[Ruscha in his studio]

Transcribed from the film produced and directed by Gary Conklin, 28 min., Mystic Fire Video, 1981.

"Hollywood" is like a verb to me. It's something that you can do to any subject or any thing. You can take something in Grand Rapids, Michigan and "Hollywoodize" it. They do it with automobiles, they do it with everything that we manufacture. It all somehow comes out of that. But it doesn't come from this little community that I live in. It's only coincidental that I live in this little place called Hollywood.

"Hollywood dreams"—I mean, think about it. Close your eyes and what does it mean, visually? It means a ray of light, actually, to me, rather than a success story. And so I play around with the ray of light rather than with the success story. I'm not interested so much in success stories or living out success stories personally. The phenomenon of the thing is just the imagery that comes out of it. If you look at the 20th Century Fox, you get this feeling of concrete immortality. The letters actually come out of this shaft that is shooting way back in the ground like this, you know, and it's all substance. But in a sense that's like a ray of light so those images are in my work.

I'm not as much interested in words as I am in the evocative power of them, rather than their poetic power. The words themselves are made up of little letters which also are visual, and they also somehow come up into a marriage of the two. There's like little strings of things, like little objects have always intrigued me and the words are the same way.

[Shot of Ruscha painting Another Hollywood Dream Bubble Popped *(1976)]*

[Shot of the evening sky]

[Montage of Ruscha's Miracle *(1975),* Large Trademark with Eight Spotlights, *and word paintings]*

[Shots of neon signs and advertisements]

[Medium shot of Ruscha in his studio]

[Shots of driving on Los Angeles roads—factories, landscapes, office towers, etc.]

[Shot of Ruscha's Bronson Tropics *drawing (1965)]*

———

221

Ed Ruscha, *Bronson Tropics*. 1965. Graphite on paper. 14⅛ × 22⅝″. Photo courtesy Ed Ruscha.

Do you often see better from a car than on foot in Los Angeles?

Well, you get the motion behind it. If you're walking, it's more contemplative. If you're driving, you have less time to think about it and so things are automatic. They're swift, see, it's almost like, whoosh! like this. They go by you so fast that they seem to have a power to them, they have more power when they're flying by you. An apartment house drawing. A drawing of the Bronson Tropics apartment house, it's like a random picking I have noticed in my travels around the streets of L.A. I've made drawings on the spot, I've taken photographs, I've done all kinds of things to record these feelings I had running around the streets of L.A.

Everything you see on the street I'm influenced by. That's what it is, it's just the iconography of the city, the way the city is. Columbus, Ohio is not that way. New York is not that way—it's not like California, it doesn't have this little silhouette, popped-up building feel. It's like a model, it's like a surface, and I'm interested in all these little surfaces along the way. And that's why I'm curious about streets in L.A., because somewhere it all comes back into my art, the idea of streets in L.A.

Los Angeles to me is like a series of store-front planes that are all vertical from the street, and there's almost like nothing behind the façades. It's all façades here—that's what in-

[Montage of Ruscha's Apartment Building drawings (c. 1965)]

[Shot of Ruscha's painting I Live Over In Valley View *(1975) followed by Los Angeles suburbs]*

[Los Angeles buildings and streets]

[Shots of billboard advertisements and storefronts]

[Driving by storefronts]

[Close-up of a red map]

[Medium shot of Ruscha in his studio]

[Montage of Ruscha's Standard Station *paintings and urban fires]*

[Driving through Mount Olympus: suburban houses, construction sites, hillsides]

trigues me about the whole city of Los Angeles—the façade-ness of the whole thing. [. . .]

Streets are like ribbons. They're like ribbons and they're dotted with facts. Fact ribbons,
I guess. That's potential subject matter to me
and so I take some things and I write them
down and I look at them forever and forever
and forever and I might use something ten years
afterwards that I had noticed before, you see.

Mount Olympus is a pretty funny place
to drive through. I really enjoy driving
through there. [. . .] Now, it's changed in the
last three or four years in that people are actually building out there again. But for a while it
was like a ravished hillside, an incomplete architectural dream of somebody's, to build all
these places that look like Rome. That's one
thing about L.A.: the degenerate things seem
to offer so much for an artist. To view somebody's indulgence and the direction of their
indulgence. [. . .]

———

"Ed Ruscha, Young Artist: Dead Serious about Being Nonsensical"

Patricia Failing

Ed Ruscha's business cards identify him as "Ed-werd Rew-shay, Young Artist." He might draw a picture of a tree on the card to prove it. Or maybe a 1950 Ford. "But I'm still amazed," *he says,* "really amazed that I can be an artist and that people will buy my work."

Forty-four-year-old Ruscha has been a "young artist" for more than twenty years. In 1963, three years after graduation from Chouinard Art Institute in Los Angeles, his first one-man exhibition was held at the nearby Ferus Gallery. Since then, there have been sixty-five one-man Ruscha exhibitions and his work has been included in more than two hundred group shows throughout Europe and America. On March 25, the first full-scale Ruscha retrospective opened at the San Francisco Museum of Modern Art; it will later travel. In conjunction with the show, Hudson Hills Press of New York has published The Works of Edward Ruscha, *a comprehensive volume designed by the artist himself. [. . .]*

Ruscha first became known as a Pop artist, painting commercially pristine images of California icons like Standard gasoline stations and the 20th Century Fox trademark. In the mid-'60s he narrowed his subject matter to single words, often rendered as three-dimensional objects that could be squeezed, poured or set on fire. From 1970 to 1972

Originally published in *Art News,* v. 81, n. 4, April 1982, pp. 74–81. Published on the opening of the exhibition *The Works of Edward Ruscha,* organized by the San Francisco Museum of Modern Art.

Ruscha stopped painting and made prints of words inked with substances like baked beans, caviar, daffodils, cherry pie filling, axle grease, chutney and Metrecal. Later he branched out into photo-silkscreening and etching, started painting on unconventional surfaces including taffeta and satin and made innumerable pastel drawings of favorite phrases such as "Honey, I twisted through more damn traffic today" and "Headlights are similar to people's eyes." He has also made two 16mm films and published fifteen amicably black-humored books.

Despite the variety of his production, a lot of people still think of Ruscha as a standard Pop artist. New York's commissioner of cultural affairs and former curator of twentieth-century art at the Metropolitan Museum, Henry Geldzahler, points out, however, that "it is difficult to pigeonhole [Ruscha's] style at all. Conceptual, Pop, Surrealist, Dada, neo-Dada, earth art—all these are, arguably, elements of his style. Ruscha can be pinned down partially by any of these labels, and yet he escapes all of them."

Ruscha prefers it that way. "The best labels are pressure-sensitive," *he says.* "They should be peeled off easily because labels pin a man down. . . . If any of these labels stuck, my career would probably be over, because fashions come and go." *[. . .]*

Ruscha is a man of medium height who tends to grin rather than smile, and whose casual attire contrasts with his carefully tended haircut. A reporter from Rolling Stone *once described him as looking "as if he would be an elegant card dealer if only he'd favor ruffled shirts."[35] He speaks politely and openly to studio visitors about his work, although he rarely seems to say what the more philosophical among them want to hear. This kind of visitor, usually from out of town, believes that artistic issues such as literal versus depicted space, the muse of mathematical composition systems, transubstaniation of word and image, non-narrative discourse, and the objectification of vernacular speech all have something to do with Ruscha's work. But in responding to questions about, say, the a priori numerical field defined in his book* Twentysix Gasoline Stations, *Ruscha tends to change the subject discreetly.* "You know, what really interested me about that project," *he might reply,* "was the sound of the number '26.' I really like the number '26,' and I wanted to do something with '26' in it."

Such behavior seems to have confounded serious critics, who tend to make appreciative noises about Ruscha's work without subjecting it to in-depth analysis. Composing a catalog essay for Ruscha's retrospective, critic David Hickey found himself "charged with the obligation of summing up a body of critical opinion which no one had been so bold as to venture. I mean, here was a guy who was about to have a retrospective who managed to generate about as much critical comment as Sonny Bono. . . . It made Edward Ruscha look like a genius, of course, to have gotten so far into deep water without having acquired any academic pilot-fish; me it made look a little foolish: kamikaze intellectual stalks white idea with snorkel and Brownie."[36]

Talking with Ruscha, one soon realizes that if there are any direct answers to questions about the "meaning" of his work, they are probably autobiographical. The fact that he grew up looking at the flat, low horizon landscape of Oklahoma, for example, left an indelible impression that Ruscha transferred to his paintings. With his middle-class, middle-western Catholic upbringing, Ruscha felt liberated by California culture and intrigued by the artist-celebrity lifestyle it could support. Also significant is the subversive conception of art and nonsense he developed along with his Oklahoma City high-school fraternity brothers such as composer Mason Williams and painter Joe Goode.

Ruscha, Goode and Williams are still close friends. "When the spirits of people you're attached to as you grow up tend to keep going along in the same direction, you tend to influence each other," *says Ruscha.* "We all seemed to grow up in the same strata too. In Oklahoma back in the early '50s we were experiencing a kind of runny-nose prosperity—we weren't sodbusters exactly. We did have the opportunity to go away to school—as far away as California—and not be saddled with the kind of Bible Belt values I grew up with—the success-and-prosperity consciousness that said you had to go out and emulate your parents. We could see, growing up in Oklahoma, that there was no room for poets and artists—absolutely no room."

No room, at any rate, for the kind of art and artist who really interested Ruscha. "I looked at a lot of pictures in books on Dada in the library. It wasn't because I was interested in developing a scholarly appreciation—I was more attracted by the titillation I got from the works I saw in those books. I was inspired by this sort of lunatic group of people who made art that ran against prevailing ideas. Their nonsense was synonymous with seriousness, and I've always been dead serious about being nonsensical."

After graduating from Classen High School in 1956, Ruscha and Williams drove to California in a lowered '50 Ford with Smitty mufflers. "California seemed the most natural place to go," *Ruscha remembers.* "New York was out of the question—it was stepping backward somehow. I suppose because of the media images we had seen, California had more appeal. The magnetism could have had to do with pure colors—the colors of the palm trees—or it could have had to do with pure ideas, like blonde girls running on the beach. I knew there was a cold intellectual side to New York, and that did have some appeal to it—but not enough. I didn't want to freeze back there. It was cold enough in Oklahoma."

Ruscha enrolled at Chouinard Art Institute, the Walt Disney–backed school that became the California Institute of the Arts in 1971. Robert Irwin, Billy Al Bengston, and John Altoon were teaching there, and fellow students included Larry Bell, Llyn Foulkes, Wally Batterton, Eddie Bereal, and Oklahomans Goode, Don Moore, Patrick Blackwell, and Jerry McMillan. Ruscha tried without success to become an Abstract Expressionist. "They would say, face the canvas and let it happen, follow your own gestures, let the painting create itself. But I'd always have to think up something first. If I didn't, it wasn't *art* to me. Also it looked real dumb. They wanted to collapse the whole art process into one act; I wanted to break it into stages, which is what I do now. Whatever I do now is completely premeditated, however off-the-wall it might be."

In 1957 Ruscha saw a reproduction of Jasper Johns's Target with Four Faces *in* Print *magazine. It was the "atomic bomb" in his training, he says.* "I saw it as something that didn't seem to follow the history of art. My teachers said it was *not* art. I didn't need to see the colors or the scale—it was just a pure, powerful image to me that came across in a halftone illustration. It was a strange fruit, and I guess I was really ready for that."

Ruscha, in fact, "never was inspired by the holy world of painting. I was always more interested in photographically oriented image consciousness—printed pages, detached imagery." *He also developed special appreciation for Marcel Duchamp's painting* The Chocolate Grinder. "It was like a mystery that did not need explaining to me. I'll never need to take an intellectual delving into that subject—not because I'm afraid to, but because I don't think there would be that much to offer over something that just has its own power. The real oddity

---

Ed Ruscha, *Su*. 1958. Oil and ink on fabric, 37¾ × 36⅛″. Collection Suzanne and Gerry Rosentsweig, Los Angeles. Photo courtesy Ed Ruscha.

of *The Chocolate Grinder* is that it has a dedication to certain classic truths about the making of a picture and the illustrating of an object and then it also has this *inane*-ness to it."

In the late 1950s Ruscha started making collages and montages and then began painting the covers of hardbound books. "I began to see book covers as juicy surface to work at and on. Books and their titles have always been important to me. So the title of my artworks is very important to me—sometimes as important as the work itself. I looked at books as canvases almost because they were three-dimensional in the same way canvases are—so on some of my later canvases I also painted titles along the so-called spine of the canvas."

Using a format analogous to a book cover, Ruscha composed one of his first word paintings, Su, *in 1958. Its two letters centered alone on a square, neutral background, "Su" referred to Su Hall, a girlfriend at the time.* "I thought of it as my painting of her and for her—my portrait of her," *says Ruscha.*

After graduating from Chouinard in 1960, Ruscha took a full-time job in an advertising agency doing layout and graphics, an experience he found to be "sheer hell." After a year he left and spent seven months traveling in Europe, where he discovered that "the classics didn't mean anything to me at all. I didn't spend much time in the Louvre. I was much more interested in visiting galleries to see what was going on. And what was going on, oddly enough, was Johns and Rauschenberg." [. . .]

[In 1962] Ruscha began moving out of his Jasper Johns phase, tightening his surfaces and painting single words like "honk," "radio," and "oof," centered on neutral backgrounds. "I can't tell you exactly why I picked those words, but I was interested in monosyllabic word sounds that seemed to have a certain comedic value to them." *Ruscha also made his first painting with illusionistic three-dimensional letters in 1962,* Large Trademark with Eight [Spotlights]. *Its subject is the 20th Century Fox trademark but, Ruscha cautions,* "it didn't mean I was really into sign culture—community graphics—as such, although I do respond to it. I think my work always came more from the printed page than from big things out there because, for one thing, none of my paintings is big. I'm thinking of James Rosenquist and how his work came directly from his experience of painting billboards for the

public. If I'd had that kind of experience, I'd probably be painting bigger paintings of bigger things."

In addition to admiring their printed and typographical forms, Ruscha was also intrigued with words because they "exist in a world of no-size. Take a word like 'smash'—we don't know it by size. We see it on billboards, in four-point type and all stages in between. On the other hand, I found out that it is important for *objects* to be their actual size in my paintings. If I do a painting of a pencil or magazine or fly or pills, I feel some sort of responsibility to paint them natural size—I get out the ruler. Some of these ideas came together and blended in the late '60s when I painted words like 'adios' and 'hey' and had cherries and kidney beans in the letters. The beans and cherries were painted actual size, but the words were still in this anonymous world of no-size."

Words may not have size but they can have three dimensions, as Ruscha demonstrated in Large Trademark with Eight Spotlights. *And since objects are generally governed by the laws of physics rather than the rules of grammar, Ruscha began painting words as if they could be subject to physical forces. In* Securing the Last Letter *and* Squeezing Dimple *of 1964, for example, compressed and stretched letter forms are held in place by illusionistic C-clamps. In* Annie, Poured from Maple Syrup, *1966, a dripping, viscous puddle momentarily assumes the form of the Little Orphan Annie comic-strip logo.*

Another genre of word-objects was the "paper ribbon" drawings Ruscha first exhibited at the Alexandre Iolas gallery in New York in 1967. In these trompe l'oeil drawings, words are formed from what appear to be strips and pieces of paper illuminated by a low, raking light that casts long shadows. Although some reviewers thought they were made with an airbrush, the drawings created a small sensation at the time because they were, in fact, hand-executed in gunpowder, a medium Ruscha found superior to pure charcoal, one of gunpowder's prime ingredients.

About the same time, Ruscha discovered another way to objectify words by spelling them out in illusionistic splashes of liquid. "My 'romance with liquids' came about because I was looking for some sort of alternative entertainment for myself—an alternative from the rigid, hard-edge painting of words that had to respect some typographical design. These didn't—there were no rules about how a letter had to be formed. It was my sandbox to play in. I could make an 'o' stupid or I could make it hopeless or any way I wanted to and it would still be an 'o.'" [. . .]

Another of Ruscha's virtuoso graphic performances resulted from an invitation by Alecto Editions in London to produce a series of prints. The invitation came in 1970, at a time when Ruscha "didn't like oil painting anymore. I had gotten interested in the idea of staining things instead, and then it began to seem natural to stain things with things that really stain, like carrot juice. It seemed simple—the direct way between A and B—as opposed to trying to *illustrate* a stain using traditional illustrator's tools like oil paint." *In London, therefore, Ruscha decided to try to make prints with organic extracts rather than traditional inks. Many candidates flopped. Carnations, for example, did not pull because the paste separated from the liquid. Cream left a slimy deposit. Tomato paste dried to a gray dust. Chocolate syrup, raw egg, coffee, strawberries and tulips, however, were among the many substances that did result in successful screen prints.*

News, Mews, Pews, Brews, Stews & Dues, *as the series was called, pleased Ruscha enormously but failed as a commercial venture. For one thing, the results were not all that visually compelling: each word, centered in Gothic script, is rendered in colors that are often surprisingly mundane considering their origin. The organic "inks" also proved to be somewhat unstable: pinks from salmon roe, for example, slowly changed to bright yellow. Ruscha tends to regard these changes as bonuses, but traditional collectors, who pay from $300 to $4,000 for other Ruscha prints, apparently did not.*

Between 1962 and 1972, in addition to publishing fifteen books, Ruscha managed to execute more than five hundred word images in various media even though he was a "young artist" only part of the time. He was also employed as a book designer and printer's devil, and from 1965 to 1967 did layouts for Artforum *magazine, then headquartered above the Ferus Gallery. In 1967 he married Danna Knego, from whom he was divorced in 1972. Their son, Edward Joseph Ruscha V, was born in 1968. He also worked on projects with [Billy Al] Bengston and ceramic sculptor Ken Price and continued his close friendships with Williams and Goode, who frequently accompanied him on drives back to Oklahoma.*

"I used to drive back four or five times a year," *says Ruscha,* "and I began to feel that there was so much wasteland between L.A. and Oklahoma that somebody had to bring the news to the city. Then I had this idea for a book title—*Twentysix Gasoline Stations*—and it became like a fantasy rule in my mind that I knew I had to follow. Then it was just a matter of being a good little art soldier and going out and finishing it. It was a straightforward case of getting factual information and bringing it back. I thought of it as making a sort of training manual for people who want to know about things like that."

Twentysix Gasoline Stations, *published in 1962, was the prototype for most of Ruscha's subsequent books. It contains black and white snapshots of gasoline stations in California, Arizona, New Mexico, Oklahoma and Amarillo, Texas—the model for Ruscha's famous 1963 painting,* Standard Station—*each photographed from across the street and identified by a one-line caption giving name and location.*

Ruscha's second topographical book, Some Los Angeles Apartments, *1965, is identical in format to* Gasoline Stations *and serves as a training manual about typical Los Angeles habitats like the Fountain Blu, Tiki Tabu, Bronson Tropics, 11 Pompeii and Lee Tiki.* Thirtyfour Parking Lots, *1967, records totally vacant Los Angeles parking lots from the air. [. . .] In* [Every Building on] the Sunset Strip, *1966, Ruscha used a motorized Nikon to photograph all the buildings on both sides of the street and then pieced together the pictures into a double strip that unfolds to a length of twenty-seven feet. Other absolutely literal examples of title-content identity include* Nine Swimming Pools, *1968,* Records, *1971, and* A Few Palm Trees, *1971. [. . .]*

Ruscha's films, ostensibly straightforward shaggy-dog stories, have a similarly ironic infrastructure. Premium, *1970, based on a story by Williams that Ruscha also made into a book called* Crackers, *stars artist Larry Bell and includes comedian Tommy Smothers and topless-bathing-suit-designer Rudi Gernreich among its supporting cast. In the film, Bell lures a girl literally into a bed of lettuce, douses her with salad dressing, abandons her on the pretext of having forgotten crackers and then signs into an expensive hotel to eat saltines in bed alone. Another form of sexual displacement underlies* Miracle, *1975, in which a slobbish auto mechanic attains salvation by eschewing his friends, his luscious paramour (played by actress Michelle Phillips) and the entire outside world to attend to the needs of the technological soul—the carburetor—of a shiny red Ford Mustang.*

The point of Ruscha's offbeat humor eludes many people, but not, it seems, his old school chums. These faithful friends share a sensibility—or a nonsensibility—that makes

---

233

one suspect that some of Ruscha's work should be interpreted as a kind of fraternity in-joke. Ruscha keeps Williams apprised by postcard, for example, of his latest creations, such as Franchise Cemeteries *and* Ave. of Disgust. *Williams in turn suggests titles to Ruscha ("John Wayne Memorial Nuclear Playground") and has recently "thought of another book I'd like to do with Ed. It would be called* Things That Worry You *and would have pictures like an eight-year-old kid with a bow and arrow standing next to your car, or a large box in front of you in the middle of the freeway."*

It was Williams, in fact, who suggested to Ruscha that he keep the journal that now serves as a kind of creative linchpin. On its pages Ruscha records phrases from books, dictionaries, the radio, magazines and conversations that may later turn up in one form or another in his work. Looking them over, he comments on some of the notations he has actually used. Slobbering Drunk at the Palomino: "That's from a Frank Zappa song." Mysterious Voltage Drop: "I read it in an electrical manual." Malibu = Sliding Glass Doors: "That whoosh they make sounds like the ocean." Talk Real: "My kid said that once to me when he was small." Hello I Must Be Going: "A Groucho Marx quote." He Walks Into A Meeting Hall Full Of Workers And Yells Out, "O.K. What Is It You Guys Want, Pontiac Catalinas?": "It came to me in a dream."

But what kind of messages are these? How should they be interpreted? In 1971, when Ruscha was clearly equating words with physical objects, critic David Bourdon wrote that "a knowledge of the English language is not a prerequisite for enjoying Ruscha's work. . . . His work is more visual than conceptual because he obviously is more interested in the transformation of words into pictorial images than he is in making literary or intellectual allusion."

True enough in 1971. But since 1975 or so, much of Ruscha's oeuvre has consisted of pastel drawings of phrases like "just us chickens" and "squeaky lil' tummies," spelled out in plain block letters on completely anonymous backgrounds. This work obviously isn't "more visual than conceptual," and no foreign language dictionary decodes fragments of colloquialisms like "just us chickens." So what does Ruscha think he's doing here?

"I'm not thinking of the literary aspects," *he says.* "I'm not a poet. I'm more of a wordsmith—like a tunesmith—than I am a writer. I go for quick, simple combinations of things. I'm not into storytelling. I'm more into just—still—exercising my own fantasies."

The artist with *Pontiac Catalinas* (1984. Oil on canvas, 64 × 64″), c. 1990. Photo: Winston Conrad.

For the last two or three years, Ruscha's fantasies have also included "grand horizontal" paintings that nudge words and phrases into a kind of cosmic dialectic. The thirteen-foot-long rectangular backgrounds of these paintings represent Panavision-like sunsets or, more recently, the ionosphere at night, and serve as stage sets for expeditions from one extreme set of concepts to another. Tiny white letters on the left end of one canvas, for example, say "wolves/explosions/disease/poisons," while on the other side of the curving globe, to the right, we find "home." On another canvas "ancient dogs barking" is lettered on the far left corner, and "modern dogs barking" on the far right.

These paintings have not been as well received as most of Ruscha's other work, perhaps because his prolific production has begun to obscure the intricate relationships between these canvases and the rest of his oeuvre. "Ed's real strength is the depth of his works rather than any of its particular facets," observes his friend Larry Bell, "and maybe this will come out in a retrospective." Ruscha's strength also derives from his ongoing infatuation with the false magic, film personalities and high-tech euphoria of Los Angeles. "Ed's a very kind person and not defensive like some artists," Bell explains, "which gives him a more fluid access to something like the show-biz milieu. On the other hand, Ed's one of the toughest people I've ever known. You have to be very tough and ambitious if you're going to make it in L.A."

As proof of Ruscha's aggressive grip on L.A. culture, critics sometimes cite his sensational painting The Los Angeles County Museum on Fire, *1965–68, now at the Hirshhorn Museum in Washington, D.C. Questions about the painting's exact political symbolism, however, tend to produce answers from Ruscha like,* "You know, what really interested me about that project was its oblique aerial perspective, which is very important to my work. It's also important because it contains another generality about what I do. It reads from the lower left-hand to the upper-right-hand corner. *Standard Station* and *Large Trademark* do too." *(And, one might add, so do the spoon, plate and clock in the 1974 "Domestic Tranquility" suite and, among others, the 1973* Insect Slant *from the "black ant and cockroach" series.) Pressed further, Ruscha admits that* "although I didn't have any particular gripe against the L.A. County Museum, I do have a basic suspicion of art institutions, period. You can engrave that in marble. But I actually feel like there's something classical and gentle about that painting. There's this nice green lawn around the building and everything's so peaceful—and suddenly there's this little flame over there on the side"—*he says this somewhat gleefully*— "that looks as if it could possibly engulf the whole building. But the fire is really like an after-statement—like a coda, as in a coda to music, which is something I find myself doing a lot in my work. And, I guess in a way, it's important that the subject is an *L.A.* museum. I've wondered at times whether if I lived in another city, my art would be different, and I suppose it would be. The iconography of this place does mean something special to me. I love it, and I've always loved it, because it feeds me and it feeds my work."

"Catching Up with Ed Ruscha"

Lewis MacAdams

[. . .] *LM: When I was over at your show at Ace, I was looking at this piece that says One-Night Stands Forever, and it hit me that maybe you've come all the way around from non-meaning to acknowledging some spiritual or emotional place in yourself.*

ER: Well, it has nothing to do with spirituality. Or if it does, it's only a suggestion at the potential humor of it. It's just that the combinations of words really struck at a kind of curiosity; that's all it happens to be. Like I did a drawing one time called *The Catholic Church* [1974]. I could never say anything intelligent about it, except that just the power of those three words, "The Catholic Church," seems to contain its own potency protein.

LM: Would you have allowed yourself that twenty years ago?

ER. Probably not. But I did do a film called *Miracle* [1975]. It was about a guy who fixed a carburetor on a Mustang.

LM: Do you feel as if you're a neutral person?

ER: I'm kind of apolitical. I guess I'm socialistic by nature. I'm less capitalistic in regards to my dealings with society, but I'm not a zealot. We were talking about

Originally published in *L.A. Weekly*, v. 4, n. 34, August 27–September 2, 1982, pp. 26–28.

Beirut, or the invasion of the Falklands, I find myself just mildly curious about subjects like that. It's just that I kind of bow to my takes on things that happen every day, and I find myself being inspired by seemingly innocent and insignificant things.

LM: When you think of L.A., what's the first word that comes into your mind?

ER: "City," for sure.

LM: It seemed as if in Seventeen Painters of the Sixties, *the work that really put L.A. on the map, that showed there was this different aesthetic this town was spawning, was your big painting of the Standard station.*

ER: But that was a painting of a Standard station in Texas. That Los Angeles thing is just free association. Would it have been any more meaningful if it had been an Oklahoma gas station? But now that I look back on it, it's beginning to get harder to find a gas station that looks like that. It's beginning to look like the '60s. That's the curious thing about that book, *Twentysix Gasoline Stations,* that the painting came out of. In the future this book is going to look totally dated; and that's the one thing I was totally against. I didn't want that thing to ever have any nostalgia value, or nostalgia potency.

LM: That's sort of the way Peter Plagens treated your Sunset Strip book—as a certain moment in time, what with Vicki Carr and The Righteous Bros. on the marquees. It's funny to see the toughest work taken in by time. It's a lesson, too.

ER: Well, I think that's probably why I don't make books anymore. It's because as I kept producing these things and amusing, entertaining myself—which is the basis of it all—I began to think that I was being viewed as an artist making books. But you see, I had liked the *anonymity* of the whole thing. The first book I did was really anonymous. And each book has an anonymity, a sort of pureness that is lost when you see the collection together. But someday I think there'll be another kind of book that I'll make. I'm not sure what form it'll take, but I feel it coming on. I don't think it'll be like the publications I've done before.

LM: Is it difficult for you to be famous? Does it cause you to be too responsible?

————

239

ER: You're forced to contend with it, with people's awareness. But when people talk about my work it's not the kind of thing that would make me bite my nails, because I am more or less a free agent in this enterprise that I'm in. I don't know. I feel like I'm moving through this whole thing very slowly. I go from one thing to another very slapdash. I'll start on one thing and stop and work on something else. There's seemingly no rhyme or reason for it.

LM: Do you have a big enterprise, prints you have to get out?

ER: No, not really. I don't have a big production. Two people who help me part-time. It's still a garage production. [. . .]

LM: In your career have you always just gone on at the same rate, or did you feel that there was a moment where it was, like, "Wow, it's happening"?

ER: Well, it's actually always been happening with me. I have all these misgivings about approaches to my stuff and all that, but I'm not a tortured soul, so at least I have somewhat of a fulfillment in doing my work. It's been kind of a long haul, actually, but one reason is because I live in L.A. And for an artist, L.A. promises nothing and delivers not much more. Whereas New York promises everything for an artist and delivers zilch.

LM: Are there works that you've done that when you finished them you realized that you'd made some point, or you'd reached some point, or some plateau?

ER: Yeah, but I've always felt that being an artist is more or less doing a variation on a theme. The work I'm doing now is just a slight variation on work I was doing twenty-five years ago, so that causes me to wonder. But I mean if you look at Picasso's work and see the umpteenth thousand little erotic etching, you might look at the last one and say, "Did he really need to do this?" Because he'd said it so many times before. It all becomes a part of a nervous hang-up, the nervousness of output.

LM: Do you feel like commercial reasons enter into what you do?

ER: Well, I wish it did, almost. Usually my least favorite paintings sell. I did a series of prints using vegetable materials—organic materials—*News, Mews, Pews,*

Brews, Stews & Dues—that I thought was going to be a resounding commercial success, but it was a resounding commercial flop. So I guess really I'm not a good judge at all.

LM: Do you ever work on commissions?

ER: Unless someone says, "Here's X money, do what you want," I tend to fall apart. I'm not really a commercial-type artist. I don't do bank paintings.

LM: What is your relationship to Hollywood? I notice that a lot of people in the movie business own your work.

ER: I'm inspired by movies, because I think movies have the potential of becoming a more powerful art form than painting because movies can talk about so much, and painting can't. Painting's kind of one-dimensional. But video, now that's one art form that repulses me. And performance art kind leaves a bad taste in my mouth. I see that they might be trying to bridge the gap between dancing and film or something, or dancing and theater. I think there's something just so dry and senseless about it.

LM: Do you feel that there are techniques that you've mastered?

ER: No, there's no such thing mastering a technique. Even if everybody unanimously says you've mastered it, that still doesn't mean you've mastered it. It all comes back to the individual mind and there's nothing that *I* feel I've mastered. Or perfected.

My art is nonthreatening in the sense that I use traditional techniques. So art, as the artist describes it, can be the use of tricks and devices, and there's no disparaging edge to the words "tricks and devices." It's just a matter of using tools to produce a certain end result. That's really what art is to me. I'm confounded by the thing still myself. But I find that the one thing that slows me down is I'm more interested in end results than I am in means to the end. In other words, getting my hands dirty painting is not as important as having the painting done. [. . .]

"A Conversation with Edward Ruscha"

Robert Landau and John Pashdag

RL & JP: Why did you come to L.A. from Oklahoma?

ER: The first thing I had to do was get out of Oklahoma. As much as I liked the place, there was no room for artists or inspiration whatsoever. This was 1956. I was attracted to going either east or west. At that time, and pretty much today, the East Coast was starched clothing and heating oil, while the West Coast was flexing biceps and health. This made the choice relatively easy. Didn't all Okies with mattresses on their cars go west, anyway? Beyond that, I seemed to be drawn by the most stereotyped concepts of Los Angeles, such as cars, suntans, palm trees, swimming pools, strips of celluloid with perforations; even the word "sunset" had glamor. West was hot. East was cold. This was new life. That was Europe. This city simply had a good story for itself, that's all.

RL & JP: How does L.A. influence your work?

ER: All my work gets affected by the things that attracted me to this town in the first place, together with the little twists in my character that motivate me. A heavenly mountaintop is not going to get the job done. This is it for me, at least for now.

Originally published in *Outrageous L.A.* (San Francisco: Chronicle Books, 1984), pp. 8–9.

RL & JP: Is the "spirit" of [Los Angeles] still the wide open spaces—freedom kind of thing that brought you out here?

ER: I think so. You can look at the sunset and see it here. There's something in the sunset. The East Coast has a sunset that is metallic. Our sunset is more "glorious." Also, after I moved here, I found that L.A. tolerates any kind of behavior or lifestyle, and that suited me fine.

RL & JP: What about humor? Take the Fine Arts Squad mural of the Pacific Ocean at Blythe, after California's fallen into the ocean—do you think a piece of art like that, taking the greatest natural disaster that could befall the place and putting it up on the wall of a recording studio, could come out of New York?

ER: I don't think so. I think that particular work is probably one of the best examples of art in the community—art being relative to the community. I know that painting and I've always liked it. It seems like there's a nail whose head has been hit, you know? Beyond that mural, I think that Chicano clothing and car styling are some of the most worthwhile contributions that L.A. has ever produced.

RL & JP: Does L.A. appreciate and value its artists?

ER: No, not particularly.

RL & JP: What does L.A. value highly? What is held in high esteem here?

ER: The freeways. Just so those cars keep moving. I'm a part of it almost every day. It's sort of like a rolling thunder parade, isn't it?

RL & JP: How would you describe the L.A. environment? You can't really say it's beautiful.

ER: Well, I think it is. It's not beautiful exactly on the surface; it's beautiful in a kind of folklore sense, and it's quaint in the sense that it has not been as hard-hit by bulldozers and blacktopping as other communities have.

RL & JP: Do you like driving?

ER: I don't dislike it. You can turn on the radio and the radio becomes the sound-track for what you see out the window. And somehow I get more from doing this in Los Angeles than I do in another city.

RL & JP: What about earthquakes? Do they frighten you?

ER: No. Earthquakes, I think, are kind of gentle and friendly. I have not been wronged by an earthquake. I don't particularly *like* earthquakes—sure, there's a certain helplessness when they happen, but if I see this window rolling back and forth like this, there's nothing I can do except laugh.

RL & JP: What makes L.A. unique?

ER: It is the ultimate cardboard cut-out town. It's full of illusions and it allows its people to indulge in all of these illusions. It's a siren calling me. I always have to come back to this city—I don't know what it is. There is plenty about this town that aggravates me—but I'm a victim of magnetic attraction.

RL & JP: What about the cultural mix?

ER: I think everybody is gradually mixing here. There doesn't seem to be rampant prejudice here, or a reluctance to get together, as far as cultures go. We all want to live in the center of the picture postcard. A hundred years from now there will be some gorgeous mono-ethnic race living here. It's probably as it should be.

RL & JP: What do you do for recreation?

ER: Drive and fish.

RL & JP: Do you think painting will ever be an outdated medium?

ER: I don't think so. It may not be the medium of the future, though. I think there may be some form of moviemaking that can begin saying more than a painting can say. It certainly has potential. That's why I like movies so much, because I think they do have a certain power of expression that two-dimensional things can't have. Painting and movies both suffer from mediocrity, though, but one will never actually replace the other. Movies are the result of involved collaboration, while painting is completely free and singular.

RL & JP: What does the term "pop culture" mean to you?

ER: Does that come from "popular"? That probably means anything that's happening today.

RL & JP: Does that give an ephemeral side to our culture?

ER: Yes. It's sort of instant this and instant that. And nothing really stays around. So what's wrong with that?

RL & JP: People tend to look at it and assume it's very superficial.

ER: Superficiality can be profound and funny and worth living for. I mean, everything's ephemeral when you look at it in its proper focus. It just happens more quickly in L.A.

Ed Ruscha, Western Avenue studio, c. 1982. Photo: Tim Street-Porter.

An Excerpt from "Art: L.A.R.T.: Edward Ruscha"

Joan Quinn

[. . .] JQ: How would you describe the work you're doing now?

ER: I'm a little calmer now. The work I do now tends to show me that I'm an adult. Although I feel immature in certain ways, I feel that the work I'm accomplishing these days is somehow making an adult out of me. It just gets simpler and simpler, I mean my views of what I'm up to seem simpler and simpler. I guess I am trying somehow to perpetuate certain ironies that go on and I've always been doing that. That's sort of the job of an artist.

JQ: That's something that people really think about when they look at your work. I think you look at words and you ask, "How does Ed Ruscha find these words? Does he have a notebook and, if he does, I'd like to see that notebook. Does he have a pad by his telephone? What does he jot down? What kind of images does he expect people to take?" From the way you're talking about maturing, it's totally clear in your mind what you're doing. I have a couple of your words at home—two "won'ts." As I start looking at the word "won't," it changes from time to time. Does it matter to you what your viewers see in the word?

Originally published in **INTERVIEW** Magazine, Brant Publications, Inc., March 1984 (pp. 80–83).

ER: Not really, because my job is not to communicate so much. I may pick something as different as cheap cocktail words or a biblical psalm.

JQ: When do you pick them?

ER: At the time that they happen. I can't control it. I recall those words that you have. The word "won't"—the most difficult thing about painting that picture was putting the apostrophe in. I hope I'm not confusing you. You see, sometimes you can study a work, like the word "the" and looking at that word long enough, it just begins to lose its meaning.

JQ: How do you deal with that? Is it the different calligraphy, the different way you space the words?

ER: I don't set out to make a statement with the word "won't." My choice is ambiguous but it's a fixed choice. In other words, the word appealed to me at that particular time, in that year, and I can't even remember why.

JQ: You don't have a notebook that says, "Such and such happened and 'won't' was the word that came out of this."

ER: No. But you see, words can come to me from those associations and experiences.

JQ: Let's say this painting of "Hollywood"—does that conjure up an image in your mind?

ER: No. This is an unfinished painting. It's unfinished and unresolved.

JQ: Well, the Hollywood sign then?

ER: The Hollywood sign is actually a landscape in a sense. It's a real thing and my view of it was really a conservative interpretation of something that exists, so it almost isn't a word in a way—it's a structure. It's a phenomenon or something. [. . .] A lot of things are simple backdrops to me. They can be backgrounds of no particular character to show what the words are all about. Don't worry kids, it's just a background—but here are some words, too.

JQ: Do you ever feel you should be fitting into the framework of a different type of artwork other than conceptual? Or a different name?

ER: No. That's why I feel I've been able to survive this mess, I've been able to ignore the isms that happen. Really, a survivor is someone who has escaped the isms or otherwise walked out on them. Why be a card-carrying member of any ism?

JQ: When I talked to you on the phone today you were doing something very ordinary and when I asked you why you said, "Artists are people, too." Did you do a painting of that?

ER: I did a little drawing on snakeskin.

JQ: Were you feeling sorry for yourself?

ER: No, that doesn't mean that at all, although I know that artists, by the mere fact that they're artists, are going to undergo some level of suffering because of the public. It's like, "Oh, you're an artist? Scratch your name on this napkin. Maybe someday you'll be famous."

JQ: It's the way people think. Does that ever bother you?

ER: Well, the public has a misconception about artists. They still have us swaddled in some kind of agony clothes.

JQ: Do you feel like you've paid your dues?

ER: No. I haven't done enough for the social clubs. I have eaten out of tin cans, so if that's paying dues, then yes. As an artist I don't know where I stand. I actually have no illusions about where I stand in the whole scheme of things.

JQ: Do you feel like you're a part of art history?

ER: I'm just a part of the community. I don't know where I fit. I don't know who my audience is. I don't know where I am.

———

"Interview with Edward Ruscha"

Bernard Brunon

[. . .] BB: Your work has often been presented as a social comment on the American way of life, from David Bourdon writing, "[Your] books may be the most authentic counterpart we have to the American Scene painting and photography of the 1920s and '30s,"[37] to Joan Casademont describing your paintings as "American idioms that reflect specific material values."[38] Do you intend for your art to be of this "unique American style,"[39] and how much importance do you put on the sociological aspect in it?

ER: In the early 1950s I was awakened by the photographs of Walker Evans and the movies of John Ford, especially *Grapes of Wrath* where the poor "Okies" (mostly farmers whose land dried up) go to California with mattresses on their cars rather than stay in Oklahoma and starve. I faced a sort of black-and-white cinematic emotional identity crisis myself in this respect—sort of a showdown with myself—a little like trading dust for oranges. On the way to California I discovered the importance of gas stations. They are like trees because they are *there*. They were not chosen because they were pop-like but because they have angles, colors and shapes, like trees. They were just *there,* so they were not in my visual focus because they were supposed to be social-nerve endings.

Originally published in *Edward Ruscha* (Lyon: Musée Saint Pierre Art Contemporain/Octobre des Arts, 1985), pp. 89–97.

BB: You said in a conversation with David Hickey that Abstract Expressionist artists "wanted to collapse the whole art process into one act; I wanted to break it into stages, which is what I do now."[40] *What are these different stages and how do you approach them?*

ER: I was very moved by Abstract Expressionist painting as an art student and still find it overwhelming that those pictures were painted in the late '40s and early '50s, when you stop to wonder what other creatures were doing with their lives at the same time. To generalize, they approached their art with no preconceptions and with a certain instant-explosiveness, whereas I found that my work had to be planned and preconceived, or rather wondered about, before being done. My subjects tend to be recognizable objects made up of stuff that is non-objective and abstract. I have always operated on a kind of waste-retrieval method. I retrieve and renew things that have been forgotten or wasted. [. . .]

BB: For the last fifteen years or so that you have been using words and sentences, they have always been painted or drawn on paper or canvas, never directly on the wall as Lawrence Weiner or Victor Burgin do. Why do you need to present a "picture"?

ER: This seems to be a question of permanence versus mobility. I am a victim of the power of the four-sided rectangle and I think it is here to stay. It seems so logical to make a mobile picture.

BB: You said of your moving to Los Angeles in 1956, "seeing all these things, meeting all these people, the whole thing was a lasting experience for me. I still have it, I always will. That's why I will never leave Los Angeles. . . . I still get lifeblood from this place."[41] *What then made you go to Europe for six months in 1961, spending two months in Paris?*

ER: Traveling away from home always gave a surge to my routine, but I've never given myself the opportunity to live anywhere but California. Why go elsewhere when you are happy with your own spot and call it home? My first trip to France was exotic and at the same time very "Hollywood." You would be surprised how similar the two places are. Going to Europe was something I was bound to do, like a necessary milestone to pass. I was into popular culture then, not the art of Europe. Going there today, I would seek out the old masters. [. . .]

———

251

—————

"Premeditated: An Interview with Ed Ruscha"

Jana Sterbak

JS: You started making books in about 1962. How did that come about?

ER: It was a reaction to seeing so many paintings at the time. The books contained the possibility of using words and photographs at the same time. I liked the fact that they were human size—portable friendly objects. I liked the idea of leafing through. I even developed a format that I liked, a format which is more or less standard.

JS: The books are composed mostly of images.

ER: They are photographs, mostly photographs that I took myself.

JS: What about the first book, the one of the gas stations?

ER: To me that seemed like a travelogue. I love the highways, I love to drive.

JS: How about the swimming pools and California?

ER: And about the lifestyle, the particular issues about how a swimming pool would look—the waterness, the ripples, a particular kind of indulgence. . . . I am not a sociologist. I have no exact method or motive in mind. I don't have to come

Originally published in *Real Life Magazine*, n. 14, summer 1985, pp. 26–29.

up with an answer: "Did I say all I wanted to say when I finished?" It's not analytical. That's why a lot of the books leave questions. I put in the questions, I want it ambiguous. [. . .]

I've always considered the books very private. They never had a large following; they've always been underground. The more books I did, the more people began to view them as a kind of collection. Whereas, with the first one, people did not know what I was up to. There was genuine doubt in their minds. I liked that, the idea of the question mark. As I continued making [the books], the question mark began to diminish because I was making a certified statement. A person had the opportunity to look at twelve of them. The books became a thing in themselves, almost an artwork. Their potency was diminished. That could have contributed to my stopping making them. When I showed the books to someone who didn't know anything about art, it was simple. They liked it— the pictures were right side up, they had captions you could believe, they were not meant to offend any sensibility.

JS: How do you come up with the phrases for your paintings?

ER: Some are found readymade, some are dreams, some come from newspapers. They are finished by blind faith. No matter if I've seen it on television or read it in the newspaper, my mind seems to wrap itself around that thing until it's done. It's strange, I don't know what motivates me, but each of the works is premeditated. I don't stand in front of a blank canvas waiting for inspiration. At one time I loved the word "ace." It meant something to me that was powerful. I made a few paintings of the word. I always like monosyllabic words like "smash" and "honk." Single words kept my interest for a while and then, later, there was only one thing to do—heap more words in. Until finally, I found myself doing a painting which says, *Study of Friction and Wear on Mating Surfaces* [1983]. I keep notebooks. The initial ideas are written out. I don't draw them, I stage them onto the canvas. I had an idea for this drawing called "Nerves." I saw it as a capital "N" and then a lot of space and then "erves" and, in between, a line. I see this thing and being a good little art soldier, I go and do it. I just put the questions out. I don't sit there thinking, "Why am I doing this?" There is no answer.

JS: When did you start using other materials than paint in your work?

ER: It must have been '65 or '66. [. . .]

JS: Is there a relationship between the substance you use and the words that go with it?

ER: No, I certainly don't look for it. It's not left up to me to make any kind of statement or pun in what I do. Just like now, I can make an oil painting with certain colors work with any kind of subject matter. The colors and brushstrokes and materials don't have to support or interpret the idea that you are trying to transmit. I don't like that. I don't like the idea that to paint the word "Mad," I better use red. That choice is instinctive; it's not premeditated as the words are.

JS: How would you define yourself?

ER: I don't know I've ever had to. Most artists are doing basically the same thing—staying off the streets. I don't feel like I am committed to any kind of heroic study. I committed myself to being an artist and I've done it for twenty-five years. It's daily routine. I don't look at myself and try to find out where I am at, I don't know where I am at. Who knows what's going to happen in the future. . . .

JS: You've no problem producing; one thing comes after the other?

ER: No, I run into dry spells. I don't make books anymore, I feel that my statement has rounded itself off. And even though I have some motivation in that direction, I am keeping it all in the refrigerator just like they've kept Walt Disney.

JS: How does the spectator fit in?

ER: That's a good question, I don't know. I'll tell you, I don't even think about it. It's not my job to do that. It's for other people to do that, maybe the critics. But I don't think it's all that necessary that the critics make the connections. Whether or not the work communicates anything to anyone is not important to me. The work is my indulgence. I don't set out to get something across. I don't think very many artists do. That's where the trouble begins, when artists try to communicate.

JS: What about Pop Art in relation to your work?

ER: It happened about the same time that I started to do my pictures. The direction of my work was the result of a reaction to Abstract Expressionism, same as theirs. I think I was more involved in the surface goodies than the Pop artists were. Warhol had a real disdain for the surface embellishment. He could look at things cold. He was able to rid the picture of any kind of sentimentality. That was great. [. . .]

JS: *What do you read?*

ER: There's a writer from England I like a lot. J. G. Ballard. [. . .] Film forms a part of my life, though I don't see everything made. I get turned off by advertising. Advertising irritates me. You might say, "Hey, that's where you get your inspiration." Well, not really. I might see a letter I like. Maybe.

John Huston is my favorite director. I don't see a lot of parallels between art and film except they are both independent art forms with the freedom for indulgence.

Ed Ruscha, *Words Without Thoughts Never to Heaven Go,* Miami-Dade Public Library. 1985. Oil on canvas on 8 aluminum panels, each 63 × 192″ within 40′ diameter circular opening. Photo: Paul Ruscha.

"A Few Words with Ed Ruscha"

Vicki Sanders

[. . .] "I came down here, went to the library spot and looked around at the opening. It was beyond comprehension. I felt smaller than a microbe."

If he accepted the Art in Public Places commission to paint a mural in the new Miami-Dade Library in the Cultural Center, it would be a first for him, and a very public one.

"Just the idea of being offered the opportunity to present something for something that was so big and maybe overwhelming in terms of space. . . ." *He hesitates.* "I've never worked on anything quite that large and in quite that curious way. [. . .]"

And so it came to pass that when the library opened in July, in its entryway was Ruscha's $140,000 mural painting, eight panels designed to rim the ring of the balcony overhead. Printed on each of seven was a word, smaller than the one before it, from Hamlet: *"Words without thoughts never to heaven go." The eighth panel was left blank, intended as a resting place for the eye. [. . .]*

"I know that some people didn't like it, but I think some people did. The major thing is the satisfaction within myself that it is a good work, as a work of art of mine, not just because it's for the public or that you can look around and

Originally published in the *Miami Herald*, December 23, 1985, p. 6C.

read the English words and understand them, making it logical and simple to accept. Not that. But [because] it works as a complete statement. I feel really good about it, and I say anybody who doesn't like it has missed the point and is out to lunch and not for real."

By the end of this spiel, he is laughing, in part because of the clichés he's playfully heaped on the end of his thought, in part because of his natural inclination to shrug his shoulders over others' opinions of his work.

"I can't analyze my audience. You never know. You can't second guess what people are thinking. This leads you to think and behave [as though] you don't have to communicate with an audience. As long as you just work for yourself, the audience will take care of itself. [. . .]"

Though he is well known in contemporary art circles, the number of his works owned by major museums is few, he says. The Museum of Modern Art has a print but not a painting, the Guggenheim owns nothing and the Whitney only recently acquired a work.

Artistic success, to Ruscha, is a process of self-exploration that can be complete only when he dies. "I haven't resolved it yet, the issue of my art. I don't know where it's going to go. Until it's resolved. . . ." *He pauses.* "Success means death. You can make that synonymous."

"ED RUSCHA: GOODBYE TO VISTAS AND ALL THAT"

Ralph Rugoff

[. . .] Ruscha moved to Los Angeles in the late 1950s. He and his wife have spent the last four years living in Sherman Oaks, a geographic experiment that will soon conclude with their resettlement in West Los Angeles.

Prior to his planned move from Valley, however, he was reached at his Venice studio and squeezed for a few thoughts on his life as a Valley resident. [. . .]

RR: Do you consider the Valley to be a unique place in America?

ER: Oh yeah. I mean, [in the '50s] the Valley was like the rest of America, except that it was just much hipper, I guess. I'm from Oklahoma originally, and it reminded me a little of that—just one-story buildings set up on a dead-level grid. But the Valley was much further along, much more sophisticated.

RR: Do you have a favorite Valley landmark?

ER: Somehow, the intersection of Laurel Canyon and Ventura Boulevard has always appealed to me. Back in the late '50s, there used to be a Tiny Naylor's drive-in there, and now it's just low, one-story businesses with a gas station right on the corner. It's got some sort of soul to it, though. But to tell the truth, I sort of gave

Originally published in *L.A. Weekly*, June 16–25, 1987, pp. 25–26.

up on the Valley when they bulldozed the Tail of the Cock [at Ventura and Cold-water]. That was one of my favorite places of all time out there, so when that happened, I felt like it was the beginning of the end. The La Reina Theater [in Studio City] was another favorite, and that also got torn down so they could put up some development.

RR: Do you feel there's no hope for the Valley?

ER: I feel like the Valley is sort of decaying. The old charm it used to have is disappearing. I read the Valley section of the *L.A. Times,* and I use that as an indicator of the whole thing. Every day, there's some article in there about something that's the last this or the last that—the last horse ranch, or the last living tree that was cut down to make way for some monument honoring trees, or whatever.

RR: Is there anything in particular you still enjoy about the Valley?

ER: I've always liked shopping out there. I mean, you can find anything in the Valley. For instance, you can find anything that pertains to automobiles, all kinds of parts and obscure things. One place I really like is Dutton's, where you can find just about every book you'd need. And everything's so level in the Valley. You can park on the street right outside the store. You can walk into that store and know your car's right out front. Well, you can't do that in L.A. anymore—you've got subterranean parking structures to hassle with. But I see that starting to happen in the Valley now.

RR: Is that why you're moving to West L.A.?

ER: The reason we're moving out is that I just felt like the bubble had popped when I discovered there's this sixty-home development park they're going to build on the top of Mulholland, right where it intersects with Benedict. It used to be just a piece of wild land that was sort of like my private little national park. I could hike up there and meditate or do whatever, and no one ever went up there at all. Of course, the city just had to sell it to some developer. I knew they'd do it, and sure enough, they've just started bulldozing that thing. Now it's going to be a big housing development. I guess any vacant parcel of land out there is considered something of an eye-sore. It's like stagnant land, and they're determined to make use of everything.

RR: Is the Valley becoming more like Los Angeles?

ER: Definitely. The writing's already on the wall. They're going to lift the height restrictions on buildings for sure, and it's going to be downtown from Tarzana straight to Studio City. It's trying to be like a big city, and if they can get that Trump Tower look, they're happy.

RR: Is there any one building or area that you find outstandingly ugly?

ER: No, there really isn't. That is something about the Valley, I guess. I mean, there's great residential sections—of all classes actually. The flats north of Ventura are particularly noteworthy. They have an appealing visual sense to them.

RR: Has the Valley ever served as a source of inspiration, or of ideas for your work?

ER: Only in the general sense that the Valley has a Western feel to it. I mean, you've got your health nuts, car freaks, every type you find in these places. And also the flatness of it. There's just nothing like it east of the Mississippi, where you've got that industrial revolution hanging all over you.

RR: What motivated you to move to the Valley in the first place?

ER: Well, actually, my wife moved there. We were separated at the time. She moved out there, and I just ended up living there. It wasn't my choice, but I've always liked the Valley. I've always liked Ventura Boulevard, and the Valley's sort of the home of jazz and car culture.

RR: Were you proud to be a Valley dweller?

ER: I guess there is some semblance of pride or something people have in living out there. It was kind of ideal in some ways, like one last little hold on something that was once somewhat rural and agricultural. But there are getting to be too many people out there. It used to be strawberry fields and pumpkin patches and all that, but not anymore. I just read yesterday where the last pumpkin patch was being paved into a parking lot. They're just running out of space.

———

"ED RUSCHA"

Fred Fehlau

FF: In the early '70s, installed in the LACMA's contemporary art galleries were three pieces that stand out in my mind: one of Robert Irwin's disks, a painting by John McLaughlin, and your Actual Size *[1962]. Interestingly, both you and Irwin continue to produce new work, while a lot of the other artists in that collection seem to be repeating past successes.*

ER: I have always worked with a theme in which I see variations throughout the years. What I do is rooted to two or three things that I'm still trying to figure out. But I'm still at it, and my new paintings are linked to things I did years ago—it's really not new to me. On the surface it appears to be much different; maybe it's the black and white, and there are less words than before, so people think I've made a change, but I'm not sure that's true.

FF: What are those two or three things?

ER: I wish I could go through them; it has to do with music, it has to do with art, of course. I got introduced early on to Walker Evans's work, Russian Constructivism and, of course, Abstract Expressionism. When I was in school, I painted just like an Abstract Expressionist—it was a uniform. Except you really

Originally published in *Flash Art*, n. 138, January–February 1988, pp. 70–72.

didn't have to wear it, you just aped it. It was so seductive: the act of facing a blank canvas with a palette. I liked painting that way, but there seemed no reason to push it any further. But I began to see that the only thing to do would be a pre-conceived image. It was an enormous freedom to be premeditated about my art. I wanted to make pictures, but I didn't want to paint. Some painters just *love* paint—they get up in the morning and grab a brush, not knowing what they are going to do, but they just have to have that hot brush moving those colors. But I was more interested in the end result than I was in the means to the end.

FF: Do you still maintain a belief in the preconceived image?

ER: Yeah, I still believe in that. But the idea of getting my hands dirty is not as bad today as it was ten years ago. There was a period when I couldn't even use paint. I had to paint with unorthodox materials, so I used fruit and vegetable dyes instead of paint. I had to move some way, and the only way to do this was to stain the canvas rather than to put a skin on it. Now I'm back to putting the skins on.

FF: What comes to mind are a lot of artists using language now, such as Barbara Kruger, Jenny Holzer, and Louise Lawler. Do you feel any connection with that work?

ER: I didn't know about these people until a few years ago. I do know Louise Lawler; she's been making art for about ten years. I haven't met the other people, but I think that it has a lot to do with cycles, and that seems to be true no mat-ter what. Things do go through a style cycle, or a load cycle, almost as if they're in a washing machine. My whole job in this scene is not to produce and sell as much art as I can; I never felt that as a goal. I've never sold out a show. I don't re-ally sell my paintings until two, three, even four years later. The impulse from the public is not shown to me, like other artists that I've heard about. I would have had an entirely different career had I lived in New York. Although I was paint-ing right alongside everybody else, I wasn't included in the Pop Art shows hap-pening at that time. I've got a legitimate bitch about that. But I do love living in L.A.—it's an outpost, like living in Australia.

FF: The language in your work seems to become literature.

———

ER: When I began painting, all my paintings were of words which were guttural utterances like *Smash, Boss,* and *Eat.* I didn't see that as literature, because it didn't complete thoughts. Those words were like flowers in a vase; I just happened to paint words like someone else paints flowers. The words have these abstract shapes, they live in a world of no size: You can make them any size, and what's the real size? Nobody knows.

FF: Those words are not verbal, per se, but image words . . .

ER: They relied heavily on the connotations and interpretations of the viewer. And they did have a certain obvious punch. It wasn't until later that I was interested in combinations of words and making thoughts, sentences and things like that.

FF: Do you see your books and the later pastels as stories?

ER: I've seen that possibility when I go back and look at things that are truly complete and not to be changed. I can't go back and work on a painting that I finished in 1965. My history is not a plastic medium—not something that I would care to link together. There have been a few people who have done that before: taken the words that I've used and tried to make sense out of it, as though I might have kept the ultimate secret to myself, which is not true. My things are really individual and not thought about in terms of communicating to a viewer over a long period of time.

FF: Words function as cultural—not organic—signs. But the word is made out of carrot juice, or rose petals. So how does the slippage between the natural and the cultural operate in relation to your use of subject and material?

ER: Well, I had no master plan in doing work of that sort. Around the late '60s I started working with those kinds of materials, making some silk-screen prints and painting with them. I needed to go off and find my own private sandbox to play in, and that was it, and those were the materials—the palette. People looked for puns or certain clarified mysteries in the work. They'll say, "Oh, carrot juice. Well, that's more humorous than blood." If you print the word "Evil" with blood, then you're obviously making a definite statement. But my work is not really about that at all. It's open, it's puffy. It has no connection to logic in that respect . . . Once I'm in the sandbox, there's a spontaneity that I'm after that really makes these things happen. My choice might be just a particular choice of the day, just like anybody who paints a picture might decide to paint one day with red and the next day with blue. Blue doesn't necessarily mean peace, and red doesn't necessarily mean evil. So those connections are moot. Still, people are going to see connections and respond.

FF: You don't care about misinterpretation?

ER: No, and materials don't necessarily have to respect the origin of the idea. I'm not taking these things with loaded evidence and loaded response to make a message.

FF: How does figure/ground or word/ground function in your work?

ER: Well, in some way, certain parts of the paintings can be almost worthless. They start to make a stage. A stage is nothing more than a backdrop for the drama that happens. Paintings of words can be clearer to see when there is an anonymous backdrop. I've always believed in anonymity as far as a backdrop goes— that's what I consider the ground or the landscape or whatever it is that's in a painting. I do have paintings of backgrounds with foregrounds that seem to be the words or the images. That's why I have this kind of lofty idea of a landscape as being a pivotal point to making a picture. And so there's a landscape that's a background, but I don't see it. It's almost not there. It's just something to put the words on.

FF: In your new work, that opposition slips away. It's no longer this on top of that.

ER: This is just another stop on the highway of my work, and I'm not sure that it makes a transition from anything I've done before. At the same time, I'm not writing my own history. So if it appears to be out of sync with other things I've done, then you might be right. But the words [titles], in that case, sort of balance the subject. I am after a kind of tension that doesn't involve simply putting large words in the middle of a canvas; it's just a different question altogether.

———

FF: How concrete are words? Are they different than a bowling ball or a suburban landscape? Does a bowling ball say bowling ball in the same way that "Bowling Ball" would say bowling ball?

ER: I never really give it that much thought—although, it has to be almost user-friendly. When I choose something I just don't see a painting of the words "Bowling Ball"—which makes my art sort of from the gut. I don't ponder whether something is going to fit a certain theory or not. It just has to have a certain something or other to make me respond to it. And for the most part it is still preconceived, although I don't make things happen exactly like I think I want to. There are always little accidents along the way. Usually some of those accidents are the best things. But it really has to be instinctive.

FF: What about your new work? The loss of words? The displacement of the words into titles rather than the image?

ER: Well, these newer works I'm doing seem to come from their asking to be titled—the titles are sort of glaring. I've always felt a title is extremely crucial. They're missing from the images in some respect. As I started to work on these things, I could see that they reminded me of some kind of narrative or story about struggle. Even the subject matter seemed to suggest something struggling up a hill, a car driving up a hill, an elephant walking up a hill. So many things going up hills. I thought to myself, am I making up a story about things going up hills, or am I just into hills? And aren't hills just some sort of metaphor for an abstract line that goes from lower right to upper left?

FF: Especially lower right/upper left. . . .

ER: Yeah. And I'm still wondering about that because I do have a thing for diagonals. That's why I think that a lot of the juice in my work has to do with abstraction.

FF: Jean-François Lyotard draws out the following progression: the cognition of an image takes place physically—just you and the thing. Understanding, however quickly that might occur, takes place with the memory of that seeing, which is a recognition. It might be that the time between recognition and cognition is very short—the recognition is the image trans-

ferred into language. Your work fouls up that recognition; you can't say that it's a picture or a word, or that's a red, or that's a landscape, because it cancels itself out.

ER: I don't know really how to respond to that. Although I think that the art world is a rather simple mechanism, it can become highly complicated by what people add to the message once they have viewed a work of art. At one time I used to think that art was strictly visual, and you're not supposed to go and dig deeper into messages. But now I believe it all has to do with tantalizing your memory. . . . The most that an artist can do is to start something and not give the whole story. That's what makes mystery. And in a sense, if you believe that, then you can almost believe that nothing can be explained, which returns us to philosophy. That, in turn, circles all the way around to just looking at paintings again.

FF: Has any work been lost in the shuffle?

ER: Well, I think my books are the toughest part of my art. Yet, my notoriety or whatever it is is not really based on that. I have misgivings about the fact that people didn't see my books as I wanted them to. I always felt like that was the dark side of what I was up against and what I stood for—the toughest, meanest art I was making. Occasionally those images would lapse over and become part of—actually—the black-and-white work I'm doing now. I remember this notion I had in school about Franz Kline, thinking how great it was that this man only worked with black and white. I thought at some point in my life I would also work with black and white—and here it is. I was into making those books and doing photographs without being a photographer—sort of media fucking—and that really inspired me. I did a book on apartment houses, and then I did a series of drawings of the apartment houses, and now I see that these paintings really are, God, just coming out of those ten little drawings I did of the apartment houses. It always seems to go back to there. Somehow, this has a lot to do with the way an artist thinks. It starts very early. I heard that Kurt Schwitters spent his life collecting subway tickets and trolley tokens; I just pictured this guy out on the street doing this—making an art out of this—and it sort of sealed it for me.

FF: You mentioned music at the very beginning. . . .

ER: Music has a way of bringing back all kinds of memories, that's one thing. It can make you nostalgic. That's a force it has. And it can also be instructive in a certain way. Although I love painting, music can be funny and it can have all these things that painting sometimes misses.

FF: And what about all these questions?

ER: Well, they're only beginnings of things. Some of them are obscure and I don't mind that. I've got nothing against questions. But then I've got nothing against cubism either.

"Rebel with a Canvas:
Ed Ruscha's Original Art Is Drawing Attention"

Chris Hunter

[. . .] Ruscha, who has prided himself on being somewhat of a rebel in the art world, is now basking in the pleasures of being an artist with a permanent display in a major municipal library. The Miami-Dade commission came through in 1985 and for the last three years, Ruscha has been busily preparing the artistic statement that will mark the interior of the new South Florida building.

"It's my first public commission," *Ruscha said, standing in the Lake Worth Lannan Museum watching his paintings being installed for the Palm Beach County Exhibition.* "It's gradually become an art for art's sake project for me. People ask me what I'm doing and I say I'm doing something in a museum. Then I catch myself that I'm thinking museum but actually, it's a library. But it really is like a museum." [. . .]

Snagging an inspirational line out of Shakespeare's Hamlet*, Ruscha has created an artistic installation that shines with his own individual style but also is a symbolic beacon for the library.*

"I've always felt like my job is not trying to communicate to an audience," *he said.* "The artist's job is to please himself and the viewers will make their own interpretation. This project has made me realize that I had to communicate to the public. Whatever I do [at the library] is with the public in mind." [. . .]

Originally published in the *Palm Beach Daily News*, March 18, 1988, pp. 1, 8.

It's clear that the Miami public commission has been an inspirational opportunity for him, but he's also surprised that he's actually doing such a respectable thing.

"This was quite a surprise to me," *he admitted.* "I didn't think I could do something like this. It is a responsibility. You've got to wake up in the morning and go to work every day. An artist's life is not really made that way, but they've allowed me to do pretty much what I wanted to do."

Ed Ruscha has almost always been able to do pretty much what he wanted, and if there's an inside joke to his use of the Shakespearean phrase for his library project, it's that Ruscha's "words" have never been without thoughts.

"I've always felt like titles are a very important part of my work," *he said.* "Sometimes the words are the title. Backgrounds are almost like a stage setting or a foil for the subject, which is a word."

Spike Jones (on stage), early 1950s. Photo: Unknown. Courtesy the Estate of Spike Jones.

"THE SENTIMENTAL MUSICAL TASTES OF ED RUSCHA"

Kristine McKenna

Ed Ruscha is often described as the definitive regional artist of Los Angeles. [. . .]
What does this favorite son hear as the sound track for our fair city?

"For me, jazz is the music of Los Angeles—perhaps because that's the music I was into when I first came here. [. . .] Of the music that's associated with this city—the Byrds, the Doors, the Eagles—the Byrds are the only ones that do it for me. I used to go see them at Ciro's on the Strip in the '60s, but I wasn't into most of that music. I guess I was sort of square. [. . .]

"The first record I bought was something by Spike Jones," *he recalls*. "His music shook the foundations of things and that made it perfect for young people.

"At that point I wanted to be a cartoonist and his stuff was the musical equivalent of a cartoon, and it seemed more accessible to me than classical stuff, which I thought of as a high and untouchable art form. I perceived painting that way too when I was young and I had no interest in fine art then. [. . .]

"I spent a lot at time in jazz clubs during the '50s seeing great people like Chet Baker, but the jazz I liked peaked out in the '60s," *he says*. "I rarely go see live music of any kind now, nor do I listen to much jazz made since then.

Originally published in the *Los Angeles Times*, June 19, 1988, Calendar, p. 6.

"I think art in all forms—including styles of music—reaches a logical conclusion at some point, and after that it's just imitators elaborating on something that's already been completed.

"For instance, there was a wave of great country singers—people like Hank Snow, Lefty Frizzell, Hank Williams, and Faron Young—that most artists of today borrow heavily from. As far as I can see, the style has run its course and died out. Of course, the corpse will continue to be repackaged in different forms to fit the standard of the day.

"There doesn't seem to be much going on in music right now," *adds Ruscha, who buys about five records a month.* "In fact, the last new artist to arrive on the scene that totally knocked me out was Captain Beefheart—he really was working on the farthest experimental edge of popular music."

Of the musicians associated with the art world—Philip Glass, Talking Heads, Laurie Anderson—Ruscha likes some, but not all.

"I like David Byrne's music, but Phil Glass gives me narcolepsy. My son's into New Wave music and he took me to see Glenn Branca and I liked him a lot. I also like Alan Vega, Lene Lovich and Bow Wow Wow. Malcolm McLaren's a fairly innovative gentleman and Bow Wow Wow's music was put together really well.

"I like reggae and all kinds of ethnic and roots music, but I can't bear the kind of wailing rock opera that people like Sting put out. I don't care too much for rap although I do like the Last Poets, whom I consider to be the forerunners of rap. [. . .]

"When I'm in the desert I listen to American music from the '20s and '30s—things like Bing Crosby and Bix Beiderbecke. That stuff is great out there because you look around and there's nothing man-made for as far as the eye can see, and you begin to wonder what decade it is.

"I guess I have fairly sentimental tastes in music, and the stuff I like tends to evoke a rather romantic notion of the America of the past," *he concludes.* "We were going at a slightly slower R.P.M. then and I like that. However, I don't see this music as nostalgic. It's as relevant to life today as it was the day it was recorded."

"ED RUSCHA"

Bill Berkson

BB: Shall we talk about how the prints are coming along?

ER: Okay. When I start one of these projects I never know what's going to happen. I'd like to be able to say I plan ahead, but I never do. So sometimes the strategy will be to take one of my paintings and make a print out of it, but it doesn't always work. I've got a couple of plates here that I've cancelled because they just don't work like they would if they were paintings.

BB: What is the difference?

ER: Well, you get one color overlapping another and then you get this color mark, and it's sort of unacceptable from that standpoint. I don't consider myself one of the greatest printmakers. I used to be more into it than I am now. But there's a bit of rust that builds up if you don't use that medium for a while. Every time I go back to do something like this I find there are ten new techniques that either have suddenly been resurrected from the tenth century or are brand new.

BB: There's a brushiness in those prints—all those horizontal strokes in Heaven *and* Hell *[both 1988], for instance—that doesn't happen in your paintings.*

Originally published in *Shift*, v. 2, n. 4, 1988, pp. 14–17.

ER: Yes, but I've always had this side-to-side paint action. I'm sort of a prisoner of this quasi-landscape idea anyway. If I go back and analyze my paintings, I see that there is a sort of ground line happening—horizontals that get into brushstrokes, that get into everything, and I guess that's what my work is made of.

BB: I noticed some stencils in the studio. Do you use stencils for the images in the paintings and prints?

ER: No. For the paintings, I transpose a drawing onto the canvas—sometimes freehand, sometimes tracing—but ordinarily I don't use a stencil. I used a stencil on the "glass" of *Hourglass* [1987] only because I really had to do it that way. But I usually work out something on newsprint, putting two pieces of newsprint together, and then trace it through to get the drawing. Or else I'll cut out a shape sort of like a stencil but then I always mark on the canvas. The tracing is just a minimal guideline to set the stage for the work.

BB: Do you consider yourself very systematic? Does one thing necessarily lead to the next?

ER: It usually does. I find myself just calling on my intuition and staying on course through a given thing. And I find myself not working in series. I envy an artist who can work in series. I've always envied artists who can do that. It takes a constitution of steel to do something like that. Instead, my work sort of trails off, and then it perks up, and down the line it will come up again. I can't say that I work in series but I do paintings that *appear* to be from the same period.

BB: How do you make up the images, or do you make them up? How do you go from the elephant to the ship to the rows of houses?

ER: It's the icon/logo concept, I suppose. Things that are immediately recognizable. The idea is that recognition and a silhouette go hand in hand. I get the imagery from all sources. I may have seen several ships and then I'll work on a drawing, change it, put some masts over here, a sail here. I never consider the drawings anything but preparatory—they're not things in themselves, that's why I don't show rough sketches. Finally, I just enhance the thing back to a silhouette position, a silhouette appearance. Then that goes on the canvas in the form of an outline, and that's where I start working. The images just come from any-where—a magazine, a photograph of an old ship.

BB: Where did the Chick Unit *[1986] image come from?*

ER: From an old newspaper photograph. I just saw the power and the rightness of it. It was just meant to be.

BB: What about the words? Do they just pop up? Or do you keep notebooks, lists?

ER: Yeah, I do keep notebooks. I write things down that I see as food for po-tential material. I also—believe it or not—write a lot when I'm driving.

BB: On your lap?

ER: Off to the side. And I've gotten so that I can communicate with myself and still drive a car and not look at what I'm writing. Lately, I've done some paintings where I've actually enlarged those handwritten things. But as far as content goes, that's the most open-ended part of my art, in that both the words and images have to be fluid and simple and unlabored and sort of automatic. Some of the images will crisscross one another. You know, if *Chain and Cable* [1987] had just come by my train of thinking two days after I came up with this idea, it would have been an entirely different picture. So there's no master plan to establish the procedure for doing a masterpiece. I do these things fairly automatically and with as much blind faith as needed to make a picture. Usually, that's fairly spontaneous. What's the reason for doing it? I don't know what the reason is.

If someone wants to look at *Chain and Cable* and say "Cain and Abel," then I'll say, yes, that is maybe a logical viewer's response. That's strictly in the ballpark of the viewer.

BB: Do you expect to do any more books?

ER: No, I don't. I've got a few books in the refrigerator, but no plans to do any. I've moved away from that. I don't know why, because I've always considered books to be the toughest part of my art. I just felt that they were a lot stronger than any of my paintings. [. . .]

———

BB: What about movies?

ER: Movies are a great medium. They might even be the medium of the future. They might make them differently in the next fifty years—I'm sure they will. But the whole idea of a single person making a whole movie is almost impossible. You have to cooperate with many people. I have to be alone in my studio. I don't have a lot of assistants. I have one assistant, and I need an assistant, but I don't need an everyday assistant. I don't need anybody around. I like being alone, and I find great satisfaction in just doing my own work. But to make a movie, to get the means to the end is so overwhelming. You might get a great product, you might not, but that's why I appreciate Hollywood and respect those people that make feature films. I hate video. I'm a dimwit in mechanics and computers, and everything is moving in that direction now. I know they can do great things. But I still like the quality of film, and everything I had to go through to make the couple of films that I did was worth it. But it's so expensive. The only way to do a movie is to do a feature in today's big world. Unique ideas are usually subjugated to small productions, and in that case the films are never seen. It's just not a spontaneous medium. I'd rather paint pictures.

BB: What was it like stepping into a character role in a big-time movie like Choose Me*?*[42]

ER: Well, I loved that. I'm not much of an exhibitionist but working on *Choose Me* was pretty interesting. The director had this role and he asked me if I'd like to play it and so I said yes. And immediately I fell into this schedule, which was really nothing at all—I worked two days on it. It was good seeing how someone else makes a movie. He had his own style, and he liked working with non-actors, too. He called it clumsiness, or spontaneity, what you can't get with polished actors. Everybody else in there was an actor except me, I think.

BB: The space and the color in your paintings sometimes look influenced by Hollywood movies. There's almost a celluloid gloss.

ER: Yeah. If I'm influenced by movies, it's from way down underneath, not just on the surface. A lot of my paintings are anonymous backdrops for the drama of words. In a way they're words in front of the old Paramount mountain. You don't have to have the mountain back there—you could have a landscape, a farm. I have background, foreground. It's so simple. And the backgrounds are of no particular character. They're just meant to support the drama, like the "Hollywood" sign being held up by sticks. [. . .]

BB: Do you read a lot? Any particular kind of literature?

ER: I don't know what they'd call J. G. Ballard. Science fiction, I suppose. He's beyond science fiction. I like him a lot. He cuts open the belly of what's going on and everything falls out on the floor. I like to read writers like him, and it's kind of aggravating that I don't have more time to do that. I read what I want to read. I think most people do that. Or I read what I want to *see*. Don DeLillo is another writer that I like, and Tom McGuane. But, see, I'm after a certain kind of book. I don't want to read *Empire of the Sun*. I got halfway through that and dropped it. It's like he's painting flowers instead of concrete bunker ramps.

BB: Do these books suggest images to you?

ER: Yeah, they do—sometimes just the images of the words they use. I've done a few paintings using verbatim words from certain sections of books. Of course the words I use come from every source. Sometimes they happen on the radio and sometimes in conversations. I've had ideas come to me literally in my sleep that I tend to believe on blind faith, that I feel obliged to use. At other times I'll see a sign somewhere. Just recently I painted a picture called *Christ Candle* [1987]. I saw a candle company on Venice Boulevard in L.A. It said "Christ Candle" and I just wrote this down while I was driving. That became a logical reason to make a picture, or maybe an excuse. You know, you don't have to have any radar or clairvoyance to interpret things. I like to know that I can have these things flow easily.

BB: Do you think anybody understands these things?

ER: Maybe not, but they certainly don't understand any more than *I* do.

BB: At a certain point, I was wondering if anyone really understood what these pictures are. Or do you understand something about them that nobody's ever said, that you're just waiting for them to come along and say? Or that you don't want them ever to say?

Ed Ruscha, *Christ Candle*. 1987. Acrylic on canvas. 72 × 72″ (183 × 183 cm). Collection Emily Fisher Landau. Photo courtesy Ed Ruscha.

ER: Occasionally, someone will spout off something that will wake me up. They might be on target or off target, but a lot of things *do* come from the outside. I don't have hard and fast rules about the way my work should be interpreted. I am not a ponderer of other people's responses. I find it strange that somebody will say, "What exactly do you mean by this?" Like they're confounded by it. That will really throw me, because they can walk across the street and look at a painting with some ink spattered at it and get some mystical message, and that baffles me. I never know what the viewer is going to think. I've sort of taken it on as my job to make things official by finishing paintings. That way I can carry on. It's a little like asking somebody why they want to stay alive.

"Ed Ruscha"

Thomas Beller

TB: To what extent do you feel your early word paintings anticipated the conceptual linguistic art that one sees quite often now?

ER: Well, I'm not the first artist who has painted pictures of words. That's been done throughout history. I don't consider my work to be that new. I've got almost no feeling for much of the work of today. I don't feel I've influenced these people, necessarily. I think it's just a symptom of what's going on in mass culture now that leads people to work this way. It's also part of the style cycle, I suppose. They know my work. But those people weren't inspired by me. But then again, I'm not immune to this idea of inspiration from my forefathers. [. . .]

TB: What was more important to you when you were painting words: the way it looked or what it meant?

ER: The content was important. More than responding to something that was poetic. I'm not a poet. Sometimes people ask me if I have poetic connections in my work; I feel it is minimal at best. I responded to contemporary life, city life; the words I picked were pulled off the street, for their street power rather than their poetry power. And of course the shape had to more or less follow the shape

Originally published in *Splash*, February 1989, n.p.

of the letter form or you don't read the word. So it was a flip-flop between those two things. [. . .]

TB: In your more recent paintings, words have at times dropped out of the paintings entirely, sometimes leaving a gap of white space where they might have been. Are you rebelling against the word?

ER: No. I think you could look at them on one hand as though they were a device, something to get me through this thing: this act of painting or this act of telling whatever story I have to make. It can suggest to you something like a censor's strip. Or it can suggest the opposite. It can suggest a space for a thought. [. . .]

TB: Do you think that [the stereotype of the artist as bohemian] is reflective of the status of the artist in the eyes of today's younger artists? A lot of text art or art that is based specifically on a certain deconstructionist philosophy rejects the notion of the artist as a guy with beads, standing on a hill somewhere, the wind blowing in his face. He's a little "off"; not insane, but just off, and he gets this inspiration for an artwork: it's not irrational, but almost divine.

ER: Very good! I like that! It's a stereotype, but even today there is some grain of truth to it.

TB: Do you think this picture of the artist is valid?

ER: Yes. I think it is a mistake for a person to enter this business of art with the idea of climbing a certain ladder or to make a lot of money.

TB: How about if it's not just money? How about the notion that making art is a very rigorous intellectual exercise and that the raison d'être of the guy on the hill is antiquated; impulse, or some quasi-divine insanity is not a valid way of making art?

ER: Well, it is a valid reason to make art. Today there is the promise of a livelihood in making art, whereas in the past there wasn't. The idea of painting pictures in exchange for little pieces of green paper has just never been a part of me. I never dreamed when I started painting that I could ever sell a painting. I was more after compatriots' approval and just accomplishing something. For a time I did this typographical work with a printer, and also some advertising to support myself. Then I began to see that I despised all of that. And I just couldn't do it. So I started painting. For a couple of years I didn't sell anything, and when I began to it was a total shock to me.

TB: The last few months have seen an explosion of prices for artwork at auction. Records were set all over, including for your work. What is your reaction to your work being swept within that upward wind tunnel?

ER: I think if these prices distorted the artist's motivation, then there would be some sort of emptiness to it all. And there would definitely be more elevator music in the art world. And there is enough of that as it is. I feel like there is too much information in the art world right now. There are just too many painters and too many paintings. Think about it. You can devise some kind of Franz Kafka nightmare of paintings being stored in buildings that are beginning to crumble from the weight.

TB: What do you mean by too much information?

ER: It's really difficult to follow the direction this subject is being taken by critics and artists alike. The art world is now a satellite dish to the community. You've still got only two eyes. And how can you possibly swallow all this stuff? Some of it is very interesting. It's worthy if you can rake through the uninteresting work. [. . .]

TB: What was it about L.A. that caught your eye artistically?

ER: It was a kind of contemporary decadence that I responded to and I suppose it had a lot to do with the car and gas stations and that sort of thing. I felt that there was a speck of decadence here that fueled me.

TB: Were you commenting on that?

ER: The statements I was making then were struggles to make. Along those lines, I think that a lot of younger artists today are able to avoid that struggle and go straight to meatier subjects in their paintings. I think that is one of the features of

———

283

younger people's art today. They are able to seize something that I felt I had to struggle through in order to see.

TB: *Why are they getting there quicker?*

ER: I don't know. Maybe because of art history. They've been able to learn.

TB: *Learn about the struggle?*

ER: Nah, they've just learned to grab for the neck faster. [. . .]

TB: *Let's talk about the dark paintings.*

ER: I think they came mostly from photography, although they are not photographically done or anything. I feel that they are related to the subject of photography. I think these works somehow share something with photography. I don't know why. I have a definite side to side horizontal brushstroke. It's part of the concept of the landscape, I guess, and I painted all my pictures like that. These newer paintings are dark and strokeless. They're painted with an air brush.

TB: *People have been creeping into your paintings. What compelled you to invoke human figures, and why have you stayed away from the human form in most of your work?*

ER: The human figure has never really offered me any future. I don't find any magic in the human figure. When it means something symbolically, almost like a logo, or a solitary thought, then I use it. Sometimes there are people an inch tall in my paintings. I'm not working the human figure as much as I am the story that's behind it. So if there is a painting of a Spanish dancer, it's more a Spanish dancer than it is a woman wearing a Spanish dress. I like the idea of taking a particular subject and not questioning its integrity, committing myself to it. It is a sort of proven artistic achievement to take an object that seems unimportant, that has no real Catholic glory, and glorify it. In ancient history most of the paintings were meant to convey how great things were; in modern painting artists have selected subjects that are almost forgotten. Everybody is looking for things that are forgotten.

TB: *What is the effect of absenting figures from your paintings? Particularly your gas station paintings, which are almost desolate.*

ER: I think they become more powerful without extraneous elements like people, cars, anything beyond the story. That's why these lines, these planes in a gas station were more important than trying to create an Edward Hopper scene. It became something for me to investigate. I was able to subtract a romantic story from the scene—I wanted something that had some industrial strength to it. People would muddle it. There was a coldness that I liked when I painted those pictures. It all gets back to humor, I suppose. And that includes a devotion to abstract art and to figurative art, I suppose I'm a product of all those things that I looked at when I was growing up. It's a mixture of it all. Where does Muhammed Ali fit into this story?

"Hot Property"

Victoria Lautman

[. . .] "Honestly, I've never felt the need or obligation to communicate with the public, and I feel most artists are the same way," *admits Ruscha. [. . .]* "Oh, some artist might think, 'Gosh, I sure hope they understand this,' but that's not part of what I'm doing. There's just no right or wrong way to approach my work, and each viewer will come with his or her own associations anyway. And that's the way it should be."

As far as Ruscha's apparently arbitrary choices for phrases to immortalize, they can originate "from memory, sometimes from dreams, sometimes from listening to the radio. But it's always been very intuitive and personal for me, and it's not about entertaining people. I've never sat down with a pad and pencil and thought, 'What can I do today?' The words that I use, their combinations, the phrases—they're all things that somehow personally affect me, that I find amusing, or ironic, or something."

For instance, the artist was driving along one day and noticed a hand-scrawled bumper sticker advising the reader to "Do AZ I Do."[43] "That just caught me. That was just perfect source material." [. . .]

Originally published in the *Chicago Tribune*, April 26, 1989, sec. 7, p. 21.

Of course, floating the words before a view of cloudy skies seems fraught with meaning, despite the humble origin of the phrase. Maybe there's a religious message here, like God in heaven talking to us poor humans. . . . Then again, maybe not. "That didn't come about from any specific design or plan on my part," *Ruscha concedes. [. . .]* "The clouds, the night-time views, the window-shadows—they're like anonymous backdrops to me, like stage sets or curtains, and I just happened to be working on cloudy skies when the whole 'Do AZ I Do' thing came about."

Just like that? That's all? "Yep," *he laughs.* "It's all so simple it's complicated!"

Still, the desire to imbue Ruscha's work with all kinds of deep messages is natural, and has had some unexpected results for the artist. When he helped organize a recent exhibition of his work in Tokyo, "there was this one painting that had a sort of Japanese calligraphy in it, but which had no communicative value at all. I just made it up to go in the background," *Ruscha recalls.* "Well, I was asked to drop the work from the show because they said, 'The calligraphy doesn't mean anything to our people.' But since I wasn't intending to communicate in the first place, what difference did it make? It was like wallpaper to me—it wasn't supposed to mean anything!" *Eventually, Ruscha agreed to omit the work, but he was not a happy camper.*

As for the artist's future in what has proved to be an impetuous market, it's anybody's guess. [. . .] Few artists ever get to witness this in-out-in-again action during their lifetime, and it must be an odd thing to observe.

"Oh, it is. It really is," *admits Ruscha. [. . .]* "But, you know, I'm totally committed to making art, so I'm not surprised I'm still here."

"An Interview with Edward Ruscha"

Bonnie Clearwater

BC: In the fall of 1989, a major exhibition of your work will open at the Centre Georges Pompidou in Paris. The show will then travel to museums throughout Europe. Do you think people will have difficulty understanding your work if they don't read English?

ER: That question has come up before. I find it curious that people have said there is a problem with the English language being used in my work. But I don't see that with any other artists' use of words. Do we see that problem with a Picasso painting that happens to have a French word like "*journal*"?

BC: Do you think it helps to have the words translated?

ER: Art is a visual, universal experience, but if there needs to be a translation for a single word that dominates a painting, then let it be. I think in a certain way the translation does help and I've asked to have the words translated on wall labels. But my work can also be appreciated for the starkness of the shapes and not necessarily for the dictionary definition. When I'm working, I some-

Originally published in French as "*Edward Ruscha: Quand les mots deviennent formes*," *Art Press*, n. 137, June 1989, pp. 20–25. Published on the occasion of the exhibition *Edward Ruscha: Paintings*, organized by the Museum Boymans–van Beuningen, Rotterdam and the Centre Georges Pompidou, Paris.

times lose track of the intention of the words—they become the foreground central subject.

BC: Not only do you make use of the English language, but your subject matter seems to relate specifically to the mass media culture of the United States. Do you think the Europeans who visit your show will understand such references?

ER: I think Europeans are particularly aware of American life and very knowledgeable of the English language. The world knows a lot about our culture. I'm always reminded of this when I go to England and see the record stores. The music industry over there is so knowledgeable about what goes on in America that they know more about our music culture than we do. They may not know my work in Europe, but it will be there to be seen.

BC: How will the European show differ from the retrospective of your work that traveled through the United States in 1982 and 1983?

ER: I'm going to show work of the last ten years in the European exhibition. It will include works that stand for the different directions I've been exploring. The oldest work will be a series of five small paintings from the late 1960s, such as *Automatic* [1966], *Vaseline* [1967], and *Rooster* [1967]. It's an area of my work that I feel has not been addressed. I just think it will make an interesting jump into my later work.

BC: The way the letters are spread apart in these small paintings makes it difficult to concentrate on the complete word. The letters seem more like patterns.

ER: Yes, these words are pattern-like, and in their horizontality they answer my investigation into landscape. Like you say, they're almost not words—they are objects that become words. I think that this pattern quality links these paintings with my later works.

BC: One of the reasons I decided to compile a catalogue raisonné of your work[44] is that certain episodes of your career, like these small word paintings, still are not widely known; and that the current interpretations of your work are based on the few paintings, drawings, and prints that are shown or reproduced over and over, like Hollywood, Standard Station *and* Large Trademark with Eight Spotlights.

ER: So many times I've seen my work capsulated. My best-known works are shown in exclusion of other works. I like the idea of each work having an identity of its own.

*BC: By studying your work chronologically, I've noticed certain tendencies. For instance, your frequent travels across America early in your life seem to have been an important influence on you, as a number of your early paintings are the names of towns—*Sweetwater, Dublin *[1959],* Chatanooga *[1960],* Vicksburg *[two versions: 1959 and 1960], and of course,* Hollywood.

ER: My early travels did affect me so deeply that they actually served as source material for me. I had wanderlust when I was fourteen. Even before that I would always travel with my family. [. . .]

BC: There's a nostalgic quality about these paintings of names of towns. Reading the list of names is like hearing a train conductor announce the names of stops along a given route.

ER: The towns that I happened to use as source material for my work, like Dublin, Sweetwater and Vicksburg, only had fleeting historical connotations for me. I had no earth-shaking experiences in these places that made me want to recall them. I liked the ring and sound of the names and they had some link with what I was interested in at the time, which was travel. [. . .]

BC: You keep referring to your interest in landscape painting. Can you elaborate on this aspect of your work?

ER: It's been somewhat of a struggle for me to get beyond the initial structure of art—I'm a prisoner of the idea of the landscape in painting and it's something I've continued to be tied to. I have a very locked-in attitude about painting things in a horizontal mode. I think I'm lucky that words happen to be horizontal, that letters follow one another with spaces and pauses and then more letters in order to make up words and sentences.

BC: *The diagonal is another compositional device you've used consistently throughout your career. You used it in* Standard Station, Large Trademark, *and* Hollywood *in the 1960s, as well as in your paintings and drawings of windows. Also the first silhouette paintings of the early 1980s are of figures, elephants, cars, etc. climbing a hill—each taking their turn as a modern-day Sisyphus. More recently, the diagonal appears in the oblique grid paintings of city lights. What is the appeal of the diagonal composition for you?*

ER: It's less an appeal than an assignment or formal problem that I find myself taking on. The diagonal comes out of the idea of motion and speed, as well as perspective. When you divide the canvas like that you always have the suggestion of speed and depth.

BC: *Your interest in the horizontal-landscape format is particularly obvious when you paint on long, narrow canvases. These paintings actually force the viewer to travel physically from one end of the canvas to the other. The experience of viewing these works is very much like traveling through a landscape. The effect is cinematic as well.*

ER: I've been influenced by the movies, particularly the panoramic-ness of the wide screen. The wide screen says something about my work. Television had no effect on me like it has on other artists. [. . .]

BC: *As your training was as an Abstract Expressionist, do you work spontaneously or do you plan out your works in advance?*

ER: Sometimes I make notations in a form of a reminder. These usually work as a springboard for getting myself involved in the work. But usually I'll stage a rough pencil idea. I don't do extensive studies for paintings. I usually work directly on the canvas.

BC: *Some of the objects, landscapes or skyscapes that you paint seem closely observed. Do you sketch from objects and nature, or do you use photographs as your main visual aid?*

ER: Sometimes the source of the imagery in my work is very specific; sometimes it's general. I don't sketch from nature as a rule. I draw from nature only when it serves me. I might make drawings of cloud formations that I can't capture other ways. I also use a camera for recording images—it can work better than a sketch—and I sometimes refer back to the photographs.

———

BC: In your paintings of objects such as marbles, pencils, or olives, you seem to be interested in the specific qualities of these objects, and you attempt to render them in their actual state and size.

ER: The word "documentation" may have some meaning here. I felt like reproducing things from nature in their real state. I've done a lot of things that were natural size. If I paint a picture of a marble, I want it to be natural size. I've had this faithfulness to the subject. This idea doesn't go through all of my work but there is an underlying direction to my work that is rooted in factual dimensions and statistics. My interest in facts is crucial to my work. Not that you'll find factual information in my work. [. . .]

BC: Your creation of [your] books seems to have contributed to the categorization of your work as conceptual art.

ER: People were so happy to see me produce such books at the time that they couldn't allow themselves to accept that I would paint a picture. This was when conceptual art was at its strongest and conceptual artists were intent on having contempt for anything material like a painting.

BC: But you remained committed to creating paintings. These straightforward documentary photographs, though, had an effect on a series of drawings you made in the 1960s of apartment buildings in Los Angeles. These were the drawings you created by using loose graphite or gunpowder.

ER: I've always done things that are soft and powdery. These drawings helped me in the direction of completing finished drawings.

BC: By using the graphite and gunpowder, you were able to achieve a diffuse effect in your drawings that's similar to soft-focus photographs. These early drawings also seem to have led you to create the recent drawings of figures in silhouette, which in turn lead to the soft-focused paintings. In the earlier drawings, though, the buildings are depicted as solid objects occupying space, whereas in the recent paintings of houses the forms seem to dematerialize into shadow.

ER: I actually used my own photographs of apartment houses to inspire me to do the drawings of the 1960s. I saw them [the buildings] not so much as

292

silhouettes, but as objects, and the treatment of them became an aid to what I'm doing today. That's why I link these earlier apartment house drawings to the recent works. They both have diffused, soft-focused qualities.

BC: Do you see a continuity in your work from the beginning of your career to the present?

ER: Whatever my work was made up of in the beginning is exactly what it is like today. There really is no difference. I find myself doing the same things and feeling the same way about a subject. I borrow from myself. I could have seen the silhouette paintings happening twenty years ago. The composition of these things [is] still locked into this problem of abstract art and how things fit together in a picture. I am a combination of someone who is an abstract artist and someone who deals with subject matter.

BC: It seems clear in your recent works that objects and words are interchangeable. In your painting Five Past Eleven *[1989], a bamboo pole stretches across the upper left quarter of a giant clock face that tilts back into space. The rod has the same relation to the background that words have in other paintings.*

ER: If I'm dealing with a foreground/background problem, sometimes the background can be anonymous but still have the look of something specific, as in this painting.

BC: In paintings such as Five Past Eleven, *do you intend for the viewer to derive particular meanings from the combination of images?*

ER: These are not designed to evoke any specific associations. I don't have a specific point of taking my inner thoughts and making other people see these inner thoughts. That doesn't happen with my art.

BC: But the clock face as background seems to force a specific reading in relation to the bamboo pole. It's not neutral like the colorfield background of some of your earlier word paintings.

ER: I've skirted the issue of time before in my work, such as in the hourglass silhouettes and clock face paintings and drawings. I've also used the bamboo pole before. The pole resembles the human finger—it has thick joints and then narrows between the joints. The pole looks like a pointing finger, as does the hand of the clock.

I think the combination of forms in these works has a lot to do with abstract art. It's going back to the use of the circle and the diagonal. If someone wants to say the painting is dream-like, I won't argue with them. There is a heavy grayness and seriousness about the work.

BC: Actually, the clock in this painting reminds me of the half-moon shaped paintings you created for the architectural lunettes in the Miami Public Library in Miami, Florida. It's as if you split a lunette in half. Even the color of the clock is similar to the gray tones of the lunettes. Did you make that connection?

ER: Well, I wasn't conscious of that until you mentioned it, but the preparatory drawings I did for this painting were of half a clock face positioned upright and face on, which looked very much like the lunettes. I felt the image was more powerful when I turned the clock into an oblique, spilling away from the picture plane. The lunettes might have been a subliminal influence.

BC: You received the commission to create murals for the library in 1985. Did you approach this public project differently from your studio work?

ER: It was the first time in my life as an artist that I was faced with communicating with the public. I realized that I could not approach this project like the works I paint for myself. I wanted to make people think about where they were, about the purpose of a library and about the function of language.

BC: The library project was divided into two parts. The first consisted of murals for the rotunda over the library's entrance, which were installed in July 1985. You painted eight panels that fit within the edges of the ring of the rotunda with a quote from William Shakespeare's Hamlet—*"Words Without Thoughts Never To Heaven Go." The second stage, which you have just completed, was for the lunettes throughout the library's two public floors. Originally you planned to use words in the lunettes that referred to the nature of linguistics, such as the conjunctives "and," "if," "so," "but," or the interrogatives "who," "what," "where," "when," "why," and "how." Did the iconographic scheme of the lunettes evolve as you continued to work?*

———

ER: I'm using some images like the ships, the maps of the world, hourglasses, and yardsticks. The images on the non-word lunettes act as punctuation and as relief from the words.

BC: *Do you feel this commission affected your work?*

ER: The project allowed me to work on a big scale. Working on so many works at once has been a real treat for me.

BC: *Over the last few years you've received considerable attention both nationally and internationally. Are you concerned about the impact of all this interest in you might have on your work?*

ER: I've had a few skids in my life, but I never fear running out of ideas. It all adds up to a collection of loose ends.

———

"THE LAST WORD"

Ralph Rugoff

In 1986, at an age when many artists have long since committed themselves to flagrant self-plagiarism, Ed Ruscha unveiled a series of paintings that, in appearance at least, were unlike anything he had ever done. [. . .]

    That Ruscha is still capable of producing challenging and forceful new art shouldn't be all that surprising, given a three-decade-long career distinguished by a consistently inventive output. What still seems truly remarkable, however, is the fact that not a single painting from the exhibition was sold.

    "It wasn't the first time that's happened," *says Ruscha.* "Usually it's taken me around six years *after* an exhibit before I could sell any of the work. I've never held anybody responsible for that," *he laughs.* "I just took it as a matter of course that most of my shows didn't sell."

    In the last three years, it seems that the art world has scurried to make amends. [. . .] It also seems clear that the art establishment is reassessing his contribution to contemporary art history. [. . .]

    Confronted by this recent surge of attention, Ruscha likes to joke that he's become the proverbial "twenty-five-year overnight sensation." *Even on the eve of his second retrospective of the decade, his skepticism remains intact.* "The whole idea of a retrospective

Originally published in *Art News*, v. 88, n. 10, December 1989, pp. 120–125.

has deep implications for an artist—mostly negative ones," *he remarks*. "By the time you've gone through the fanfare of producing something like that, your career has shut down. And *then* what do you do?"

The fuss about his recent work has left Ruscha slightly nonplussed. "I don't feel that my message to the world is any different now than when I was painting bright, colorful paintings with words," *he comments*. "I'll admit they have an edge to them, but that's just because people usually associate darkness with somberness and fog.

"One thing these paintings have made me deal with is the idea of figurative art, and they may have moved me to consider a slightly different approach to solving some issues that I've always been up against. [. . .]"

The fuzzy-edged quality of the silhouette paintings—many of which appear to suffer a nocturnal dropout of visual detail—is an effect Ruscha achieved by using a spray gun for the first time. "I've always had a prejudice against using an air gun, but these paintings just couldn't be done with a brush," *he explains*. "I wanted to make a strokeless painting." *[. . .]*

[Although] clearly generic in character, the silhouettes manage to express an enigmatic, chilly poignance. [. . .] "I think a lot of artists see ambiguity as one of the things about art that has some strength to it," *Ruscha comments*. "Paradox and absurdity have just always been really delicious to me. The intangible gets to me, the subjective gets to me, the emotional and the intuitive get to me." *[. . .]*

While he has been routinely included in nearly every contemporary head count of prominent artists, Ruscha's work nevertheless met with curious resistance from the Eastern art establishment—partly because his unorthodox, idiosyncratic approach to art-making made his work hard to classify. Without the convenient tag certifying membership in a Major 20th-Century Art Movement, his art doubtlessly appeared less attractive to museums and collectors worried about owning the right piece of art history. [. . .] Not only did major Eastern museums decline to purchase his paintings, but his work—ghettoized as West Coast Pop—was also excluded from key group exhibitions. "I was insulted in a few instances," *Ruscha says*. "I was never in many of the major Pop art shows that happened in the '60s or '70s because it was perceived as a New York–based phenomenon. Later the same thing happened with my books—after these artists

———

297

from New York began getting into that, it was suddenly decided that concept art was something that developed in New York."

Not even Ruscha's 1982 retrospective made a big impact on his reputation. "Even when I had that show, none of the museums bought works out of that, and I didn't sell anything, either. And I was sort of at a point where I needed to," *Ruscha adds.* "But there was just no outlet at all. Every artist I knew and everyone in Leo's [Castelli] stable was selling out shows, except for me." *[. . .]*

It's probably no coincidence, then, that his recent reevaluation came about after the debut of his silhouette series—works with the kind of somber gravity appreciated in certain European art circles. Yet in preparing for his Beaubourg show,[45] *Ruscha found himself facing the same obstacles that have dogged him throughout his career.*

"I've had about thirty shows in Europe, but the people at the Pompidou were still telling me they didn't really know my work," *he says.* "They were trying to get me to show only the golden oldies they were familiar with, which would have meant putting together another retrospective, and I don't want *another* retrospective. They say things like, 'Maybe if we have paintings that say *less* words, because, you see, the translation is a problem.' And I'd say, 'My God, man, how can you possibly say that and then have shows of Jean-Michel Basquiat, who's got millions of words in his paintings? Do you understand *those* words any more than you do mine?' [. . .]"

Despite the critical success [of the painting Five Past Eleven*] and the fact that it was snapped up by the Hirshhorn Museum and Sculpture Garden in Washington, D.C., Ruscha calls it a* "troublesome painting. There's something too placid or maybe grandiose about it. It has a visual strength, but the real deep stuff in there—I wonder where it is?" *Ruscha shakes his head.* "I just don't think it's going to take me anywhere." *[. . .]*

While art writers have often sought autobiographical traces in Ruscha's work, [. . . he] avows that his sources of inspiration are more immediate.

"I might overhear something in a coffee shop or read something in a catalog or a J. G. Ballard novel that gives me an idea," *he says.* "Art's about the glorification of *something,* though in my case it's not necessarily the common object. It might be the power of the word or words that I'm glorifying. For instance, right now I have this idea that 'white fury' means something to me. I know what 'white' means and what 'fury' means, but why does 'white fury' mean something to me? And why do I have to make a painting out of it?"

Given his career-long preoccupation with language, it's tempting to see Ruscha as a forerunner of '80s text-and-image artists such as Jenny Holzer, Barbara Kruger, Mitchell Syrop, and Richard Prince. Ruscha disavows any connection. "I think those people operate in a totally different sandbox," *he says.* "We may be knowledgeable of the same sources, but I don't feel myself linked to their work.

"A lot of the art movements that have happened recently, like Neo-Geo, haven't really gripped me. These artists may be sincere, but they're not totally revolutionary and they don't have the social impact the Pop artists did." *[. . .]*

He claims that his future plans are vague, although he says he's bent on "making some paintings just for myself. But I don't have a waiting list of words or a backlog of ideas to work from," *he hastens to add.* "Right now I don't know what I'm going to do next. And I like that. Much of the time it's like I'm operating on blind faith," *he explains.*

"It may be there's some sort of emptiness or stage play at the roots of my work. Or at least it may be some kind of final solution," *he hints somewhat cryptically.* "The truth is, I'd be happy just being a patch on Hans Hoffmann's painting pants," *he grins.* "The way I see it, I'm just a little art victim. I'm a soldier for art with a job to do."

"Conversation with Ed Ruscha"

Bernard Blistène

BB: *It has been said that you are the artist of Los Angeles as Manet was the artist of Paris. What do you feel?*

ER: That's almost too much to swallow. Comparisons are strange answers to things, but I don't claim to know more about this city than any other artist. I'm not a native of Los Angeles. I'm from the midwest, the southwest actually, from Oklahoma. When I came here it was more or less an extension of my life there. Everything was horizontal, but this was like a garden of Eden compared to Oklahoma. [. . .] And I still love this city, but I'm frustrated by it. It's a love/hate relationship.

BB: *So you are a frustrated man?*

ER: Well, you, know, I like to get out of town. I like the open areas. I like where there's no city. I spend a lot of time in the desert. Over the past twenty years it's just harder and harder to live in this city. [. . .]

Originally published in *Edward Ruscha: Paintings/Schilderijen* (Rotterdam: Museum Boymans–van Beuninger, 1990), pp. 126–140.

BB: But why so insistently painting when, obviously for you, there were other possibilities?

ER: Well, it happened in art school: I totally bought the life of an artist, lock, stock and barrel. I knew I was going to be an artist in some way or other. At first I wanted to be a commercial artist. I learned sign-painting and painted many signs commercially. [. . .] I couldn't say what I wanted to say in any commercial art form. It was impossible, so I committed myself to painting. It wasn't even my choice, in a sense—I'm a victim! I saw that there were things to say and work to do, and I wanted to do more with my life than work for someone else. I like the idea of working for myself, alone. I've always liked that. The climate at that time, too, provided a certain camaraderie with friends and fellow artists—all of us doing similar things. So I began to meet more artists, more painters, and I could see I was just born for the job, born to watch paint dry. [. . .]

BB: Is your work about evocation?

ER: I guess the idea of noise, of visual noise, somehow meant something to me, and still means something to me. The idea that you can say a lot in a small given area somehow has always intrigued me, and this seems to be one of the principal guidelines in my work. I never forget that I have a given space in which to make noise, or lose sight of the idea that it is going to echo whatever I feel.

BB: When you say that you like to make visual noise with your painting, is this some kind of definition?

ER: It is. It's a freedom to insult people or assault people.

BB: So now I understand why you are not a writer. It is a question of impact.

ER: Yes, I never wanted to write. I prefer the economy, the directness, of visual tools, rather than communicating as a writer. There are some similarities, but my words are always instant choices.

———

BB: In your work I find a kind of chiasm, a cross between what you paint and what is written on the canvas, whereby what is written on the painting never refers to the image: what Duchamp called an intentional distortion.

ER: Very true. I think of it that way myself sometimes. There is a vast separation: I see myself working with two things that don't even ask to understand each other. I like the emptiness of things at the same time that I like things that are power-packed.

BB: Yes, but you mix both kinds of reality—they intersect. Is it perhaps a question of not being able to say what you see, and vice versa, a kind of collision?

ER: Yes. Despite the fact that I use words, I work in and on a non-verbal world, and this is the irony. [. . .]

BB: For me, the irony in your work is that in spite of the attentive, formal approach, there is a strong impression of immediacy and improvisation.

ER: I believe in intuition and approaching things as instant gratification. Just do the things you want to do, make the kind of pictures you want to make. [. . .]

BB: The process of your painting is becoming more complex—and more sophisticated. I am thinking of the black paintings, for example. Would you agree with this?

ER: Perhaps, but that's not by design. It's not as though I sat down and did some mathematical calculations and saw that the only way for me to go would be black and white. I'd rather keep the paintings fluid and spontaneous and free. The longer I am at it, the less I want to look at my work historically. I don't want to have to go back and appraise myself. I'm doing different work now, but I still feel that it is rooted in the oldest things I was inspired by. [. . .]

BB: Can we come back to language and the manipulation of words? The language you use is so "spoken" that it stops me from speaking when I look at your paintings. For me, the impact of your work has much to do with a kind of relocation from movies and books to the canvas, to the extent that I am blocked from having the kind of speech I might normally have with a painting; and this, I would add, is not a bad thing. Something which we might otherwise say about painting no longer comes into play.

———

ER: My work doesn't come with a set of instructions. There are no rules for looking at my paintings. They come, as I have said, from my intuition.

BB: *Questions of language have become central to the century. It seems to me that you have wanted to bring about a distinction in your work between what we would call in French "la peinture" and "le tableau." You never cease to work with the possibilities which remain open regarding, so to speak, the painting which can be read and the book which can be seen. Is it at this point that, for you, language becomes subversive? And is this the reason why your books have become a form of subterfuge?*

ER: My books were very hot items—it was hot art to me, almost too hot to handle. I liked the idea that my books would disorient, and it seemed to happen that people would look at them and the books would look very familiar, yet they were like a wolf in sheep's clothing. I felt that they were very powerful statements, maybe the most powerful things I've done. I'm kind of considered part of the mainstream of art history now. My work is not revolutionary, but the books that I did were, at that point, a can opener that got into something else. My books were art objects to me, but a lot of people chose not to even accept them, and for this reason they have always been underground—and still are. I consider my books to be strictly visual materials. I even perceived them as bits of sculpture, in a way. They were three-dimensional, they were thick. I even painted on the sides of my canvases for a few years to accentuate the idea that this was a three-dimensional thing. I would make a painting that said "Radio," for example, then paint the title on the side. In an odd way, it was like a book, and so my paintings were book covers in a way. That's it, I do book covers. If you make a book cover and put a word on it, then it's immediately accepted by people, but if you do so in painting, then it's sort of disorienting. And isn't disorientation one of the best things about making art?

BB: *Would you say that this sliding between two things, that these transpositions, are at the heart of your sense of irony and the absurd?*

ER: Absurdity for its own sake is rich. The selection of something absurd or the absurd handling of an absurd subject has attracted many artists. We have "bad" painting, we have "absurd" painting. Artists forever have been trying to do things that are unacceptable. That's the nature of being an artist: to do things that are unacceptable . . . and would I change the natural order of things?

BB: Do you think that sometimes your work refers to a certain kind of surrealism? I mean, for example, Magritte or even Dalí?

ER: Not really. There are some sympathetic waves of thought maybe, but my work is more tied to the frustrations and decadence of city life—the light bulb, more than the candle. I saw Magritte and Dalí after they were forbidden. I saw them as art history, so that meant something else to me. But the forbidden things . . . artists always want to do things that are forbidden. They want to be tough, they want to break the rules, they want to bring on this absurdity and when it's done right, it can be truly beautiful.

BB: We have spoken about city life. When you come from Europe, the first thing you learn is that in Los Angeles no one walks, everyone drives. I think of your work, therefore, as a huge field in which you drive—and of the canvas as a kind of windshield! Would you accept this kind of reading?

ER: That's a notion. . . . Yes, that could very well be true—the automobile and space and all that, these have a lot to do with my work. If I didn't drive, if I lived in a place where there were no cars, I'm sure I would think about things entirely differently.

BB: And, taking this idea a little further, regarding the way in which you handle space and illusion, is there not something in your work of the drive-in?

ER: That's great, I'll accept that . . . a drive-in. *[Laughs.]*

BB: Can we speak now about your work in terms of uprootedness, of displacement?

ER: Uprootedness, displacement. . . . I don't know where my work fits there. . . .

BB: Have you seen Stranger than Paradise?[46] *For me your work feels a bit like this film.*

ER: That's a compliment. Yes, it's true, the film deals with a sort of lost world, without refuge. But if you are going to push me in this direction, I would have to say that it is difficult to compare a painting with a movie. With a painting you don't get a running story-line from beginning to end, you are confronted instead by something smack, face-on, something which doesn't move. And yet movies, the screen . . . these have always been closely related to my work, and that's why I am so involved with them.

BB: *Without a doubt. And photography?*

ER: Yes, there's a certain power to a photograph. The camera has a way of disorienting a person, if it wants to, and for me, when it disorients, it's got real value. Movies and photographs are great art forms because they offer so much on a flat screen, on a flat surface. [. . .]

BB: *By combining words and images, words and colors, you run the risk always of literal readings. Yet you continue to short-circuit such literal interpretations. Do you think this is due to a kind of paradox; to the pursuit, if you like, of the subversive image?*

ER: I am careful not to be literal, not to offer this other option to anyone. If I paint a picture of the word "cool," I don't use a lot of blue or other cool colors— instead, I find myself deliberately taking another route.

BB: *To bring about the juxtaposition of two things which have no relation to each other, except in being together on the same canvas or on the same screen?*

ER: Yes, and sometimes it's about oddness. I've always had a deep respect for things that are odd, for things which cannot be explained. Explanations seem to me to sort of finish things off.

BB: *For the present generation, you are a key figure. You have taken a real freedom with many things. Your art has a phlegmatic quality which expresses itself superbly in the mediation between words and painting. Your work is not tragical-romantical, there is nothing in it of the hari-kari which is characteristic of the work of a good number of your contemporaries. On the contrary, what comes through is a sort of pleasure and coolness, a supreme detachment.*

———

ER: Well, the idea of getting pleasure from art is part of it for me.

BB: *It is, however, an idea which has been rejected by a number of your contemporaries.*

ER: Perhaps, but take Matisse and Picasso—they were not tortured gentlemen, as far as I know.

BB: *Not at all, but they avoided confusion before it had a chance to arise. Can we speak, though, of artists who are important for you? There is often, as you know, the temptation to see in your work a resemblance to the work of Edward Hopper.*

ER: I don't know why, but I've always found his work to be kind of institutional, not modern—it's the reverse of modern. There's something too obvious, too clean about it . . . too cosmetic. But you are right, people do compare my work with Hopper's, because of the gas stations and other useless comparisons which I don't find at all accurate. I don't dislike his work. There are some classic paintings which were timely, which summed up the 1930s—these paintings are historic, you respect them for what they are, but the real meat of his work never got me. I never responded to that at all.

BB: *Do you think that your work is an expression of its time, as you recognize Hopper's was of his, and is timeliness a subject for you?*

ER: You know, for a good long while, I felt like the art world moved along so slowly and that it had little to say; while movies, on the other hand, seemed to offer so much. Now I think painters are saying more than filmmakers . . . which is strange for me in a way, because my paintings have a closer relation to movies than to painting.

BB: *The first thing to be said regarding making movies is that there is always a range of constraints. But beyond this question of a mediation between cinema and painting, I feel that your work, in the context in which you do it, is emblematic of a particular America which remains, for us, an exoticism.*

ER: This is never a question in my mind; and yet my paintings do come out of an American sensibility, out of urban frustrations which are characteristic of where I live. My work has no connection to Europe. There is no doubt that my paintings, to a degree, feed on movies, and yet I have stayed a painter. I guess you could say I am interested in the possibilities that remain in a time which tends to favor the moving image. It's a paradox, but I find that painting offers more possibilities than movies, perhaps because making a film is such a formidable undertaking. There are always so many people working on it. But I am surprised that the cinema, which is such a young art form, hasn't questioned its own foundations to the extent that painting has. As I said, it's perhaps a question of medium; it's easier to bring off a painting than a film. This is also why I prefer to stay alone with my paintings.

BB: *From time to time you use culinary metaphors, you speak about cooking, and you have included various culinary ingredients in your work—vegetable juices, carrots, spinach, chili beans—to, as it were, "prepare" your paintings.*

ER: That's true. I guess making art is a bit like working in the kitchen: there are all these vegetables. I'm always looking at ways to concoct new things, I use different elements, and I feel I have to surprise myself, while at the same time staying faithful to my art.

BB: *Can we speak now about the size of your paintings?*

ER: Proportion is a lot more important to me than size. A large work will overpower you in a certain way that a small painting cannot. I dream of getting into paintings that are vertical, that are narrower than they are high, but most of my proportions are affected by the concept of the panorama. Like I say, I'm a victim of the horizontal line and the landscape, which is almost one and the same to me. So I've eliminated a lot of unnecessary sky and unnecessary ground. I try to focus on where the sky meets the ground so that you have a stretched-out version, something panoramic—a panavision format. I find myself always coming back to this horizontal idea. Back in the early '80s, I was doing these paintings that were very long and skinny. Then they became more than paintings, they became objects, and were taken out of the common, friendly—let's say, user-friendly—shape of a painting. I guess maybe I'm trying to put more time and mileage between one end and the other.

———

BB: Continuing this notion of the panorama, of a cinerama or panavision, it seems to me that your work is nourished more by the thought and reflections of certain artists such as Robert Smithson—whom you knew and with whom you were at various times closely associated—but, in contrast to such artists, you wanted to locate this way of thinking strictly within the framework of painting. As I see it, the alignment of your work with Pop Art has been confusing, and it is even more evident today that your work has closer links to the thinking of land artists, or even certain conceptualists such as Lawrence Weiner. In fact, the sources of your work are always to be found outside the pictorial field, and it has become your task, as it were, to transpose or transplant them.

ER: It is always too simple to reduce an activity to a category. I have drawn from everything which is around me. This is maybe what you call freedom, or is a part of your definition of exoticism.

"GETTING A READ ON ED RUSCHA"

Suzanne Muchnic

[. . . The exhibition Edward Ruscha: Paintings *is touring internationally . . .] before winding up in the city that has become so much a part of Ruscha's identity. [. . .] During an interview in his spacious Venice studio, the fifty-two-year-old artist appeared to have taken the blitz of popularity in stride.*

"If I had been more involved with the hub of the art world it might have affected me more. But I've been in L.A. for a long time and that has helped me. I hid out here, so I didn't get spit out with some art movement. That allowed me to stay around longer," *he said.*

"It's a real fickle situation. There are so many cycles. I've always been prepared for the possibility that my work might dry up and no one [would] want to see it. A long time ago [fellow artists and I] used to say that if we had to drop the whole thing, we could do it without taking any demerits for it. But I've worked so long—about thirty years—if I can't handle it now I wasn't made for the job."

As if listening intently to what he just said, he added emphatically, "I was made for the job." [. . .]

As for his popularity in Europe, Ruscha figures that he simply got swept up in foreign captivation with all things American. "You see it all across the board. If you want

Originally published in the *Los Angeles Times*, December 9, 1990, Calendar, p. 3.

to know about American music, go to England. There are James Dean fan clubs in Tokyo," *he said.*

People from other countries "are genuinely interested in what is going on in America. That may be one of the factors in choosing my work," *he said.* "They see me as curiously American, as opposed to other artists who have a more international look."

Foreign interest in America is not news, but for Ruscha it is a turnaround. "I ran into difficulty in Europe a few years ago because of the words in my work. People said the audience couldn't speak English and the words couldn't be translated because they were loaded with innuendoes peculiar to American experience. Now that curtain has lifted," *he said.* "They are more curious about what artists are up to. I guess it's the American sense of freedom that fascinates them. Europeans are more bound by convention. There's an explosion of artists in Europe, but they seem to be involved with common causes—social, political, but also the visual influence of painting. [. . .]"

Preparing for the show has caused a flurry of activity on the quiet industrial street where Ruscha works. An electronic gate moves back and forth to admit visitors. Inside his clean, white, warehouse-like studio, he points out a scale model of the museum's galleries, which he has used to plan the installation. An assistant answers the door and helps with physical labor. The telephone rings every few minutes. Not exactly peaceful, but Ruscha indicates that the situation is far from normal.

He moved here five years ago after twenty years in a shabby courtyard complex on Western Avenue. "I needed a place with four big walls to work on the Miami commission, and this was perfect," *he said, explaining that the studio formerly belonged to his Los Angeles dealer, James Corcoran, who used it for storage and special presentations.*

When the excitement dies down, Ruscha is a "pretty regular" *working stiff.* "It's more or less a routine. I bring my lunch pail to work. As long as I have an excuse to do something, I have all the time to do it. I've been doing it for so many years that I've forgotten why, and that's probably as it should be. You have to treat art like a baby—commit yourself to it, set aside time for it. If you don't, you have problems. [. . .]"

———

The words and images in his art come from various sources—printed and spoken works, ordinary objects, experiences and memories. Ruscha's abiding love of words has something to do with an early interest in printing and typography, however.

"I developed a kind of typography that I call Boy Scout Utility Modern. It's not about the history or range of typography. It's the kind of thing a carpenter might apply to making a letter form. I like it for just that reason. I'm more interested in words than how they are made, but I like them to look homemade. Some people wear shoes that say something; some people wear shoes that don't say anything. I use a typeface that doesn't say anything. Everything just comes together to make the words," *he said.*

"Sometimes I feel like I'm doing book covers for mysterious stories. Or story titles, though that is not my intent," *he mused. Paradoxical combinations of words and images come from* "deep cynicism about where I live and what I do," *he said, but he has no formula for success. If he did, he probably wouldn't trust it.* "I've been so galvanized by the art world and I have so many feelings when it comes to art that I think it's the automatic thing, the intuitive thing that has the power. [. . .]"

Still, there are essential elements of his art. "The quest for paradox has always gripped me as an artist. There has to be negative conflict. Disturbing things have an attraction to them. The idea of subversion is a powerful subject. It's not a question of making pretty pictures. That's not what art is all about. [. . .]

"All my images have a connecting link in a continuity. I'm not sure what that link is and I don't really care. It's like contemplating a toothpick," *he said.* "Art for me is the act of making it. Reasons behind it are completely secondary. The mysterious element will never be uncovered and that's as it should be. The day I go to a Freudian analyst [to figure it out] is the day I should have my head examined."

"A Conversation between Walter Hopps and Edward Ruscha, Who Have Known Each Other Since the Early 1960s, Took Place on September 26, 1992"

Walter Hopps

WH: Ed, do you remember the address of the first place you lived when you arrived in Hollywood from Oklahoma?

ER: I lived on Sunset Place, near Lafayette Park. That was when Mason Williams and I came out here in 1956.

WH: Was there a house later, in Hollywood, where more of you lived?

ER: Oh, yeah. That was 1818 North New Hampshire, right near Barnsdall Park.

WH: The Division Street house and studio—

ER: Division Street is a place in Glassell Park, one of those obscure communities.

WH: What was that address?

ER: 3327 Division Street.

WH: For some reason these addresses, the names of these places stick out in my mind, and they turn up in your work.

Originally published in *Edward Ruscha: Romance with Liquids* (New York: Gagosian Gallery/ Rizzoli, 1993), pp. 97–108.

ER: Well, I guess streets do. Streets come up in my work. Division? How about Electric? But Division Street was my first art studio.

WH: Where did you paint Sweetwater?

ER: That was done at 1818 New Hampshire Avenue in Hollywood in about 1958, while I was in school.

WH: The first painting with a word in it that I can remember was Sweetwater. *Do you remember any before that?*

ER: I don't know when my first word painting was.

WH: When did you go to Spain, to visit the town of Lorca?

ER: Oh, that was in '61.

WH: I was curious—so that was after Sweetwater?

ER: Yes, it was.

WH: So, in the beginning there was the word, and as best we can remember it, the word was Sweetwater.

ER: Yes. Sweetwater was a town in Tennessee that I hitchhiked through when I was going down to Florida in 1952. Dublin, Georgia, was another town . . .

WH: There's a small painting that's called Dublin.

ER: And a large painting.

WH: A small collage painting and the large painting—both Dublin, Georgia.

ER: Yeah, Dublin, Georgia. It figured in my memory somehow, this great hitch-hiking trip I took through the South. There are other examples. Those two towns, Sweetwater and Dublin. And Vicksburg. Vicksburg, Mississippi.

WH: Vicksburg, Mississippi. Probably the third important place and word painting.

ER: That was one of my first paintings—the first painting I sold, anyway.

WH: The first painting one sells sticks in one's memory.

———

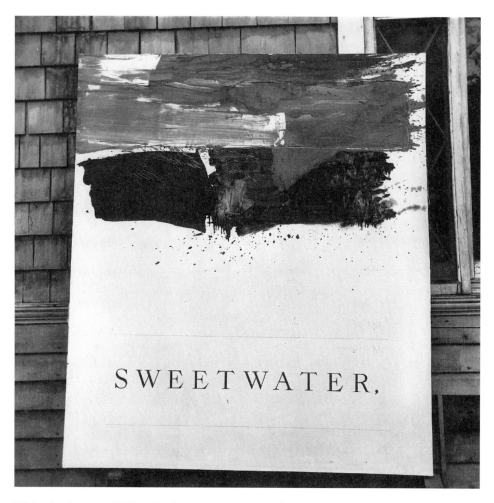

Ed Ruscha, *Sweetwater* (1959. Oil and ink on canvas, 60 × 48″, destroyed) leaning against the house at 1818 N. New Hampshire Avenue, Hollywood, 1959. Photo: Ed Ruscha.

ER: Yes, it does.

WH: I think it had a little squashed. . . .

ER: *Box Smashed Flat* [1961] is the title of the painting. It's a rendering of a Sun-maid Raisins box smashed flat. I was into the violence of things then, smashing. That was painted about 1960, I think.

WH: Box Smashed Flat *and later* Actual Size, *a painting of a can of Spam flying through space like a rocket—I think the early astronauts were referred to as being in a can of Spam up there in space—those paintings were in the show at Pasadena that we did in 1962, called* New Painting of Common Objects.

ER: That's right. My first exhibit, actually, the first show I'd been in.

WH: Do you recall—I was stuck for a poster for that show, in '62, that fall, and I thought you might design one. You were standing in the office and said, "Oh, it's really easy," and you hit the yellow pages and we called up a poster company . . . .

ER: Majestic Poster Company.

WH: You got the guy on the phone and you asked me, "What's the copy? How big do you want it?" And we came up with a size, I don't know, 36, 48 inches high. And you said, "What's the copy?" We just read it to the man over the phone—the artists' names, the title, the place, and so on. And then you turned to me and said, "What's the style?" And I said, "I don't know," and you turned back to the guy on the phone and said, "Make it loud."

ER: *[Laughter]* That's what we got, didn't we?

WH: And back it came, in red, yellow, and black.

ER: Red and yellow and black. That's right. Yeah, that poster came off very well, didn't it?

WH: Yes—instant design. Before all that, I visited the Division Street studio, prior to '62. And we went in the back room, and you had come back, I guess, from Spain—a trip abroad—and you had books in the back room of that studio, to which you'd affixed photographs. And there were words you were beginning to apply to the books. Tell me about those works.

———

315

ER: Well, I worked as a printer's devil for about a year, and somehow picked up a love for printing, and printing in books. And I suppose I consider myself a painter, not a sculptor, so maybe it was my way of getting into the third dimension, in the sense that books are three-dimensional. I was working with oil paint and photography, using real photographs, making constructions. I feel it was never truly resolved in any way. I'm still painting books. So what have I learned? *[Laughter.]* I doubt if any of those books exist today.

WH: They were wonderful. There was another wonderful object that involved typography and words then. In that Division Street studio, early on, circa '61, just as we're moving toward '62. It was a Ball mason jar, maybe a quart jar, and you filled it with black paint and poured it out so that the interior was black, and you had the date, I think "1938"—

ER: Exactly.

WH: —scratched into the black paint, very neatly. It was like a little magic trick. I wondered how on earth you managed to scratch in that date.

ER: You know, it was an attempt at realism. It was three-dimensional. The shape of a Ball mason jar at that time was identical to the shape of a 1938 Chevy. There was something about the curves of it that resembled a '38 Chevy. And somehow I made this connection with the year, which for some reason has always been meaningful to me. Why, I don't know. I was born in '37, so I have no personal recollections of it, but the '38 somehow just stayed with me. I'm not sure what it is—it's a snapshot out of time.

WH: Some of the earliest photographs of yours that I can remember were of signs. When did you start taking those photographs?

ER: Which signs?

WH: I think of the visit you talked to me about, that you wanted to make to Franz Kline's studio. You admired Franz Kline.

ER: Somehow I made a connection with Franz Kline's work. I had taken photographs of a market sign on the corner of Alvarado and Sunset, where the Burrito

King is, and they were dilapidated neon signs that were no longer in use, and the sign just sat at the top of this building. I drove by that place every day and looked at that sign, which had a kind of mystical connection to me somehow. I started photographing it, then I'd transpose the photograph to something, mount that down on something, and try to make that into something else. And so I was working with a photograph of that sign, and somehow it was a gesture that was spontaneous.

WH: There were several. One I remember was the sign called "La Brea." Large, steel frame on one of the old '20s or '30s buildings.

ER: Down on Wilshire Boulevard and La Brea.

WH: And you'd made several prints of that, one of which you were at pains to see if it couldn't be given to Franz Kline. Did you ever try and give him that photograph?

ER: I think what I did was mail it to him. It was a very insignificant gesture, I think, not really extraordinary.

WH: It's a good photograph. You gave me a copy of it.

ER: I can't remember what my intention was there—like, "Hi, I like your work."

WH: Anyway, we still have a copy of that particular photograph.

ER: Oh you do, do you?

WH: Yes.

ER: Then there is one in existence?

WH: There is one in existence. We'll have to check the Kline archives to see if he ever received his print.

ER: *[Laughter.]* Yeah, photography had a reality to me then. When I grew up in Oklahoma, photographers were nerds. They were either nerds, or pornographers, or both. Then I saw Robert Frank's *Americans.*

WH: Which began to be current in about 1958.

ER: That's about when I saw it. Then I also started seeing the work of Walker Evans, which had a profound effect on me. I loved his work. I started seeing the world of photography, which I never knew anything about. Then I saw Man Ray's work. All that came about during school. But photography was always considered a secondary medium, and yet it had so much potential, I thought, for a painter. [. . .]

WH: Was it in Los Angeles where you first saw museums? Or other cities you visited?

ER: Well, I took a trip when I lived in Oklahoma in '55. I drove with my parents down to Mexico City. My sister was going to school there and she was going out with an architect. At the time they were celebrating the fiftieth anniversary of the Society of Mexican Architects, so they had a big, lavish ball there in Mexico City, with pigs stuffed with apples and all. Mexico City was the most "cosmo" place I'd ever visited. I met Luis Barragán and went to his home, and saw the architecture of Mexico City, and that was the first cosmopolitan thing that I'd ever done in my life.

WH: This is off the track, but how on earth did you meet Barragán?

ER: Well, the architecture thing, and my sister's boyfriend was there.

WH: Oh, the personal connection.

ER: Yes. But I knew I wanted to go to art school anyway. [. . .]

WH: You've taken good advantage of blank pages in certain of your books, to get the right thickness.

ER: Well, I've had to.

WH: So the first words were really places. Sweetwater, Dublin, Vicksburg. Places that struck you in your travels. Then here, settling into Los Angeles, in some of your early prints, interestingly, we find the Division Street name and address. We also find the incidental typography that's on objects that you depict, such as the Sunmaid Raisins box or the Spam can.

———

ER: Sometimes it was a faithful reproduction.

WH: *Exactly. And then the words from signs come in—Standard, Twentieth Century Fox. And on an early print, the word "gas" from a gas can. Again the cars and the mode of travel. For Monet or Renoir, it might have been the name of the little boat they were using to row across the Seine or whatever. But then phrases and disembodied words finally take their place in your paintings. Can you think of when that began? The liquid words and so on, where you pick up phrases? Adios. What's the connection, suddenly, to disembodied words that strikes you?*

ER: Well, those paintings I guess are another stop on the highway, and a very distinct stop. They're unique unto themselves as much as those books were unique to themselves. In the beginning all these things would overlap. I'd be doing things with photography and then also doing paintings at the same time, with words, and so it was like following blind faith, and I let that guide me, and I found myself doing monosyllabic words—"Oof" and "Smash" and "Noise."

WH: *Ah yes, of course. The expressions or exclamations. Those came before the liquid words, of course.*

ER: They were more architectural or architectonic, straight lines, and they had a conventional typographic family reference.

WH: *Those words began to work with a typography that was keyed to thoughts about the words themselves, like* Boss *was in a different typography from* Oof *[1962–63].*

ER: And quite often it didn't make a difference. It was what was happening at the time, and my instinct, as it began to work, would make me choose one over the other. It was not intentional for a word to have an attitude itself. I didn't have to follow a course, I had no rules for this.

WH: *So the connection between typography and word was spontaneous and determined on the spot, much as de Kooning might spontaneously, so to speak, change a gesture.*

ER: Splash something here, or change a gesture. Very much the same way. For that reason I didn't really concentrate so much on preparatory drawings. I envisioned a painting and then painted it. It was quick. There was much less room between my mind and the painting.

WH: Perhaps the obvious precedent, prior to your use of specific words and phrases in your painting, would be those we see turning up a little earlier in Jasper Johns's work, where for the most part the typography is absolutely neutral. Or almost neutral. Johns tends to use, in his earlier work, the same kind of stencil over and over, where in your case the touch and approach to how you handle the specific typography changes very much in the paintings of those early days.

ER: Yes. They go from one stylistic attitude to another. [. . .]

WH: Again, in these early, single-word paintings in the very early '60s that turn up in their varying typographies and various textures of paint, occasionally you used French words.

ER: Well, there I was, traveling in France, and I would see a sign and I would make a painting of it. *Metro* [1961] or *Boulangerie* [1961]. And I painted some pictures like that when I was in Spain—*España* [1961]. I was like a kid on his first trip to the new world, or the *old* world. [. . .]

WH: When did the liquid words start, where there's a sort of deep space?

ER: That was about 1966, I guess, and I had just seen the end of the road with a certain kind of painting I was doing. I don't know why it happened, but close-up views of liquids somehow began to interest me. And then I started making little setups on tables, and painting them, using syrup, and studying what happens when you pour syrup out, or turpentine, or water.

WH: What are some of the words?

ER: Adios, desire, mint—I painted two paintings called *Mint* [both 1968]. There's one called *Eye* [1969], one called *Cut* [1969]. *Pool* [1967]. I did only a few drawings from that idea—somehow I couldn't do drawings, only paintings. For the same reason, I've never been able to use a photograph in a painting. With the exception of those books where I actually affixed a photograph. And to me drawings have always been for themselves, not studies for paintings. Those paper tape drawings that I did—with one exception—I never did paintings of them.

Ed Ruscha, *España*. 1961. Oil on board, 14⅞ × 14″. Photo courtesy Ed Ruscha.

WH: The really exotic fluid materials, odd materials to make drawings in their own right, I guess, came after the liquid word paintings, where you used stains; for example, that portfolio of Stains.

ER: Well, I sometimes refer to it as my "romance with liquids" period, for lack of a better title. After I finished painting those pictures—that was around '68, '69—and for a whole year I couldn't paint. It was 1970 and I didn't do any painting. It was the idea of putting a skin on a canvas that began to irritate me. I hated paint on canvas. And so "staining" came out of that. Instead of applying a skin of paint to a canvas support, I would stain the surface, so it was another way out of this box I'd painted myself into. I was in a corner and this was the most logical thing, and it involved the concept of liquids. Now where does that come from? That's a very broad subject, but liquids have played a part in my work, just like diagonals have played a part in my work, as well as abstract painting.

WH: That's true. There was a lot of straight line, hard-edge geometry that was very strong in the work in '62, '63. By '63 there is Twentieth Century Fox [Large Trademark with Eight Spotlights], *all the architecture and typographic devices of* Fox *and* Standard Station. *You're rendering. It's a very controlled process. And the minute* Adios *appears—given the fluidity of working with a liquid—it attempts to, with unusual liquid, render out a word. And a whole different freeform aspect is literally in the works.*

ER: Disturbing, isn't it? It just completely turns its back on the other way of thinking. But maybe not. [. . .]

WH: In your studio here today I was surprised and delighted to see you working with books . . . a good number of years to Division Street. *But you're working with stains at present, is that right?* [47]

ER: Mmmm, I'm painting on these books.

WH: Painting.

ER: Yes. I'm painting on the book covers. I guess I'm just looking for another support. Maybe I'm moving away from the canvas, but I can't predict. I still paint on canvas, but I think there's another shift about to happen somewhere, maybe not so radical, but at least one that I know I will want to stick with.

WH: Here's an odd question. Have you ever done a painting of a word or phrase that you really hated? You like the painting or you like the work, but there's something irritating about the phrase or word?

ER: There is a work that horrifies me at every glance. It's called *Johnny Tomorrow* [1984]. I keep it under wraps because I find it so offensive to look at, and yet I admire the notion behind the words. I believe I'm a cynic at heart.

WH: How do you mean that, that you're a cynic at heart?

ER: I have a—what do you call it—positive negativism, or negative positivism. It's pessimism about the state of the world. I respond to all these things and I generally take a pessimistic attitude about them. That probably makes me a cynic.

WH: Let me give you something an artist said. A wise old artist, when a young man in Germany, referred to our state of affairs as "a foolish, fucked-up world," one of the great Dada phrases. This was Richard Huelsenbeck in around 1922, who later became a distinguished psychiatrist in New York City under the name of Dr. Richard Halbeck. But Huelsenbeck the Dadaist was forever proclaiming, "We proceed in a foolish, fucked-up world." Does that make any sense to you?

ER: Well, yeah, it does. It might be very similar to the way I feel. So many opposing conditions in the world makes for no sense, and I'm constantly wondering why I get up and do what I do, and everybody else, why they wake up and do what they do.

WH: Your attitude is not very different from that of Bill de Kooning or Franz Kline, who with extraordinary joy and pleasure and great anxiety proceeded to make their work.

ER: That's the only thing that's left, is to make your work, and that's the way to escape this world as it is. I love it, don't get me wrong.

WH: One of the great typographic messages that I ever saw was among the ruins of an abandoned hotel structure. I took Dennis Hopper there to see it, and we meant to go back

———

with an 8 × 10 view camera and photograph it, somewhere over near Glassell Park, on the eastern side of Los Angeles. Somehow, somebody had the idea in the 1930s, or actually probably in the '20s, before the crash, to build a grand hotel up in the hills of Glassell Park. The idea is absurd. And in that ruin there was this tremendous encrustation of graffiti we found in the early '60s, where bums and kids had hung out or camped out for the night. It was not easy to get to, it was away from public access. Overriding all the other phrases and words and scrawlings, in huge block letters, was the phrase "FUCK THE WORLD . . . AND FUCK YOU IF YOU DON'T LOVE IT."

ER: *[Laughter.]* Good one. Yeah, I hope you got that one.

WH: *We never managed to get back in time. A couple of years later we go back and it's a demolition site, the whole thing had been razed.*

ER: Well, that's graffiti at its finest, isn't it.

WH: *I think so. "FUCK YOU IF YOU DON'T LOVE IT."*

ER: I was in an outhouse last week that said—someone had very carefully lettered, in beautiful florally scripted letters "THIS IS THE FINEST LITTLE SHITHOUSE IN THE WORLD—JACK BARTON."

WH: *That's great anonymous poetry. Another sort of disembodied question: You've been a pioneer, one of the real pioneers, of this curious use of typography and words as being very much essential to what a painting or drawing is going to be, or can be. And once you've done it, such work becomes what painting, drawing is. Apart from Jasper Johns, are there any others—whose work you enjoy—who've also used words and phrases as part of their visual art?*

ER: Well, there've been so many artists who have used words throughout the centuries really, but the ones I enjoy are mostly from the twentieth century. Say, Kurt Schwitters. [. . .] Duchamp had quite a sizable influence on me from a pictorial standpoint and from an emotional standpoint. Arthur Dove also. [. . .] Mostly the collages. [. . .] And Joseph Cornell. I like Magritte's work, but it didn't have that much of an influence on me.

WH: *Among your contemporaries is there work you enjoy?*

ER: Yes, there is. There are a lot of people of the New York School that I like and I even collect some of their work. Donald Baechler is one. I find that the younger the artist, the more emotionally charged the work is. It might be that young artists have absolutely nothing to lose on any front.

WH: *Curiously, later in the 1960s a number of artists began to use language—and it's a very different base than your art—as a kind of visual conceptual art, whether Joseph Kosuth or Lawrence Weiner. Do you feel any affinity to that pursuit at all?*

ER: Although their work seemed severe and drained of entertainment, I related very well with them on personal levels in our various friendships. But they use instructional language, while my work is pictorial by comparison.

WH: *It's a superficial similarity.*

ER: It is. And we've been identified somehow in the same quarters because of our books, I guess. But I think that was viewed largely as a New York conceptual phenomenon, and I was not really part of that movement. But attitude, yes. There are some teachings they respond to that I do too.

WH: *What's the first work of Duchamp you ever remember seeing in reproduction or in the flesh?*

ER: Well, in reproduction, *Nude Descending a Staircase.* [. . .] And there was a picture of a church that he painted.

WH: *Yes, early on. In Blainville. It's a very sensuous painting, Ed, and the love of materials that you use so very sparingly in that pictorial quality of your work I think really sets you very essentially apart from a lot of the artists who do use language typographically in the visual arts today. I'm just curious—among the more hardcore neo-Conceptualists or post-modern younger people, is there anything that intrigues you there? In, say, Haim Steinbach's work. . . .*

ER: No, but maybe Meyer Vaisman—he's done some good things. But I have to go back—Louis Eilshemius is another artist I am curious about. He seemed to have a very personal vision, not part of any movement.

WH: He was championed by Duchamp.

ER: Is that right?

WH: Eilshemius would have been lost to the world, particularly his later, kind of vision-ary works of the floating women and so on, had it not been for Duchamp's championing of him, with Sidney Janis and others. It's very curious.

ER: You know, the Abstract Expressionists had a very pure art form. I saw them making pure art and I loved what they were doing, but I saw finally that I couldn't travel on in this language, I couldn't make abstract paintings. I couldn't paint like those people, and I loved it so much. It was powerful. But then I had these other things from the earlier part of my life. I got influenced by this guy Ernie Bush-miller, you know? The cartoonist.

WH: Right. What was his cartoon? "Nancy," wasn't it? Sluggo and Nancy?

ER: Yeah, Nancy and Sluggo. Cartoonists got my attention as a child. Basil Wolverton. [. . .] There seemed to be a world of possibility out there for pho-tography, cartooning, or maybe humor, and abstract painting. Maybe they all came together in one story. But I didn't just eliminate everything in my history and study only fine art. It didn't happen that way. Later on I started visiting mu-seums and went back into art history, but I was still there with popular imagery, I guess. Commercial, popular imagery. And then, of course, the more I paint, the less I know about myself.

WH: I remember Robert Motherwell—back in '57 when I helped Tom Leavitt with the Motherwell retrospective at the Pasadena Art Museum, perhaps the better days of Mother-well's art. Motherwell was so cultivated, so thoroughly sophisticated in the world of twen-tieth-century painting; he knew more, in the bookish sense, about other art than perhaps any of his contemporaries. And he said there is nothing like the paralysis of facing a canvas and knowing all the work, knowing emphasized, of Matisse, in each gesture you make. In one sense Motherwell's cultivation with so much work was paralyzing for him.

ER: Well, I'm glad I don't have to face that. It would make the hand very heavy, wouldn't it? To have art history, the entire art history, on your back and on your hand.

———

WH: Prior to his famous Nude Descending a Staircase *of 1911, Duchamp approached the subject in this strange, somewhat related painting, clearly of a woman. And he said he liked the painting very much, but he had such a curious emotional take on it. He said, it's so strange about that painting, she was climbing off a trolley, a streetcar in Paris, and she was so ugly, I found her repulsive, disturbingly ugly—this is Duchamp saying this—and he sort of shuddered when he said, "disturbingly ugly"—and yet he said, "I only saw her for a second, and I so fell in love with her that I made this painting. Isn't she an awful look-ing woman? But I love this painting." I just wondered if there's ever been one of your words or phrases that gave you the shudders, and yet you liked the work.*

ER: In the mid-70s I did a work using the words "psychedelic-Indian-guru-New Mexico-fadeout-photo-realism" to suggest a kind of painting style preva-lent at the time. The thought is hideous to me, but the work is rather nice. A lot of the words and terminology, phrases that I use in my paintings, are not really my vision of a perfect world. They're not my vision of anything that matters deeply or realistically or morally. I have specific paintings that I have good feel-ings about, and some bad feelings, because of the way they're painted, I suppose.

WH: The new paintings that I saw in New York—what was it, L.A. Tool and Die *[*Blue Collar Tool and Die, *1992] and* Telephone *[1992]? Were those imagined or had you seen those locally?*

ER: I go to the desert every week and I've been seeing a building out there on the way to Palm Springs that says "tires," which never made an impression on me, and when I painted this picture I realized that's the same building I've been looking at for all this time, and I've never noticed it enough to paint a picture of it. I'm not that kind of artist—it has to happen subliminally, through the back door. So I painted this picture, and there it is—*Tires [Blue Collar Tires, 1992].* Those are my "T" paintings—Telephone, Tires, Trade School, Tool and Die. It's like a vision of a modern world, a futuristic world, about what architecture and things are going to look like.

WH: So Tires *was a specific place that suddenly found its way into a painting. What about* L.A. Tool and Die—*is that a real building somewhere?*

ER: No, it's not. Just the phrase "tool and die" is enough to handle itself.

WH: Absolutely. It's very strange when you say "T-paintings." I don't think you could possibly know what I'm going to tell you now. Do you know that, as far as I know, the very first word that Duchamp ever used in an artwork is "the." A very curious drawing, or a kind of drawing where the use of a word is essential to the work. It's a "T" work. When he was coming on the boat from France to New York for the very first time, in 1915, he did a work called The. *The American article somehow fascinated him. It's his very first American work, conceived on the boat, coming to this country.*

ER: Oh, America must have hit him right between the eyes.

WH: Oh, yeah. He loved New York. From 1915 on, Duchamp was as wedded to New York City as he was to France. But it just always struck me how that little work, conceived like a curious letter, was a conceptual drawing. And its title is The. *We found it buried in files in Arensberg's papers, when I was working on that show up there in Philadelphia. He used to let me just hang out there and rifle through everything, without being formal, and this popped up. And it's now in the catalog. It was in the Pasadena show, but I think everybody just missed it.*

ER: Really? Well, how big is it?

WH: Standard letter-sheet size. But it's not just the work. Again, explore the catalog and come on this thing—and you'll see what he did. I reproduced it. But the thing is so kind of homely, so nondescript, that I don't think anyone paid any attention to it.

ER: It's one of those quiet little sleepers in the back of your mind.

Elizabeth Armstrong

EA: It has often been said that Duchamp offered your generation an antidote to the painterly aesthetic that was so prominent at the time.

ER: I don't think his effect was any stronger on my generation than the generation before. Even in his own time, people were fascinated by him and learned from him.

EA: How did you first know about Duchamp? Was it through art school?

ER: I think it was in a book, a reproduction of the *Nude Descending a Staircase*. It was as if there were an asterisk on that picture; his *Nude Descending a Staircase* was such a spectacle at the time that you remembered it for that. That was part of its value. Then, there were my teachers in school, who were more along the line of Abstract Expressionists. These people admired Duchamp, but probably didn't like his work; they couldn't see it for its true value. So he was only marginally mentioned, but all the students knew about him.

EA: You have said that your teachers were often disparaging in their remarks about Duchamp. Did that have a certain appeal to students then?

Originally published in *October*, n. 70, fall 1994, pp. 55–56.

ER: Yes, it did. And it probably had precisely the effect that Duchamp would have liked to have had on students, and that is to be a rebel. He was against a kind of academic slavery that artists went through who followed a traditional path; he was for the spirit of revolt.

EA: Did his rejection of painting, and especially of the retinal in painting, cause you to reevaluate your approach to art early in your career?

ER: It just made me aware that there was another way to think about things. Finally, the ultimate mystery of his work is its value. It's hard to be taught how to look at Duchamp's work; it has to be felt somehow.

EA: You once said that your books were the most Duchampian of your work.

ER: I feel that the spirit of his work is stronger in my books than in anything else. But I don't use him as a reference; he's just so much a part of my history and my art—as he is for so many artists.

EA: You were once quoted as saying: "If Marcel Duchamp hadn't come along, we would have needed to invent him." *Could you elaborate?*

ER: The art world was ready for that revolution, and fortunately for Duchamp he was the one who wigged us all out. I may be giving him too much credit: but he discovered quite a bit just through his investigation into things. And he was a nonpainterly person in a painterly world, who was able to make his views be known without being an intellectual, being in fact a very simple man. I think that had he not existed someone sooner or later would have "discovered" many of the things that he did.

EA: What do you think is Duchamp's most significant contribution?

ER: That he discovered common objects and showed you could make art out of them. He was also one of the first artists to use electric motors to create motion in art. He played with materials that were taboo to other artists at the time; defying convention was one of his greatest accomplishments. Plus he always looked his Sunday best.

EA: Is that important?

ER: Yes, as a way of countering expectations. We were used to paint-splattered pants and all of that, and he would always be in a suit and tie.

EA: Did Walter Hopps's Duchamp retrospective at the Pasadena Museum of Art [in 1963] have a palpable effect on West Coast artists?

ER: Well, the opening was attended by all of the artists that were on the scene at the time, and maybe some intellectuals too, as I recall. The very fact that it was his first retrospective was very important. Some guy said, "Duchamp's finest work is his use of time." The very fact that he quit painting, yet throughout his life was interested in so many things. He used his time so well.

"PRONOUNCE HIS NAME REW-SHAY"

Guy Cross

GC: What artist, sculptor, photographer, writer out there impresses you? And, are you easily impressed?

ER: *[Laughter.]* Well, I'm sorry to say that I'm not too easily impressed by anything. The things that do impress me are not so much the work that's being done today, but historical work. Work that I've never noticed before, but has been under my nose the whole time.

GC: Like?

ER: Like James Ensor, one of the first abstract painters who ever existed. Ensor was into abstraction and fantasy in 1870. Arthur Dove [. . .] and Kurt Schwitters. [. . .] And, of course, Marcel Duchamp. [. . .]

GC: What's your work about?

ER: I'm a collector of all kinds of inspirations. My work is not so much about what the pictures look like; it's more like a collection of motivations, and a result of my following a procedure that I started thirty years ago.

GC: Could you talk about this procedure that you've followed for thirty years?

Originally published in *THE Magazine*, v. 3, n. 1, July 1994, pp. 19–21.

ER: First, it's being curious about my own motivations, and then it's having some kind of program to begin with. Like, if you're going to paint a picture of flowers, you better know it! You have to have some sort of *tension,* and possibly, some kind of negative environment.

GC: *Martin Friedman wrote: "With the silhouette paintings, Ruscha seems to have entered another dimension. It's like he's walked through a mirror." What do you think about that?*

ER: I think that any writer has a certain license to say anything they want. Friedman also saw my work as a sort of Doomsday approach to the world. What he's doing is offering suggestions to people about how to perceive art. This is not only legitimate but is necessary to somehow connect the artist to the outside world.

GC: *Not all of your work has words in it. How does one read a piece like* Brother, Sister *[1987]? There are no words in the painting, just a murky and blurred image of sailing ships on a horizon.*

ER: They're not about my experience because I ain't a sailor. The ship is my interpretation of a picture of a ship rather than a ship. It's like a painting of an *idea* about a ship.

GC: *So your paintings are about ideas rather than paintings about painting?*

ER: Usually they are. But there's always an exception that's going to break the rule. No rules, no exceptions.

GC: *You've been involved in the art world for over thirty years. Because of your position as a successful artist and because of the length of time you've been involved in the art world, do you ever feel as if you're isolated, or living in some kind of rarified atmosphere, like a rock star, or any other kind of media star, where people really don't tell you the truth?*

ER: I do feel somewhat privileged when I compare my life to other people who are in trouble, but satisfaction and success are never reached. It's never reached.

GC: *Do you have any fears about your financial future whatsoever?*

ER: Yes, I do. I find that it's increasingly fickle out there. People will drop old concepts and go on to new concepts and thus go off with new artists and leave

---

behind old artists. When you're an artist there's a gestation period and you can be dropped or you can fade at any time along the way. There's no security and there are no promises of security. Nobody promised us a rose garden.

GC: *What's the deal with "East Coast artists" versus "West Coast artists"?*

ER: If you live in New York you have a much better chance of having an audience if you have talent. The critics and the collectors somehow deeply believe that an artist has really committed himself to the seriousness of the whole subject if he lives on the island of Manhattan.

GC: *In a loft for $4,500 a month.*

ER: Yes. Of course, you can also live in Brooklyn, but that's like living in East Germany. I think that there's a great deal of prejudice within the intelligentsia about artists who don't live in New York City. They see it as a handicap to not live in New York City. [. . .]

GC: *Do you ever get stuck when trying to make art, and if so, do you make art for an imaginary audience to help you get past being stuck in the creative process? For example, "What would Franz Kline think of what I'm doing?"*

ER: Yup. I think that what you're speaking about is one of the finest reasons an artist could ever have, and that is, to please people that he admires. If you can somehow reach another artist, then it's quite an accomplishment. Peer approval or the accomplishment that attracts someone you admire is a step that leaves you much farther ahead than before.

GC: *Who really understands your work out there?*

ER: I might say that Dave Hickey has a grasp of my work, and he's out there. [. . .]

GC: *You're an artist who has modeled in ads for Gap, who we see featured in glossy magazines like* Esquire, *who is an art star, who was a part of the L.A. Boys: Ed Moses, Billy Bengston, Joe Goode, Larry Bell, et al. What is the difference between the art world then as opposed to now?*

ER: It was more vital then. It was lots more fun than it is today. It had to do with the friends I was with and the motivations I had then. The rawest, rawest of nerves were exposed in the early '60s when I was young and the world was brand new. As I developed, I was able to go through that period that a young artist goes through where you just "kamikaze" things. You can throw out anything, and you have nothing to lose. But after you become more mature you see that your work is going to move along and develop in a certain way that is *not* going to contain the freedom that it once had. You can have pictorial freedom forever and ever, but the intellectual freedom is less.

GC: Do you feel that there are a lot of people out there who are heavily influenced by you, people who are copycats?

ER: I don't find anyone *copying* me. Well, I don't know—there's a few. I don't know their names, I've just seen their work. I'm surprised that my work is not more imitated. And I'm relieved! I'm very relieved.

GC: Larry Clark, James Dean, Neal Cassidy, Bob Dylan, and Ed Ruscha. See any correlation?

ER: All ramblin' souls?

———

"PANORAMIC ART AT LIBRARY ELUSIVE BUT IMPRESSIVE"

Steven Rosen

[. . .] The seventy panels of paintings [in Ruscha's murals for the Denver Central Library . . .] cumulatively create, in the artist's words, "a rolling historical landscape" of the West. [. . .]

Born in Omaha and raised in Oklahoma, he was intrigued as a child by stories and images of the West. And that has served as an inspiration for this work. Early on, he painted murals of the Oklahoma land rush. "I did them in third and fourth grade on brown wrapping paper on the schoolroom wall. Everything comes from childhood, indirectly. [. . .]"

Originally published in the *Denver Post,* August 26, 1995, p. E-08.

Ed Ruscha, installation view of the insert-panel murals in the Denver Central Public Library. 1994–1995. Acrylic on canvas; large panels: 73½× 102″, small panels: 73½ × 30″. Photo: Gary Regester.

———

"LIBRARY MURALIST SLOW TO PRAISE . . ."

Steven Rosen

Since the Denver Public Library trumpets its new building as a "masterpiece," you'd think an artist of Ed Ruscha's stature would be ecstatic to have his epic, seventy-panel painting located there.

Instead, he has barely anything at all to say about it. "It's amazingly functional," *is the best he'd say about the building, designed by Michael Graves in collaboration with Brian Klipp.* "I guess it's been made to fit in with the situation here, but I'm not an architecture buff.

"This is not an artist-architect joint venture in any way. I didn't approach this to integrate my work with his [Graves's] building. If he had his way, I would not be his artist."

Originally published in the *Denver Post*, August 26, 1995, p. E-08.

"Art Museum, Library to Feature 'Word' According to Ruscha"

Mary Voelz Chandler

[. . .] Paintings in The End *[1995], on view [at . . .] the Denver Art Museum, are cast in the mold of movie end-frames. [. . .]*

The End, *though, is also symbolic of the completion of Ruscha's $450,000 public art commission for the city, a seventy-panel mural that draws meaning from Western images, voiceprints, birds, astronomical symbolism . . . and words. [. . .]*

Inspiration for the work came from his youth, he said, from murals made on brown paper. "I don't paint horses and pioneers. I paint the idea of horses and the idea of pioneers. I'm the product of communications and propaganda." *[. . .]*

"I've been painting words so long that I can't remember why I do it," *Ruscha said [. . .] during a break from hanging* The End. "It's just another stop on the highway."

That road has taken him from an Oklahoma childhood to life in Venice. Along the way, "I've been exposed all my life to movies in a state of deterioration." *At one point, that prompted Ruscha to paint a work called* Scratches on the Film *[1993].* "Now I'm painting scratches on the film. I think it's beautiful the way film shows scratches."

Originally published in the *Denver Rocky Mountain News,* September 10, 1995, sec. F, p. 82A.

But more often, he just wants to play with words, pull and push them into new shapes. "Fundamentally, I'm an abstract artist. I respond to primal, basic aspects of art. The horizontal line. The vertical line. The works here are a series of manipulations using verticals and horizontals. I want to see things stretched."

The pieces in The End *are linked by one typeface, an Old English style with a Gothic flavor familiar to many from the masthead of the* New York Times. "There was something naturally old about it. It seemed to fit with the conclusion of a movie." *(Ruscha [. . .], in other works, has used a style he calls Boy Scout Utility Modern, a* "clubby, clumsy typeface that looks like it was designed by a phone company lineman.") *[. . .]*

Somehow, Ruscha said, dealing with Denver—"the wild west, to me"—*sent him in a different direction.* "I usually don't do something as illustrative and thematic. But what a perfect place to explore these ideas."

"Hollywood Decks the Halls: Ed Ruscha"

"A lot of my ideas for my art come from the radio," *says Venice Beach–based artist Ed Ruscha, whose channel of choice, 88.5 FM, picks up two distinctly different stations.* "I like the texture," *he says.* "It's best when it's music overlapping talk, or talk over talk. [. . .]"

Originally published in *Elle Décor*, December/January 1996, p. 168.

———

"THE RETURN OF A NATIVE SON:
PAINTER ED RUSCHA RESURFACES IN L.A."

Michael Duncan

[. . .] MD: Your new paintings mix fragments of Thomas Guide maps with L.A.'s hazy night sky.

ER: Yeah, I'm showing big paintings of intersections and streets of Los Angeles with black [speckled] backgrounds that look like the inside of your oven. I guess I've always been intrigued by oblique perspectives, like aerial views. There's something about a tabletop . . . taking a viewer up in the air, so you can look down from an angle.

MD: Out in the desert, do you find yourself thinking about L.A. again?

ER: I have a love/hate [relationship] with this place. Back in the '60s and '70s, I had a more naïve view of Los Angeles. During the '80s, I had a hate period, like I wanted to get out of town. Never really moved; didn't hate it that bad, I guess, or I wouldn't have stayed here. [. . .]

MD: Do you ever find your love of the city returning?

ER: It's constantly evolving. This place has got so much anxiety. The whole thing's built on paradox anyhow. I may hate something but it still inspires me to

———

Originally published in *Buzz*, May 1998, p. 42.

make a picture. I love the nature out there, but the desert doesn't inspire me to paint, as such.

MD: What do you make of the art scene here now?

ER: There was a real doldrums in the early '90s. The art community had the jitters. But it's coming around again. Now it seems like everybody's on fire. These cities—why is it that cities make for such interesting art and artists?

———

"CONFESSION IN CHELSEA"

Jeffrey Hogrefe

"I didn't get along with Catholic school," *said Los Angeles–based painter Ed Ruscha.* "I went one year. I had some trouble there, and my parents decided that maybe I shouldn't go back. It was some silly little thing in the first grade. I took a pocketknife to school with me, and it created a big furor. Something as innocent as that. Merely the fact that I took it with me and showed it to somebody. Then, it grew beyond control, and I had already had my fingers spanked with a ruler before by Sister Daniela. It just got so that I didn't like to go to school because I would always have to face her and I was miserable."

Eight of Mr. Ruscha's paintings are on display in a show called Three Catholics: Warhol, Ruscha, and Mapplethorpe *[. . .] at the Cheim & Read Gallery in Chelsea. [. . .]*

Speaking of his seminal word painting Sin *[1967], Mr. Ruscha [said],* "I never believed in this, 'You are sin. You are dead for eternity.' The imagery, though, I always thought was very seductive. Just the smell of incense, the icons and marble floors, and all those foxy vestaments and everything had some sort of allure." *[. . .]*

"If anything, I left the so-called spiritual awakening behind when I left Oklahoma," *Mr. Ruscha said.* "I'm not trying to say anything religious."

Originally published in the *New York Observer,* May 11, 1998, p. 26.

"Lightening Up the Getty"

Kristine McKenna

[Interview with Ruscha and John Walsh, director of the J. Paul Getty Museum.]

[. . .] KM: What are the rewards and difficulties of working with a living artist, as opposed to historical material?

JW: I usually deal with dead artists, which is more convenient because there's less material you have to make sense of; plus, they can't talk back. With Ed, the amount of material is overwhelming and it just keeps coming. As nice as Ed is, he makes you work, too. His paintings can't be taken at face value and you have to do some thinking in order to experience them, because Ed lives by his thought. Being part of that for a while has been a kick—and, as anyone who's met Ed will attest, he's a really hospitable guy. He always made me feel welcome in the studio and he's extremely well organized—museums should be so organized.

KM: What does it mean to you to be exhibited at the Getty?

ER: When the Getty was under construction my assumption was that it would be a facility for antiquities, so I'm surprised to find myself here. Some people think of it as a stuffy place and yes, they do show old art, but even the most progressive places can be stuffy and many a fine tune is played on an old violin. And

Originally published in the *Los Angeles Times*, May 24, 1998, Calendar, p. 4.

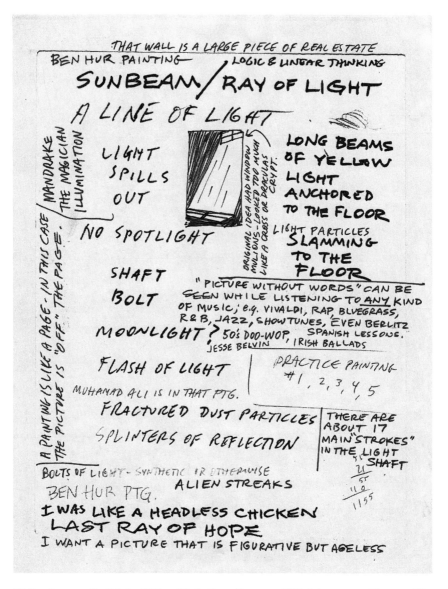

Ed Ruscha, notes for *Painting Without Words,* Getty Center. c. 1997. Ink on paper. Courtesy Ed Ruscha.

John isn't stuffy at all. John doesn't look like an athlete, but having worked with him that's how I've come to think of him—he has a phenomenal amount of energy. His position is very demanding, and my show was just a fraction of what he has to deal with every day, but he was open and available to me, and put in long hours making sure the show looked good.

KM: When the Getty commissioned you, Ed, to make a work for its auditorium, were there any parameters you were asked to work within?

ER: There were none, and when I first visited the site I felt like a headless chicken. As to why I decided to paint a shaft of light, all I can say is ideas come from nowhere and are produced by everything an artist is about. I've been doing this light shaft business for a while, and when I look at this version of it, I can see Muhammad Ali in there, and there's also me putting my socks on in the morning. Everything I'm about is in that picture—and that's something I could say about all my work.

JW: We gave Ed no limitations, but the limitations are built in because the commission was for a specific wall with specific light conditions. The project was overseen by former Getty Trust president Harold Williams, independent curator Lisa Lyons, Getty executive vice president Steve Rountree and myself, and it's hard to imagine four more different people. But when Ed brought in four big pastel studies for the painting, we were unanimously convinced. One thing I immediately loved about the proposal was that it would be a depiction of light, but would also have some of the power of the real thing. I also loved that it was going to be in a Richard Meier building. No living architect has made as much of a mystique of light as Meier has, so there's a certain audacity in putting a painting about light in a room flooded with self-consciously architectural light. That's pretty cheeky.

ER: I didn't think about Meier or his handling of light, and my project wasn't architecture-sensitive. It was, however, sensitive to the light in that location. I had a computer shadow study done of the site and I can tell you what the light in that area will look like at any time of year. I didn't work from those studies though, nor did I work from a photograph. This is an imaginary jumble of light, so I allowed myself poetic license in terms of cropping and positioning. You might say, "if you're going to give us a light shaft, how about the whole thing?" but it didn't work when I made it scientifically correct. It's a much more powerful picture cropped as it is.

KM: John, when you decided to curate a show of Ed's work revolving around the theme of light and you began researching it, did you find an abundance of work that could potentially be included, or did you really have to cherry-pick to pull a show together?

JW: There was more than enough work. When we saw sketches for the painting several things about it struck me as unusual: It's large, it doesn't have jokes or words, and it exploits the notion of radiance in presenting what appears to be a dark room invaded by a shaft of light. Because I'd known and loved Ed's work for years, I was surprised to learn he'd been stowing in these ideas long before the Getty got to him. There's no way I could've known it, though, because Ed has lots of work that's never been published and few people are aware of.

The idea for the show really shifted into focus when Lisa Lyons and I spent a day going through the slides of Ed's work dating back to the early '60s, paying special attention to painting. Midway through that visit Ed said, "You might be interested in these—I showed them twenty years ago but they haven't been out much," then he pulled out a huge flat file. Out come eight big pastel drawings of light bursting through clouds and casting great shafts of light downwards. My field is older art, so I'm looking at this stuff thinking this looks like an Italian Baroque altarpiece, or Rembrandt's Annunciation to the Shepherds. *I asked Ed what they were called and he said, "This is 'The Miracle Series'" [c. 1975].*

KM: Ed, is this the Catholic in you emerging? You're also currently in an exhibition on view through June 27th at Cheim & Read in New York, called Three Catholics, *that pairs your work with that of Andy Warhol and Robert Mapplethorpe.*

ER: Yeah, I can't deny it. I was raised Catholic, and I've been warned it's impossible to leave that behind. I've taken my own road in this thing but it probably does permeate everything I do, and I see traces here and there—Catholic literature, for instance, has been littered with images of light shafts for centuries.

KM: *A current of irony has always coursed through your art; does the subject matter of this body of work preclude the possibility of irony?*

ER: It's not as evident in this work, which is possibly more sober than the rest of my stuff. At the heart of this work too, however, is some sort of paradox that I don't understand—and that's what fuels my art.

KM: *In much of your work you've handled light in a manner reminiscent of René Magritte: Both of you create compositions that depict mysterious objects hovering in an eerie, existential void. Has the Surrealist treatment of light been a reference for you?*

ER: No. Things like that patch of light on the floor over there *[gesturing across the room]* have been more a source of inspiration. I'm intrigued by the fact that it sort of has no character, yet it's there, and I use things like that as a kind of anonymous background. I've been working with sources like that for years, and I'm still asking myself about the reality of those things.

KM: *Is there anything recognizably regional in the way Ed handles light?*

JW: *One could make the case that the paintings evoking celluloid light projections have a regional flavor. There's one in particular, with the words "The End" in nice gothic letters, like the end of some historical romance, that feels sort of L.A.*

One of the first miracle works is a twenty-eight-minute film Ed made in 1975 called Miracle *that we're screening in conjunction with the show. It's set in a garage and centers on a filthy mechanic working on a Mustang. In a series of cuts, he gets cleaner and more lucid, and in the final scene he's wearing a pristine white lab coat and has solved the problem. The "miracle" of the story is that we're given no indication of what brought about his transformation.*

Finishing up with the question of regionalism, Ed may dismiss this, but I can't look at Picture Without Words *[1997] without thinking of artists of his generation like Bob Irwin and James Turrell, who've made installations with light. Ed doesn't make a depiction of light so much as he makes an embodiment of it, but I think they all share an appreciation for the significance of light as a creative raw material in Southern California.*

ER: We might be getting into dangerous territory if you align me with artists who've taken this light business to its most serious end. Jim Turrell is a good friend and we agree on lots of things, but his approach to light is completely different from mine. His approach is more pure than mine, because he goes back to the source. I stop the source by making a painting out of it, and have no interest in the peculiarities and science of light itself.

KM: As an art student in the '50s, were you told it was necessary to work out an ideology about the treatment of light in painting? Was that part of the curriculum?

ER: Not at all. In previous periods that was definitely something they did—they did light studies and fiddled with the *camera lucida* and so forth. When I went to art school the course of study was, however, much more classical than it is today. These days they don't even have figure drawing and art students sit at computers. It's future world—which isn't to suggest I mourn the passing of the mode of study I had.

KM: For centuries light was employed in painting as a metaphor for the divine, and was interpreted as an avenue to the worship of things not of this earth. That changed with Modernism, which presented aesthetic experience, and the art object itself, as the thing to be worshipped. Now that conventional notions of religiosity have been expunged from art, what is the symbolic meaning of light?

ER: It's interesting you use the word "avenue," because the painting I made for the Getty isn't an "avenue" painting that will lead me to paint more light shafts. It's an end painting. I don't see more light shafts in my future because I've taken it as far as it can go.

KM: Do you intend that the shaft of light be interpreted as a metaphor for a miracle, or is light itself the miracle?

ER: I'm tongue-tied on that one.

KM: In a 1991 review of work by artist Wayne Thiebaud, critic Adam Gopnik commented on Thiebaud's use of "a chalky, melancholy light, which seems to have been bottled sometime in the 1930s in a small Midwestern city, and has been spilling into American painting ever since." One assumes Gopnik is referring to the light that washes over work by artists such as Edward Hopper, and has its roots in the art of Winslow Homer and Thomas Eakins, among others. Do you feel yourself to be a part of this tradition?

ER: Those artists actually painted light, whereas I'm painting an idea about light. Another difference is that those artists painted from life, while I've been more influenced by magazines and popular culture—my inspiration is often second-hand. I have a standing appreciation of those artists, yet I can't look at any of them and say "this is where it comes from." I'm influenced by living in the world. Yet, my interpretation of the world is filtered through art, so I guess I have to say I do belong to that tradition—so there you go.

JW: I think you can trace Ed's handling of light further back than Hopper, to the Luminist tradition of Martin Johnson Heade, which has links with transcendental thought, that of Ralph Waldo Emerson in particular. Luminism espoused a belief in an imminent, higher force embodied in the wonders of nature, which are there for man to contemplate for his own betterment. That's an interesting counterpoint to the Catholic belief in divine intervention in human affairs expressed by bursts of light—and miracles!

Look at Fitz Hugh Lane's sunsets over the sea, the sun casting golden light over all of God and man's creations—that was a mid-nineteenth-century depiction of nature that survived well into the twentieth century. Ed approaches this territory through popular imagery, and reflects the ironic point of view of a late-twentieth-century artist. In what spirit will people take Ed's paintings of light? How will they be interpreted? That's where the voice of the twentieth century makes itself heard.

KM: What's the most difficult kind of light for a painter to wrestle with?

ER: Probably Caravaggio's light. I think that might be harder to pull off than my light shaft. I don't have objects or people.

JW: On the other hand, Ed's light has to stand alone and do all the work—there aren't even any words to help. One of my favorite pieces in the show is a painting with that same shaft of light and the words "An Exhibition of Gasoline Powered Engines." It's hard to imagine two more disparate elements than this light shimmering with spiritual allusion, and a bunch of machinery. In that piece Ed undercuts the potential solemnity of the light; in the Getty painting it simply reveals itself.

———

KM: Is a painter always courting notions of beauty when he deals with light?

JW: He's certainly courting conventions about beauty, and I think Ed's work occupies that territory. This isn't unmediated light; this is light that evokes thousands of paintings and graphic images. When Ed painted sunlight bursting though clouds, he wasn't thinking only about the physical world; he was thinking about all those pictures that have conditioned us to accept sunlight bursting through clouds as something miraculous.

KM: The painting of natural light has associations with landscape; do you consider any of your paintings landscapes?

ER: Yes I do. A work like the Standard gasoline station, for instance, is definitely a landscape. In a sense I approach all my work as if it's a landscape, in that there's a background, a foreground and usually some other nonsense going on—lots of times it's words. The background-foreground thing is an ever-present issue for artists, and this is my response to it. It's landscape once removed. You could certainly say that about paintings I made in the '60s and '70s of searchlights and so forth, and I'm maybe saying the same thing in the Getty painting that I said in those.

KM: And exactly what is it you're saying?

ER: I'm telling my side of the story.

JW: [Laughing] She thought she saw pay dirt there.

———

"FROM RUSCHA WITH LIGHT"

Reed Johnson

[. . .] As its title semi-ironically suggests, nothing much is spelled out in Ruscha's Picture Without Words, *a monumental acrylic painting that recently went on permanent display at the [Getty] Center in Brentwood. But its spare elegance hardly means the work is devoid of symbolism or emotional content. [. . .]*

"People might think when they see this painting that there was a subject in mind, or rules, or limits," *said Ruscha [. . .].* "They just showed me the space. They didn't say, 'Make it holy, make it loud, make it colorful.'

"I appreciate those sorts of commissions," *he added wryly. [. . .]*

Picture Without Words *is one of three major commissions for public spaces at the Getty Center, which opened to the public last December. The others are Robert Irwin's [. . .]* Central Garden *and Alexis Smith's* Taste *[. . .].*

Collectively, these contemporary works help establish a dialogue with the Getty's pre-twentieth-century European treasures, underscoring the tensions between classical and modern, permanence and impermanence, in [Getty Center architect Richard] Meier's designs.

It seems Ruscha had these tensions somewhere in mind when he set about planning Picture Without Words *after receiving the commission in December 1996. Among the works in* Ed Ruscha's Light *[a complementary exhibition at the Getty, featuring works*

Originally published in the *Daily News of Los Angeles*, July 10, 1998, p. L27.

exploring the theme of light in the artist's work] are a series of five pastel drawings he made as studies, with variations on the motif of light projected through a window-like opening. Also included in the exhibitions are the results of a test Ruscha made using a spray gun to lay down thin acrylic strips of paint in various pastel hues, which coalesce into the single beam of Picture Without Words.

"I've found that I have to make these steps in order to make the progression from one thing to another," *Ruscha explained.* "I knew that I wanted something that was ambiguous, but timeless. [. . .]"

———

"Seeing Things Age Is a Form of Beauty:
A Conversation with Ed Ruscha"

Tracy Bartley

[. . .] TB: Is contemporary art only for contemporary times? Because of the ephemeral nature of many contemporary artists' materials, is it probable that no matter what effort we undertake, a spotty record of our twentieth-century cultural heritage will survive?

ER: Materials, by their nature, are already decaying. Almost any art material you select is going to somehow decay over time. Even if you think about a writer and words, words in their own way decay over a period of time. They're thought of differently today than they were in the seventeenth century.

That's not the sunniest way to look at things, but art materials are no different. When you think about hard materials like marble, bronze, and other sculptural materials, they all undergo this transformation that you just have to accept as being part of the thing. Oil paint is another example of something that's continually degrading. The sun or light of any kind is going to affect it and add age to it.

It's like how we maintain the human body. We knew the human body is not going is live beyond eighty or ninety years. We could be looking at the human body years from now and come no closer to preserving it than we knew

Originally published in *Conservation, The Getty Conservation Institute Newsletter,* v. 13, n. 2, 1998, pp. 10–11.

Ed Ruscha's "Picture Without Words, 1997." Auditorium Lobby, Getty Center, 1997. The
J. Paul Getty Trust. Photography by Grant Mudford.

about or pondered at the dawn of civilization. It's going to decay. When it comes to art, you look at traditional materials that have stayed relatively the same for hundreds of years—the way they mixed paints, ground pigment with linseed oil, and carefully followed recipes—and yet ravages of moisture and sunlight and time all give you the problems that you have to face with conservation.

TB: Do you notice this with your own work?

ER: I notice it in little ways. I've done things before that are inherently problematic—what conservators call inherent vice—like using Scotch tape. I knew when I made my collages that the Scotch tape would be the first thing to go. And, sure enough, it was. Even some paper I worked on at one time has totally disintegrated without having been exposed to the elements.

I've been documenting Sunset Boulevard for many years on 35mm film, and I've called Eastman Kodak to search for ways to preserve film and store it. Everybody seems to have ideas about what to do. And I know that film is a fugitive material—maybe even more so than paper or other supports.

TB: Film has its own set of problems. Besides the material issues, there are the technological issues: as technology evolves, the film projector that can show your film may become obsolete.

ER: Exactly. I made these films in 1970 and one in 1975, and I haven't done anything in film since then, and I go back today and the language has completely changed. [My films] still work in a projector, but the stability of the dyes and all that makes up the color—they're probably changing even though I keep them in a controlled situation.

No matter what kind of material you use, it's going to face that kind of thing. Now, what artists want, well, that's another thing. Some artists just absolutely do not care about preservation of their work. And sometimes they say they want it to be destroyed—like Tinguely's machines that destroy themselves.

TB: Do you think that artists have a responsibility to ensure that their work has a future?

ER: I don't know. Anybody's approach is a valid one, as far as I see it. You might find artists who say, "I don't want my work to be around in 150 years." Well then,

---

I say, "What's the purpose of the whole mess if you don't want anything to be around?" It's like taking your most precious heirlooms and throwing them in the trash. If you want life to end, well then, end it.

I don't do it out of any heart-thumping responsibility, but I do feel that my work should be preserved as much as possible.

TB: Do you want to see the work maintained as it was when you finished it, or do you accept the fact that it has a life of its own and is going to change?

ER: I accept it. Here I am: I've lived it, and here is the way I look. And so paper is going to look the same way. I like that look. You can look at a Kurt Schwitters collage and you can tell that those papers are really from the '20s, and they've aged, and the inks that were used on the papers have aged. This makes up what it is today. It would be strange to look at a collage done back in the '20s if you saw it like it was when it was made. You'd be disoriented. You'd say, "My, this looks clean." The colors would be real crisp and bright, and the paper would be bright white. Paper just changes with time. When you look at the paper, you see that it has aged over the years, and that actually makes it quite what it should be. It's lived an age, like a person who's eighty-five years old.

TB: Do you think that the change in materials can go too far and you can lose what the piece originally was about?

ER: Well, yes—then you ask yourself how well you could preserve something like that. Should you take that piece of paper that has a collage on it—and all the other materials including the adhesives used to paste them down—and hermetically seal it in a chamber of some sort, like an anti-aging chamber? You'd still have the problem that seventy years had passed. Something would look different from how it looked when it was made. When I see paintings on paper that were done even in the '50s—Abstract Expressionists' work, where there have been years for the oils to migrate into the paper—the stain looms out, and you see that. Seeing things age is a form of beauty. I'm always looking at paintings and works on paper from years and years ago, and I really kind of appreciate the aged look to them.

———

TB: If something deteriorated to the point where it couldn't be shown, would you want it remembered through photographic documentation? Do you think that it's important that there's documentation in cases where materials are transient?

ER: I do have things that were destroyed for one reason or another that I photographed, and I feel good about that. The idea of documenting to preserve a record of what you've done is a valid one, and I've done it for a long time. It's very presumptuous, though, in a way—how do you know how valuable this thing is to the public? Why should I save it? For that matter, art is priceless and worthless at the same time! As an artist, I've accepted the idea of caring for my work—to ensure the longevity of the work. I've done that, but I'm not a fanatic about it.

TB: So you wouldn't let it determine what material you chose or how you work?

ER: If I did, I wouldn't have used a lot of materials. I did a lot with food that changes. I don't think it's an obligation of the artist to choose materials that are lasting. I just don't think that's important. You can make work out of straw—you can make work out of air, if you want to. You're the artist! That's the freedom of the whole thing. An artist can make anything out of anything. You can use cotton candy.

Somebody once gave me a gift that was a fresh fish on a plate. It was a birthday gift. And he had written around the outside of it and I thought, this is such a great gift, I love this gift. So I put it in the freezer and kept it frozen for twenty-five years! It stayed in pretty good shape! I finally got rid of it. It was beginning to migrate, let's say.

TB: With your painting at the Getty, Picture Without Words, *did you think about the issue of longevity?*

ER: I sure did. And the issue is not really complete, as far as I'm concerned. The sunlight makes slashes across the painting that change all the time. And of course, over time, as we know, that can affect the piece. There are shades in place, but they let slivers of light through.

―――

Considering longevity also dictated what kind of support I would paint on because if I had painted it on canvas that was stretched onto a stretcher, over time it would sag because of the weight of the canvas. You'd be restretching it every two years. So we arrived at this idea of putting the canvas onto a flat, hard surface—we chose aluminum—and that really made the most sense. That's one example of trying to do something that preserves or maintains an image in the most prudent way.

All you can do is address these issues as best you can. I did an independent evaluation of the location. I do that with commissions. I spoke with the curator and several conservators. I tried to assess the spot on the wall and the conditions there. Light was the main thing, and the weight of the painting.

TB: I suppose the longevity of the work is an issue for any commission you undertake.

ER: I did a commission for the Miami Public Library, a whole series of paintings. This was in 1986, and I went back about two years ago, almost ten years later, and I noticed as I walked in that all my paintings were okay. Everything looked basically like it did in 1986. But something told me that ten years had passed. It's weird. There are no scuffs on the wall, it's all very clean, the paint is all the same color—but it's like pushing open a door that doesn't work the same ten years later; even though the door works perfectly, it doesn't work the same. There are degrees of subtlety on objects that have a few years' life on them, and I noticed that going inside.

I don't know what it is—it's something in the air or something. It looks like it's ten years old. Furniture looks that way. I think paintings look that way. Works on paper and sculpture are the same. It's very curious, amusing. The whole aging thing is amusing to me.

―――――

"Collecting Our Thoughts"

Ralph Rugoff

[. . .] "A museum is an authority figure and a subjective taste-maker that throws events serving free hors d'oeuvres. This is the opinion held by many younger artists," *observes Ed Ruscha, who once expressed his feelings with his drawing* I Don't Want No Retro Spective *[1979].* "Later on, these same artists begin to see a museum as a valuable archive center sympathetic to the showing, collecting, and documenting of their work."

―――――――――――――――――――――――

Originally published in *Vogue*, March 1999, pp. 300, 304, 308. Published on the occasion of the exhibition *The Museum as Muse: Artists Reflect*, organized by the Museum of Modern Art, New York.

―――――

"THE WEATHER OF PRINTS: AN INTERVIEW WITH EDWARD RUSCHA," JULY 16, 1998

Siri Engberg

The following interview took place at Ed Ruscha's studio in Venice, California.

SE: I want to begin by asking you about the idea of editions—making things in multiple copies. How did you feel about that process early in your career?

ER: I was first introduced to printmaking in an etching class at Chouinard. This was in the late '50s. I immediately liked the way it worked, the way the ink went on, the whole curious production of making a print. We would never really get around to making editions. We would just make a proof and play with the thing, then change it a little bit and make another proof. It was a good chemical mix of students; everybody seemed to be jived about it and excited. We would even sneak into the school late at night, and some people would work all night so that they could have use of the press. But at no real time did we address the question of making an edition or making a proof and then doing an edition from the

――――――――――――――――――――

Originally published in *Art on Paper*, v. 4, n. 2, November–December, 1999, pp. 62–67. Published on the occasion of the release of *Edward Ruscha: Editions 1959–1999* (ed. Siri Engberg), a catalogue raisonné of prints, and of the exhibition by the same name, organized by the Walker Art Center, Minneapolis.

proof. It was more of an introduction to how to make a matrix, or how to make a plate or an artwork that could then be done that way.

SE: Your first lithographs were made before your first book. Did the process of making those affect or influence the bookmaking?

ER: No, I was jumping into a different body of water there. I knew that the books were going to have this industrial look—a commercially printed appearance I felt they needed to have. The first lithographs were examples of a frenzy of drawing and smudging—the sort of thing the photographic books really didn't have. They were just completely different.

SE: You've talked about the fact that your work is, as you say, premeditated in many ways, rather than made through spontaneous action. Is that attitude reflected in your print-making?

ER: At the time I started working with prints, I was not really involved in the premeditated image, but later, I could see that having this notion ahead of time was the only way I could work. That really came out in my painting. And in the books, too. They had to be premeditated.

SE: Tell me about your early experiences working in graphic design and as a printer's apprentice—studying different printing techniques.

ER: That had an impact on me, not so much technique-wise, but in terms of imagery. At the printer's my eyes would light up when I saw mistakes. I also remember test proofs, where they would use something that had already been printed on and then print something on top of that. The layering of mistakes and tests and make-ready images that were printed one on top of the other in no particular fashion—I liked that.

SE: How do you see the prints fitting into your work at large as you look back on the editions, the books, the paintings?

ER: I think my entry into printmaking came by way of invitations. In a lot of ways I had to be encouraged to make prints. I think a lot of artists are that way;

———

they would rather make their paintings and sculpture, although they would certainly make a print if somebody would just say, "Come and make a print." But I only had that happen in a couple of instances. In one, the Standard gasoline station print [*Standard Station,* 1966], Audrey Sabol, a woman from Pennsylvania who saw some work of mine, called me and said, "I would like to make a print with you." This was totally her creation, not mine, and I responded to that. She agreed to pay for the edition if I would send her a certain number of prints. It was very altruistic. She wasn't a hustler. She wasn't a print dealer. She had her own ideas about what she wanted to do. She just completely left it up to me, and she paid for the production of the thing. I sometimes think I would never have done that print unless she or someone like her had come along. Likewise, the Tamarind Foundation would give artists the opportunity to work for a period of two months and do as many or as few prints as they wanted to produce. I liked it for that, too. There it was, there was the workshop, the time quotient was all figured out.

SE: And the expertise, certainly.

ER: Yes, they had master printers. They explained that if I had two images in mind, we'd do one, and they'd pair me with a master printer and that person would see that print through. If you were going to start another one, they'd give you another printer, a different person who would see that print through. So I liked that. I was rolling along there, and I had a few ideas in my mind. It was a cooperative effort, like making prints and multiples is, certainly. That's really the nature of the game.

SE: How do you feel about working collaboratively with workshops on your prints?

ER: I love the idea of working alone in my studio, making paintings and drawings and so on. Working with a print is a different sort of thing; it requires some sort of sensibility or responsibility. You have to be there at a certain time and all that. It kind of keeps me on edge and in line at the same time.

SE: There's a regimented aspect to making prints.

———

ER: There is, in that if something breaks down and I have to repair it, you know, I should be there to repair it, and let's get the plate back together and go on. It was a scheduled type of activity that I wasn't completely used to. Working at Tamarind or Gemini or some of these shops required that commitment of time.

SE: *In most of your editions, you have worked with fairly straightforward printmaking techniques. You don't seem to combine multiple techniques in a single print.*

ER: I never did like that. I knew early on that I couldn't use, let's say, a photograph that I had used from a gasoline station and make that into a lithograph or an etching. (Actually, when you look at it, I have done that on occasion.) But it is the same thing with drawing versus painting. Some of my drawings I could never make into paintings and vice versa. So a drawing to me was always an end in itself and not that much of a study for a painting. And paintings were just in their own sublime world. I didn't media jump.

SE: *But with the organic screenprints in the early '70s, you blurred the boundaries a bit more between drawing, painting, and printmaking.*

ER: Yeah, I did the *News, Mews, Pews, Brews, Stews & Dues* edition. I also made some paintings that were organic materials put onto unorthodox supports like rayon and taffeta, moiré, that sort of thing. Printmaking and painting sort of overlapped one another there, but usually they don't. When I did prints, I more or less saw them not as reproductions—like they've often been perceived through history—but as something else.

SE: *You seem to have a certain reverence for the whole experience of looking at prints. I notice you've created fascinating boxes and portfolios for many of yours. Stains, for example, is in a bible-like box. The Insects are in a box with dirt encapsulated on the outside. How important to you is the "package"?*

ER: Well, I have give and take on that. Sometimes you might say, "Well, what does the artist really want to have happen?" My idea is not to make sure that people get a work of mine and put it up on the wall right away. I'm quite happy to keep prints in drawers. And I like the idea of keeping them put away and then bringing them out to look at. Maybe it's like an old Japanese idea or something about the storage containers for works.

SE: What has your experience been using various printmaking techniques? Crown Point Press, for example, specializes in etching; Tamarind, of course, in lithography. Do you go into a project knowing what medium you'd like to create your imagery in? Or does the image come first, and then you choose a medium to execute it?

ER: Sometimes it's that way. Sometimes an image I have in mind will work in almost any print medium. And then sometimes it won't. Conventionally sure ways of making a print might be that if you want solid, pure color, you do it in silkscreen. If you want scratchy lines and foul biting and a sort of automatic look to it, then do etchings. If you want an appearance of a crayon drawing, then do a lithograph. But God knows what makes me decide what I want to do.

SE: After your first printmaking experiences, how did you begin to explore other techniques?

ER: At one point, I began to think, "Maybe this silkscreen idea is not going to serve me for where I am at this particular time—I don't want these real solid colors. I don't want pristine, chromatic areas." So I would end up drifting off to somewhere else.

SE: But was that partly a reaction against other artists who were using that same medium? Like Warhol, for example.

ER: Maybe, except he used it in a very awkward way, which had great style. And also he was doing it in painting, which was a very work-specific kind of thing. His silkscreens were his paintings. Yet, today, they archive them as paintings, although they were strictly silkscreens.

SE: Prints on canvas.

ER: Yeah, they were prints on canvas. And that made all the difference in the world and even amused him. He liked that—the very fact that if you put it on a piece of paper, and then take the same image and put it on a canvas, the canvas was worth more.

SE: In the 1960s, what were some of your thoughts about prints as commodity—the idea that they were salable items?

ER: Some of my friends who were more cynical said, "Look, prints are just a way to make a buck." And yet, it never was a way to make a buck, because you could make these editions and never really sell them. There was no master plan, and there was no surefire way of selling these things in any market. It only happened gradually, and then people began concentrating on doing prints.

SE: You came into printmaking at a time when there was a whole resurgence of interest in that medium. Many of the artists working in New York were making prints, a lot of workshops were starting up. You were working in L.A. at Tamarind and Gemini at a time when they were in their heyday. What was that environment like?

ER: Tamarind was more of a strict operation than Gemini because they wanted the artist to accept the responsibility of the deep meaning of this process of lithography. Of course, you could take that and throw it out the window, too. Some artists tried—like Bruce Conner made a thumbprint, which June Wayne just rejected, I guess. That was a minor little scandal that happened about the time I was there. And yet, when you think about it, a thumbprint is a perfect print image, isn't it?

SE: Absolutely.

ER: Why wouldn't it be acceptable? Well, Wayne looked upon it as too smart-alecky. But anyway, the great difference between that and Gemini was that Gemini was ready to work for any artist, to produce anything that they wanted to make a multiple out of. So I thought that was a brave thing, to try to get into that world [of multiples]. They would make something three-dimensional if you wanted. They would do cups of coffee for you if you wanted to call those editions. They had all the expertise right there to find out about those techniques that were not really even thought about before. So here we had someone like Claes Oldenburg, who was doing these floppy, move-around objects and reliefs with plastic materials. Gemini was getting into plastics. They were getting into glass. So you could make anything. Then at the same time they worked with artists who just wanted to make lithographs.

SE: Would you say that your prints have a certain look to them?

ER: No, I wouldn't. They might be easier to look at if they did, I don't know. The overallness of them—I somehow don't know how I feel about it. I think that sometimes they're so disjointed, so unlike each other, that I wonder. Well, they're all coming from me, yes. They are, but they're isolated examples of what I happened to be involved in at that time. I'm not trying to write my own history by having these things all look magically like one another. They kind of tend to jump around, I guess.

SE: Do you think very much about scale and size when you're working on paper?

ER: Yeah, it's kind of like how you wake up in the morning, and you look out at the sky, and you see what the sky looks like: if it's gray, you might feel one way; if it's sunny, you might feel another way. In the studio it's almost the same way. My reasoning is like an involuntary reflex.

SE: Can you talk a bit about some of the editioned photoworks you're doing now that draw upon imagery from the early books?

ER: Well, I haven't worked with photographs and books for a long time. Originally on my first book, *Twentysix Gasoline Stations,* I felt like I had something that was really almost too hot to handle. And I liked it for that. And then I developed the next book, which was the fires [*Various Small Fires*], and then the next book, which was apartments [*Some Los Angeles Apartments*]. So then they started speaking to one another. I remember that when the first book came out, people didn't know what to think.

SE: So would you say that the works that you're making now are nostalgic?

ER: Well, this is another way of seeing an image that I've done before, but I like it for that, too. It's just like a new medium. It's a new door to walk through. [. . .]

SE: [. . .] Are you still photographing Sunset Boulevard?

ER: Mmm-hmm. I do it about every, on average, two to three years.

SE: *And the photographs are for your own use, your own personal chronicle?*

ER: Yeah, I just put them in a lab and salt them away. I just feel like sometime in the future I'll be able to do something with them, but I don't know.

SE: *An L.A. time capsule.*

ER: Yeah, I have a belief in this idea of the time capsule. I like that very much. I had that same feeling when I first photographed Sunset Boulevard in 1966. I've seen, over the years, young people saying, "God, that's ten years ago you did that." And yet ten years ago is not that much. This is thirty years ago. But to some people ten years is a vast, long time. Time, as a property, seems to be important to me. You may not see it in all my work, but it is, I guess.

CONVERSATION WITH EDWARD RUSCHA IN HIS STUDIO,
VENICE, CALIFORNIA, OCTOBER 29, 1999

Alexandra Schwartz

AS: The questions I'd like to ask you are intended to fill in some of the gaps in previous interviews you have given over the years. You have mentioned before that Futurism had a significant influence on your work. What interested you about the Futurists?

ER: Some of the "to hell and back" dogma and the sort of nihilistic approach to life. And the absurd idea that war is a beautiful thing. I mean, I found it comical, not something to follow necessarily. Although I think that the artists within that group were really great artists.

AS: Were the industrial aspects of Futurism of interest to you?

ER: Yeah. The idea that the automobile is more beautiful than a horse. Or tipping your hat to the machine age. Mechanical things being seen as beautiful objects that you adore and worship. This was a very powerful way of thinking for the artists who got together at that time in history—when was it—1910? They had their leader, Marinetti. He was an absurdist. I suppose that I began to see this absurdism in other forms of life later on. You might say Spike Jones was allied with Marinetti. I was also influenced by the artists themselves, the guys like Balla and all the rest of the Futurists. But Dadaism had a greater effect on me. Absurdity and paradox had real meaning for me as an artist.

AS: I've heard you talk about the idea of your books being mass-produced, of not being artist's books in a traditional sense. I was wondering how Stains *fits into that, if it fits into it at all. In some ways it is more of a traditional artist's book.*

ER: It is definitely a *livre d'artiste,* whereas my other books are *not* that way; my other books are more industrial and photographic, rather than touched by the artist's hand. *Stains* was more or less a handmade book of the type that I had at times talked against and expressed dislike for. But then I found myself making an object that had the touch of the artist.

AS: What steered you in that direction?

ER: Well, I think it comes back to painting. In my painting at that time I felt that I was applying a skin to a canvas—skin that sits on the surface of a canvas—and the staining was a departure from that. It was a relief, in a way, from putting a skin on a surface. I liked the idea that some liquid substance can penetrate a piece of paper, and it's got sort of its own volition and its own movement. It's slightly uncontrollable, and I guess I like that. I was thinking along these lines in the late '60s and early '70s, making paintings that were also done in this way—where you take a wet substance and put it on a support.

I think with *Stains* there was no latitude for any kind of manipulation of the image. In other words, the stains were exactly what they were stated to be. They were like a little droplet in the middle of a piece of paper; there's no gestural opportunity, no opportunity to do anything else besides simply dropping the liquid on the paper. These stains were actually not applied by me. I liked the idea of producing this book by hiring a group of people to produce these stains with only the guideline that they centrally locate the stain in the middle of the paper—with the exception of, I think, coffee and tea, which we dipped the corners [of the sheets of paper] into. But I didn't want to have the opportunity to put a Q-tip into chili sauce or something and then swab it in any particular fashion. The more you swab it then the more it begins to look like art, and I didn't want it to look like art. I wanted it to look like a stain.

AS: You've talked a lot about Duchamp in the past, and in being interested in the idea of

———

371

the readymade in your books and elsewhere. Given that, I'm surprised you haven't done more three-dimensional objects. Is there any particular reason for that?

ER: Well, the third dimension, to me, has always existed; I'm not just a two-dimensional artist. But a book, sitting face-up on a table, has a spine. The spine might be real thin, but it is a surface, which makes the book a three-dimensional thing. It's not just the cover that I'm after in my books, it's the whole thing. When I did my paintings, I continued to paint around the side of the canvas; sometimes I would paint the word that I had painted on the face of the canvas on the side of the canvas, too. I was looking at it almost like a book with the spine and the face. To me that's three-dimensional, although in our world of thinking, it really doesn't qualify as sculpture; it qualifies as two-dimensional art that's on a wall.

AS: Did you ever make any sculptures when you were a student?

ER: Yeah, I did. I did some metal scultpure, tin can sculpture that I welded together. I took a welding class. And I did some plaster works that involved wood. They are all destroyed now, but I was vaguely interested in sculpture. But it didn't provide encouragement to me to continue with anything three-dimensional, so I never got into it.

AS: I saw the reconstruction of the Chocolate Room *[originally constructed in 1970] at the Walker.*[48] *In a way, you could consider that three-dimensional.*

ER: I looked at it as an installation, as a walk-in room. Those were the limits on what I had to do when I was invited to the Venice Biennale. There was also an opportunity to do something with silkscreen printing, and there was an opportunity to have this one room there to myself. So I was weighing the one and the other, and that's really how the *Chocolate Room* came about. At the same time, I had just come from London, where I did that portfolio called *News, Mews, Pews, Brews, Stews & Dues.* And so the *Chocolate Room* was tightly connected to that, like an extension of that, except it was like a total "Sensuround."

AS: Were you interested in Minimalism at all?

ER: I thought it was beautiful, but it was too dogmatic. It didn't offer any room for spontaneity or shift of thought.

AS: For a period in the late '60s, you weren't painting. This was at a time when many other artists were turning away from painting, as well. Did you feel you were part of a broader current happening at the time?

ER: No, but I was moving away from painting at that time, not finding a window of opportunity for myself in painting. Not that I wasn't *able* to do it, but I think this happened at the same time that this skin-on-a-surface idea came to me. I was frustrated that I was applying this skin to a surface. And so, if anything, I worked out of that by doing my stain paintings, my organic paintings, and doing that *Stains* book. Then I sort of got back on track. But I think there was one year—1970—that I didn't do any paintings.

AS: You are often categorized as a Conceptualist, and I know that you're resistant to that. But in your 1992 interview with Walter Hopps, you said that there were some teachings that the so-called Conceptualists responded to that you also responded to, and you were close to such "Conceptualists" as Robert Smithson and Larry Weiner.

ER: Yes, I like their art very much. But the idea of *pure* Conceptualism puzzled me, because I felt like it was impossible to make a statement with a work of art that didn't have something to do with the visual. And so if they were describing Conceptual art as being a thing that had no visual reference, then I would say, "Well, where are the Conceptual artists?" They *all* have visual statements. If Joe Kosuth does a chair against a wall, that's a style. Lettering on a wall—all those things that he had done—all had a style to them.

AS: A lot has been made of this New York/Los Angeles split that occurred, but it seems like there was a lot of intercommunication between artists on both coasts. Was there a distinct community among people around the country who were looking into similar things? How did you come in contact with one another?

ER: I met these people through the gallery scene somehow. But New York is considered to be the essence of any movement, and anybody else who didn't live in New York was not really part of it. There have been lots of artists' book exhibits and such that I haven't been part of; I maybe should rightfully be irritated for that. But many art movements were always seen as New York phenomena for some reason or other, and I didn't live in New York. A lot of people would think that there was some sort of conspiracy theory, that everybody was down on people who didn't live in New York. It's an ongoing question. But the Conceptual artists, at least, all basically lived in New York.

AS: I was just reading something that Mel Bochner had written around 1970, where he talked about your work. It's curious that in spite of all these back-and-forths, so many art historians insist upon some kind of regional split.

ER: Yeah, there is a regional split. I think a lot of people from New York resent people from other parts of the country and treat them like they're smart-alecks or something. "How dare you try to be an artist and not live in New York?" *[Laughs.]* But I personally like the idea of visiting there rather than living there.

AS: Early on, when you were asked about the photographs in your books, you insisted that you were not a photographer, that your photographs were just part of the larger work—

ER: —I contradict myself!

AS: Everyone does that! But starting in 1989, you started doing prints from your books. What changed your mind?

ER: I felt like I had a child that had grown up. You can do something in 1963 and then you look at it for twenty years and say, "Where has this child gone? What is it? Has it grown up?" I don't look at all my work that way. But I believe in this idea of waste and retrieval. Things that are gone from you—that you're not interested in—you retrieve those things and look at them once again and you want to make something of them. I wanted photography to be a special medium, and it always exposed itself through my books. And I like that; it's like a step into the void, taking away from the idea of its being a photographic print. I began to change over the years and feel like maybe the photographic print is not so bad after all! And so I suppose that's some of the reason that I began making these prints.

———

AS: *Do you think you might now start making "straight" photographs?*

ER: Oh, yeah. I'm not burning to do this, but I know that there's some room there for me to step into that involves photography. And that's about all I know. I'm not searching for anything, but I think it's something that's always been at my feet. I think I'll get into it again, where I actually go out with a camera and shoot pictures.

AS: *How did you start doing the paintings of city streets that you're working on now?*

ER: You know I always like to go back to *Ophelia* [by Sir John Everett Millais, 1851–1852]. In that painting, you're looking down on this woman in a sort of aerial oblique manner. Aerial photography has always been riveting to me. The idea of seeing something from the air—not where you look at something directly from up above—but where you're looking at something from an angle. It's something that moves me as an artist. I see it in my work lots, and so it was just kind of a natural thing that I began to gravitate towards, and then finally make some of these paintings. They almost look like what these streets might look like in the year 5000 or something.

AS: *How do you mean?*

ER: Well, like these are patterns for streets that once existed in the world. I like the idea of making no value judgments of these particular streets that I'm intersecting in my mind, and also that I have some kind of personal connection to these streets. They mean something in my history of living in L.A. Intersections of conduits can easily be seen by the aerial view of a city. I'm looking at these in the abstract, and then also I'm bringing it back to reality by making these real streets that intersect each other.

AS: *They remind me of grids that other artists have done, like Mondrian.*

ER: Well, yeah, Mondrian. He's certainly a player in the density of art. I think people began to relate to his work by the simple titling of his work. *Broadway Boogie Woogie* immediately puts you up above, looking straight down, directly down onto this city. When you read that title—*Broadway Boogie Woogie*—it changes the

---

Sir John Everett Millais, *Ophelia*. 1851–52. Oil on canvas, 60 × 80 cm. Tate Gallery, London 2000.

Opposite page, top: Ed Ruscha, *The Los Angeles County Museum on Fire*. 1965–68. Oil on canvas, 53½ × 133½″ (136 × 339 cm). Hirshhorn Museum and Sculpture Garden, Smithsonian Institution. Gift of Joseph H. Hirshhorn, 1972.

Opposite page, bottom: Ed Ruscha, *St. Crosses Ave*. 2000. Acrylic on raw canvas over board, 19⅛ × 28⅞″ (48.5 × 73.3 cm). Photo: Paul Ruscha.

abstractness of that picture. If it had been "Abstraction #4" or "A Period of Gestation" or anything other than "Broadway Boogie Woogie," then it would have kept his paintings in the realm of totally abstract. While he was an abstract artist and saw the beauty of abstraction, he brought it back to conventional reality by titling that picture "Broadway Boogie Woogie." People began to notice that, and pick that work as a kind of a symbol of modern life. You can almost see the little cars moving up, the little square shapes. My work is more "pictorial," I guess, and less abstract than his. But Mondrian was a mover, an influence on my work. Although I didn't make Mondrian pictures; actually, I made more de Kooning pictures or Franz Kline pictures than I did Mondrian pictures. I didn't emulate him like I did, say, Jasper [Johns]. And, not to digress, but Kurt Schwitters was probably one of the most influential people for me.

AS: You made some collages early on. Are they still around?

ER: Yeah, I've got a bunch of collages that I did back in the early '60s that were heavy into Dadaism. There it is again: waste and retrieval. You find something that's been thrown out on the street and you bring it back and do something with it. It's a common tactic. I'm guilty of using all the techniques.

———

"PROFILE: THE PAINTINGS OF ED RUSCHA"

Susan Stamberg

[. . .] SS: Ed Ruscha [. . .] has fans in high places and paints words in high places, [like] that West Coast icon, the Hollywood sign.

ER: My studio was in Hollywood, and I'd look outside the window. And if I could see that sign, I knew that the air was pretty clear; otherwise, too smoggy. So it was a weather indicator for me, and I looked at it so many times I said, "Why don't I just paint a picture of it and shut up."

SS: A long, rectangular canvas, vivid orange sunset, in silhouette against it, the letters H-O-L-L—you know. [. . .] Ruscha did it in 1977. He calls the painting The Back of Hollywood. *It looks like a very hot day in movieland, [and] a little unnerving.*

ER: Sort of apocalyptic in here, isn't it?

SS: Yes. The sign, which in reality is white, you've made black. [. . .] And the sign, which in reality you read from left to right, here you've turned around.

ER: Yeah. So you're up on top of something looking at it from a different angle.

Transcribed from a broadcast of *Morning Edition*, National Public Radio, July 11, 2000. Broadcast on the occasion of the exhibition *Ed Ruscha*, organized by the Hirshhorn Museum and Sculpture Garden, Washington, D.C., and the Museum of Modern Art, Oxford.

SS: *Ruscha specializes in different angles, different takes on the familiar. He says he's telling his side of the story.*

ER: An artist has to kind of dig and not rely on things he's searching for, but things that are already there.

SS: *Things that are there and that intrigue you in a particular way?*

ER: Yeah. Intrigue me enough to make me want to say, "Make some art out of it somehow." *[. . .]*

SS: *Cézanne painted apples. Pop art pioneer Andy Warhol painted soup cans. Ed Ruscha, a decade younger than Warhol, paints words, the still life of our day.*

ER: Well, it might be. It's popular culture, and for a long time it was ignored. And then when artists began to realize that you don't just have to look at paint splashed on a canvas or flowers painted on a canvas—you know, there are other things in the world, too.

SS: *[. . .] 1963,* Standard Station, Amarillo, Texas: *big canvas, five red-and-white gas pumps, looming red sign—Standard—white roof, everything immaculate against a black, black sky. Ed Ruscha paints gas stations?*

ER: Well, I've seen enough of them and, I guess, bought enough gas.

SS: *Do you think of yourself as a political painter at all?*

ER: No. Not in the sense that I would want to affect any kind of moral change or anything like that. It's pure painting to me. It's what I'm engaged in, and I really haven't deviated from that.

SS: *I ask you because it's a gas station, you know, and you could put in a little pollution.*

ER: Yes.

SS: *It's a very pristine canvas.*

ER: I know. Some people read that into it. And they say, "Well, the gas station is symbolic of this terrible thing that we're part of." And, you know, it's part of the frenzy of modern life, but it's bluntly displaying this imagery without any kind of social commentary.

SS: Ed Ruscha was in Washington for a week as the Hirshhorn retrospective opened. [. . .] So being in the nation's capital, would he now go home and paint our most famous marker, the Washington Monument?

ER: No. I mean, it's not like I have a laundry list of icons that I'm going to go down and capture. It hasn't really happened that way. It sort of happens by being exposed to the kind of anxiety and neurotic anxiety of the city and popular things that come off the radio and in movies and all of that.

SS: [. . .] At the Hirshhorn, a brochure accompanying the Ruscha retrospective describes him as an artist of restless curiosity. Agree?

ER: No. No. I'm pretty conservative and I don't think of myself as being "restlessly curious," no. Those are just words to me. I'd rather paint them than interpret them.

SS: So if you were to describe yourself and it wasn't to say, "I'm an artist of restless curiosity," what would it be?

ER: Well, I might just say, "Look, I'm just another member of the food chain." *[. . .]*

PART THREE

BITS AND PAGES

In this immense city of London only one piece of art attracted me — Of all places, located in the British War Museum, oddly misplaced but that fact made it even more interesting. It is ~~an~~ a bust of Mussolini in some Kind of Kitchen pottery glass — looks as though ~~from ay~~ spun from ~~as~~ a potter's wheel. From every level on a single plane you see two faces of "Il duce".

August 17, 1961, on a trip to London.

The best thing about any creative urge, passion
is that it _happens_.
　Arguments about plastic values are
senseless from my point of view - plastic
values are found every moment - they grow -
we cannot use as a guide or measuring
stick those things that have happened
in days gone by. Cubism has nothing
for me except for the fact that I KNOW it
~~they~~ occurred. Shapes, colors, lines,

August 17, 1961, on a trip to London.

April 2, 1963.

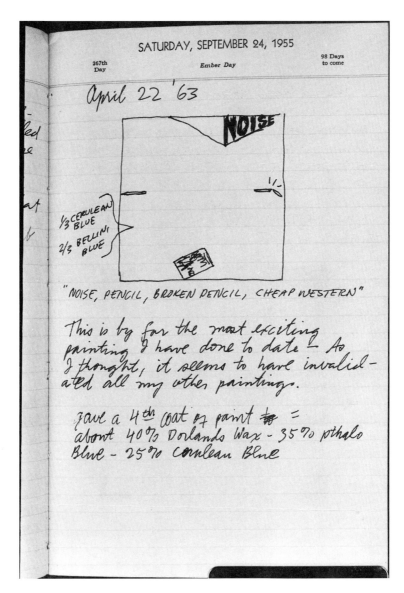

April 22, 1963.

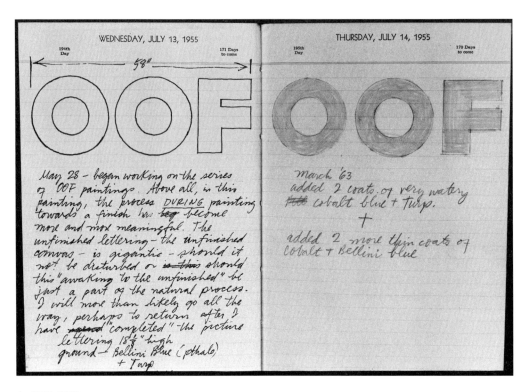

April 22, 1963.

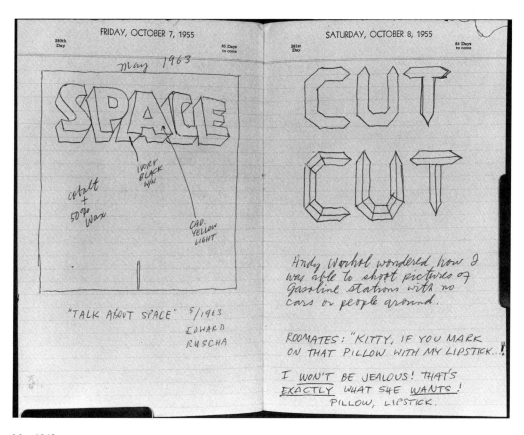

May 1963.

GETTING
OLDER
BY STAYING
HEALTHY
IS
INVARIABLY
FATAL

NOT MEANT TO FRIGHTEN CHILDREN

LOVE THIS WK CAUSE IT'S NOT DEMANDING

CAUSTIC ANXIETIES

VOID OF INTENTIONS

HEAVY BREATHING - PUFFERY

USING UP ALL THE AIR IN THE ROOM

NO DETAIL TOO SMALL
TO OVER LOOK

BAD
CONFUSION

NARCOTIC ATTRACTION

WELCOME
TO MY
SOUP
KITCHEN

'DISRUPTIVE COLORATION'

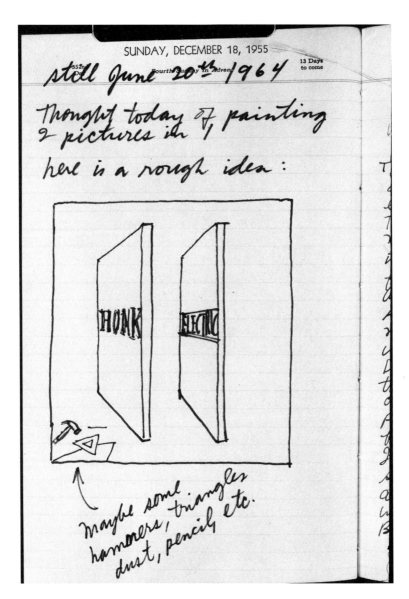

June 20, 1964.

PUT MYSELF ON
ADMINISTRATIVE LEAVE

I WAS LAID UP W/

GLORY AND MONEY
OUT THE WINDOW!

DULL FROM BEGINNING TO END
BUT LOADED W/ ENTERTAINMENT

OUR COMEDIES ARE NOTHING
TO BE LAUGHED AT   SAM
                          GOLDWYN

STREETS ARE SAFE IT'S THE
PEOPLE WHO MAKE THEM UNSAFE
                    PHILADELPHIA MAYOR FRANK RIZZO

YOU NEED KICKING BY A
JACKASS - & I'M THE RIGHT
ONE

PAT HIRO $

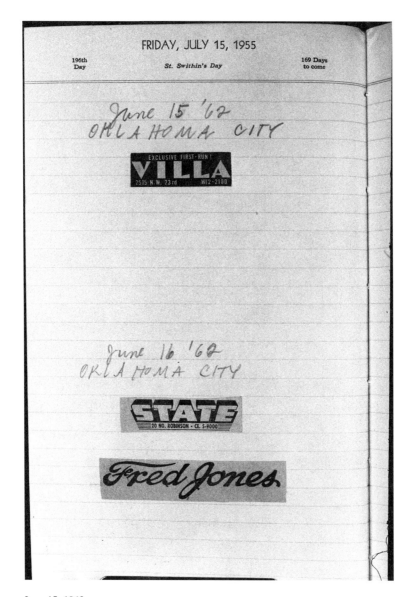

June 15, 1962.

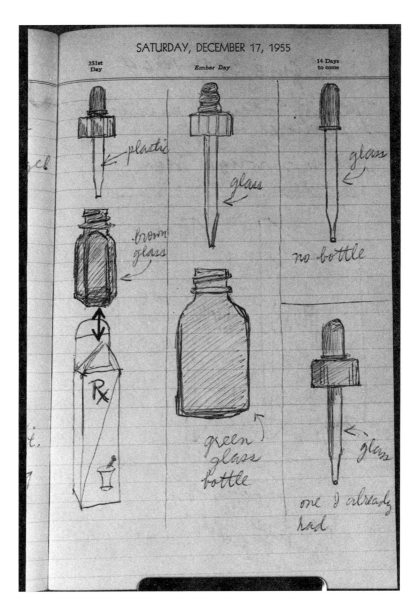

Sketch, June 20, 1964.

CROWN VICTORIA: IT'S GOT
RONALD REAGAN ALL
OVER
IT.

SHRINE TO MERCHANDISE

LIFE – IT ALL WENT BY IN AN ABSTRACT BLUR

COOKIE CUTTER KOREAN CONDO

MEGA STEREO MALLS

HWY 60
MOBIL BLAINE ST.

YOU'VE GOT LOVE TO BURN

I LIKE TO PLAY
ROBINSON CRUSOE
3 – 4 TIMES A MONTH

DO ING IT.

I THOUGHT I'D DO IT.

YES, I DID IT. I WENT

AHEAD & DID IT & NOW

IT'S DONE.

T I N A

WENDY S.
LIPFLAPPER

IF I TREAT YOU KIND OF GENTLE
THEN BABY TREAT ME THAT WAY TOO

WAITING UNTIL NOON

BRING ON THE CLOWNS

EVESDROP ON YRSELF

HOTTER THAN A BARTENDERS BUNION

MEAT MOTORS AND MULES

PERCY
MAYFIELD
BABY YOU'RE RICH

"GRIN & DIET"
ALLEN JONES
TELEGRAPH TO
ME IN
TAMPA

COLOR?

HEY, I HAD NO CHOICE IN
THE SELECTION OF COLOR FOR THE
FOOD PRINTS --- HOW DO YOU ALTER
THE COLOR OF CAVIAR OR AXLE GREASE?

YOU SEE CONFORMITY FIRST IN ART.

GET MAGAZINES IN FOREIGN LANGUAGES
& RUN ACROSS INTRIGUING PICTURES & NOT
BE ABLE TO UNDERSTAND THEM.

CORE OF MY AESTHETIC
IS THE SHAPE OF 48 FORD GEARSHIFT KNOB
                    VS
                CHEVY   "   "

THINK OF CELLOPHANE & ITS TRAUMA WHEN YOU
TEAR IT OFF A PACKAGE. SPLITTING ATOMS
RELEASING 53 KINDS OF GASES. FRACTURES OF
POLYMERS RIPPING APART IN ATOMIC SHEETS/PLATES
OF CRYSTAL FORMATIONS DISLODGING AND
TUMBLING IN AIRFLOWS THEN FALLING TO THE GROUND.

                        SOMEONE
                .....WILL ANYONE GET BACK TO ME ABOUT ABOUT THAT?

I BELIEVE
AN INNOCUOUS PIECE
OF INDUSTRIAL DESIGN
CAN SHAPE YOUR
ATTITUDES OF THE WORLD
IN MY CASE THAT COULD BE
THE GEARSHIFT KNOB FROM
A 1950 FORD SEDAN.
IT'S THE LITTLE
THINGS THAT
MATTER.

L.A. MOVIES

MOVIES GREAT ART FORM

VERTICALLY
WHIPPED PIECE
OF CELLULOID
LIGHT PROJECTION
GIVING THE
ILLUSION OF A
LANDSCAPE…
A STORY
AN IDEA
AN IMPRESSION

VARIOUS BOXERS LIKE
SUGAR RAY ROBINSON
MUHAMMED ALI
WILLIE PEP
MUSICIANS LIKE JACKIE
McLEAN, SPIKE JONES,
FRANK ZAPPA
MOVIES, RADIO BUT
NOT TELEVISION

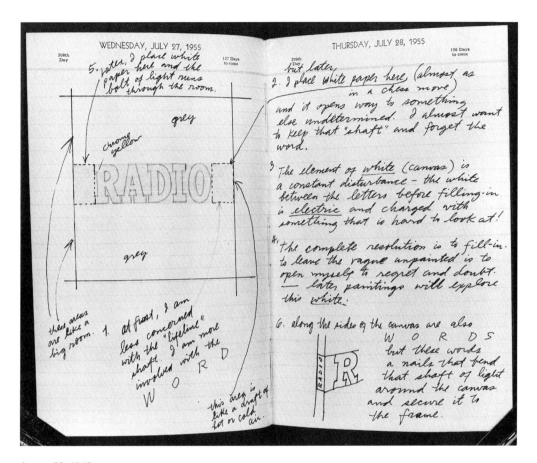

August 25, 1962.

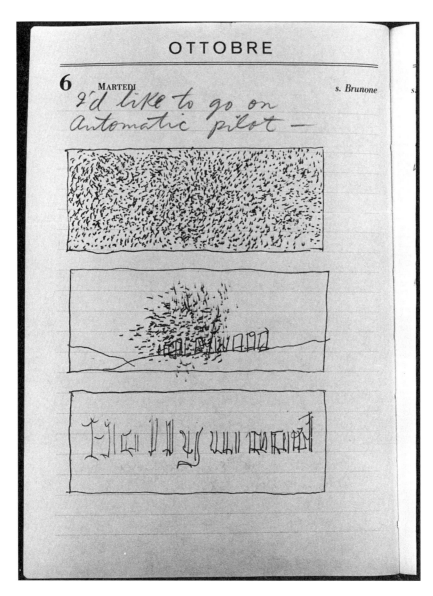

June 1971.

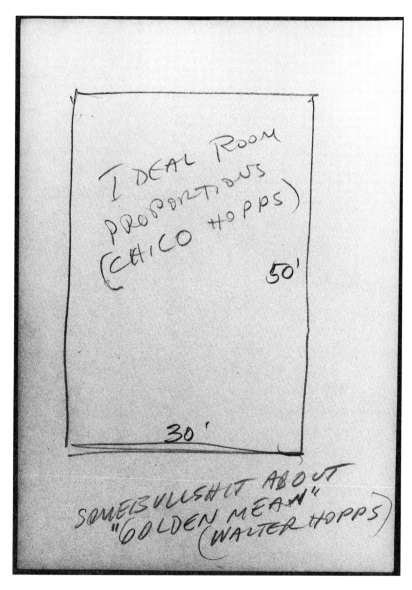

1994.

CONTINUITY
FOAM

INDUSTRIAL
VACUUM
RAILS

THERMOPLASTIC
DISCONNECT
SWITCHES

CUTTING OILS

HYDRAULIC CIRCUIT
BREAKERS

FLOAT SWITCH

HIGH INTENSITY
CENTRIFUGAL
SPOTLIGHT
SWITCHES

BLAST
RESISTORS

HYDRAULIC PADLOCKS

14T 32T 70T 167B

COMPRESSION
CHAMBERS
AND
REACTION VESSELS

SUGAR TANKERS
AND
BEEF BEDS
BEEF ON BEDS
STEEL CLAMPS
A CHROMIUM RELEASE
MECHANISM

ALUMINIZED AIR-VENTS
DEFECTIVE SILENCER UNITS
MAGNESIUM PIVOT BARS

JACK QUINN

BALES OF
ELECTRIC CABLE WERE
HEAPED ON THE
UNMADE BED.

IRON
PIVOTS

KITTY LESTER
HOPE, ARK.

STRAIGHT
LOVE LETTERS FROM
MY HEART

BEFORE
EVERY TIME BIG PROJECT
GO THRU A PERIOD OF SHOCK

ATLANTA GA
RALEIGH NC
MOBILE, ALA

BARELY REGISTERS ON THE PRESTIGE
METER

SWIMMING IN JELLO

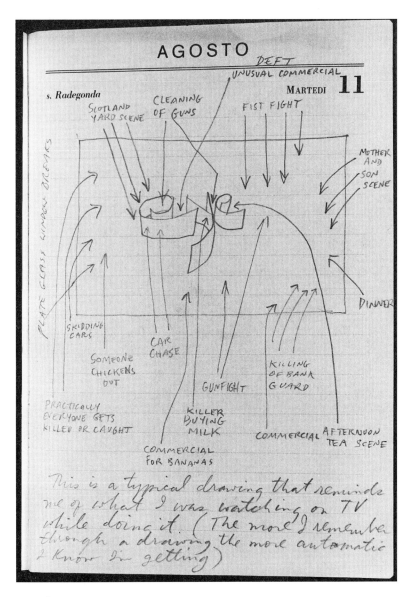

December 1970.

BREATHING PAINT
IN UNVENTILATED ROOM

EAT YOUR SPINACH

YOU WASTE OF SPACE

SAME LOOK ON MY FACE
WHEN I WENT TO DIVORCE COURT

MARGO LEAVIN

UNACCEPTABLE
LEVELS OF MICRO-
SPECIFIC
EXAMINED BADNESS

I AM IN
SUCH A
MOOD

THERE I AM
A DETAIL
IN THE
SCENERY

**OLD
CAR
WRECKS**

CRUEL EVOLUTION / GENEALOGY

ARCHAEOLOGIST

ARCHAEOLOGY VS. ROMANCE

"BLVD CALLED SUNSET" PTGS.

UTILITY POLES & METROPOLITAN CURBING
DRIVEWAYS, RAMPS, ACCESS DRIVES

AS WE ACCUMULATE MORE & MORE ASPHALT
                ROAD   CONTINUAL
& CONCRETE DIVIDERS   LANDSCAPING
                        METAMORPHOSIS

THE PICTORAL EVOLUTION OF
CENTERSTRIPS AND CONCRETE STREET APRONS

SUNSET BLVD. I SEE IT AS
A CRUEL EVOLUTIONARY FORCE
OF CONCRETE CURBS AND
ROMANCE
ARCHAEOLOGY AND ROMANCE

                    1-800-877-4848

TURTLE WAX ON MERCEDES'
   VANITY FAIR = ROYALTY FLASH & TRASH

Drawing, October 8, 1961, on a trip to Paris.

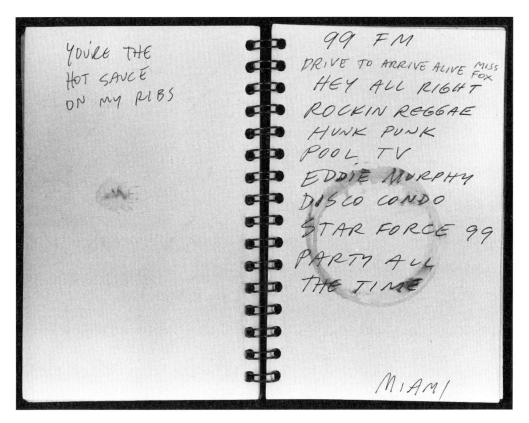

Spread from notebook (read top to bottom).
Radio DJ Talk on 99 FM radio, Miami, Florida, 1985.

YALE

IF YOU COULD FRACTIONALIZE IT...

KETTLE DRUM = BEST WAY TO SYMBOLIZE THE DESERT

ENOUGH TO GAG A MAGGOT

MY PARCELS N1/2 SECTION 25

YOU BEEN TAKIN' CARE O' BUSINESS?...EVER'DAY EVER'NIGHT

POPPED OPEN LIKE A
PAIR OF UMBRELLAS

HEMORRHAGING
MONEY

AUTHORITIES – FUNCTIONARY

ASPHALT
CONTRACTOR

FEATHERS ARE FLYING

HEAVYWEIGHTS,
HEAVYWEIGHTS
GIVE ME
YOUR EARS
M. TYSON

WOULD YOU FAVOR ME
W/ YOUR DEPARTURE?

SOUR METAL

I PICK
I PICTIFY (W/ MY PTGS)

I SEE ATOMIC POSSIBILITIES
IN THE ROTTENEST SCUM

SEEKING POSSIBILITIES

McGUGGENHEIM
CORKSCREW
LIKE A NIGHTCLUB

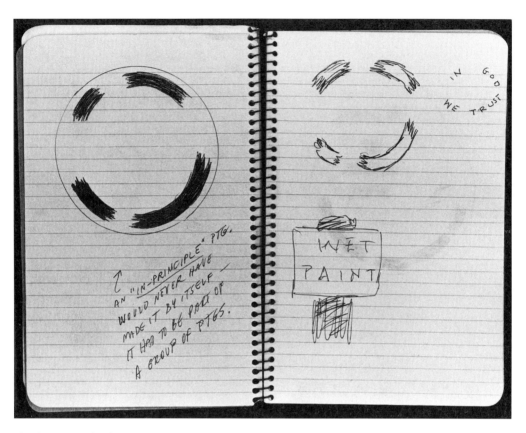

Sketches in a notebook, 1996.

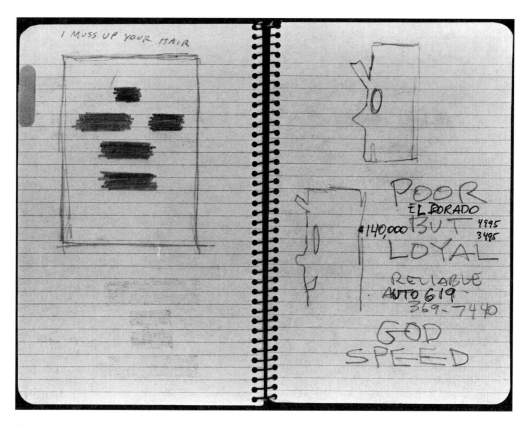

Sketches in a notebook, 1996.

WOULDN'T TRADE IT
FOR ALL THE
HAIRSPRAY
IN TEXAS

INVISIGLASS

ASIAN GOLF-COURSE COMMANDOS

THE WORLD OF PLASTICS

ASIAN COUNTRY & WESTERN THEME PARKS, INC.

ALL MAJOR FOODS WILL BE
IRRADIATED COMPOUNDS

MUSH'RMS 'MIND ME OF
 'TOMIC BOMBS

    THE
ATOMIC SLIDERULE

TEMPLE OF TRUTH

TEXAS
HAIRSPRAY

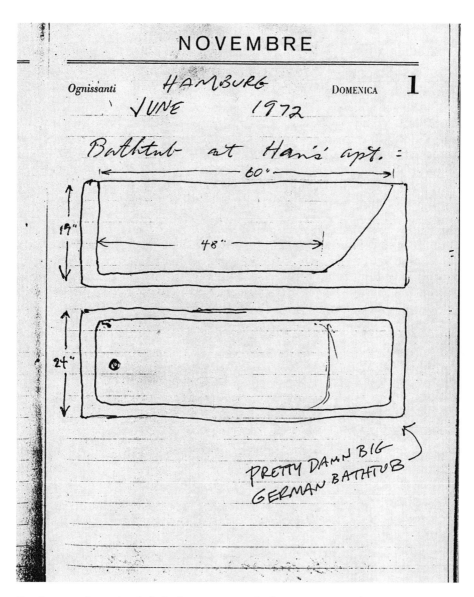

Drawing upon discovering the bathtub in Hans Neuendorf's apartment in Hamburg, Germany, June 1972.

NIGHTMARE OF JUNE 1, 1984

I had checked into a hotel room somewhere in mid-Manhattan that was situated in five or six buildings that occupied an entire block with little parkways in between the buildings. Some of the buildings were like old school structures and while I was trying to find my room I realized you could not gain access to half of them. There were doors with no handles, some windowless walls, but all the people seemed content and having a good time. Most people didn't know where the elevators were or gave vague answers. My room was on floor seven. Making my way back to the front desk I found it closed. Finally, I located the elevator but people were beginning to pile up, also waiting. Someone tried to pick a fight with me but I got out of it although the atmosphere was not tough. This hotel got recommended by many people. It was one of the best in New York if not that expensive. (The man at the desk avoided telling me how much the room cost so I never found out.) I left the elevator to ask what was the matter but everyone was too busy so I headed back to do some more waiting. There were now about 6 – 8 people waiting and had been there for about _ hour. These people were not the least bit fazed by the wait. Just then the door opened and out steps Claes Oldenburg. He was very young and handsome and was wearing a zoot-suit without the coat – pants up to his armpits. I threw my arms around him and he was extremely friendly and even put me in a good mood. I said something like "Claes, you look great this place couldn't be that bad!!" He beamed with a big smile and greeted me warmly then moved on. His elevator was unfortunately going down so when he left I had more waiting to do while the other people were not the least bit bothered by all the time the elevator was taking. My luggage had gone to my room hours ago. The look on everyone's face said I should be very, very lucky to have a room at this great New York hotel.

Still no elevator. Occasionally a face would appear of a person I recognized like an old but distant friend but too hazy to identify. No one waiting for the elevators got impatient or upset. Some of these people just cheerfully drifted away. Still no elevator. I waited watching all the busy people around the lobby. As I was coming out of this dream I said to myself, "Just like anything made in America, it's not made in America." I never got to my room.

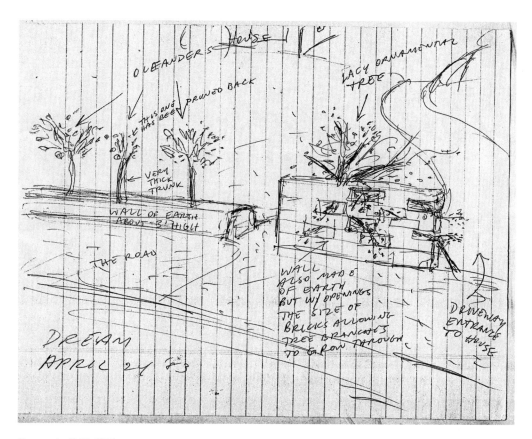

Dream, April 24, 1983.

Sketches in a notebook, 1985.

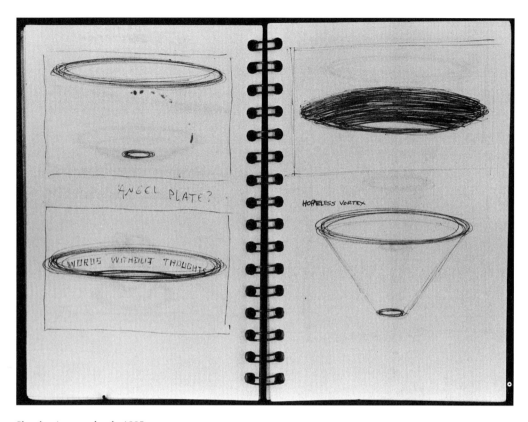

Sketches in a notebook, 1985.

PTG.
ART IS NOTHING
MORE THAN
GRAFFITI PANELS

HE WAS AT
HIS ZENITH IN
1950   (SPIKE JONES)

.

I'D RATHER WATCH
SYNCHRONIZED SWIMMING...

TUBS & BUBBLES

BUTTERDUCKS

BABYCAKES

OLYMPIC PROFILES
SAPSPLOITATION

PEOPLE WHO EXPLOIT =
"SPLOITARIANS"

THE OLYMPICS IS
ALL ABOUT US (NETWORK)
TELLING YOU ABOUT
THE OLYMPICS

PRESENTATION IS THE
SUBJECT
NOT THE OLYMPICS ITSELF

ATHLETES ARE ONLY
A SMALL FRACTION OF
THE ACT
THEY SHOULD BE THE
ENTIRE ACT

PEOPLE EQUATE
BUD LITE HOME DEPOT
WITH GOD & COUNTRY

RELIGIOUS
CRYING
ANGEL
MUSIC

THEME FROM "ROCKY"
SAPPY CHARIOTS OF FIRE TUNE

A DIAMOND IN THE ROUGH

FORGOT I WAS USING OIL PAINTS

RADIUM DYES

I WAS 14 BEFORE MY MOM LET ME IN THE HOUSE

← ZIPPERS LONG AND SKINNY →

A RATHER LARGE EMPTY IDEA

LIVING ON A LIGHT CRUST

AN ATTEMPT TO SET UP A RIDDLE

A CERTAIN HUMOROUS PESSIMISM

INTRICATE TYPES OF VISUAL NAUSEA

GATES PREVENT UNAUTHORIZED ENTRY

EVENTUALLY THINGS CHANGE

THE GREATER THE EMPTINESS THE GRANDER THE ART

IDEA ALCHEMY

HISTORICAL BLIND SPOTS

WASHERS -- THEY INCREASE HOLDING PRESSURE

I WAS LOOKING AMPHIBIOUS TO SAY THE LEAST

LEMON JUICE IN THE FACE

MUSIC = INCENTIVES ARE ENORMOUS

BREEZERS = LITTLE STACKS OF NOTES, ARTICLES

FUTURE EXPERIENCES

STICKS OF GOLDEN LUMBER

ACTIONS SPEAK LOUDER THAN WORDS

TREAT THE CAUSE AND NOT THE SYMPTOMS

HORIZONTAL SWIPES

WHAT'S YOUR UTILITY QUOTA?

FEASIBILITY STUDY

FLUID PROGRAMMING

YOU CAN SWALLOW MY PRIDE   (ZAPPA)

MEDIOCRITY ON THE MARCH

INTENSELY CASUAL

LIVING AMIDST HAMBURGER TRAFFIC

TRANS-PANAVISTIC

OBEDIENCE RANCH

STREET ICONOGRAPHY

EXCURSION INTO COMIC FORLORNESS

JUSTIFIABLE PARANOIA

SO THIS IS PARIS?   HOT EXCHANGE

IT WAS ONE OF THOSE, YOU KNOW, STRUGGLE FUCKS

LITTLE BITTY, TEENY WEENY, ITSY BITSY, STEEL SHAVINGS

OKLAHOMA CREDIT CARD (RUBBER HOSE)

WILL SOME ONE EXCUSE ME WHILE I…I…I…

SHE'S CHARBROILED -- SHE NEEDS NO KINDLING

SHE'S AN OPEN FACED STEAK SANDWICH

MY ART HAS NOTHING TO DO W/ QUALITY PER SQ. INCH

I'M WORKING HARD AT MAKING ART COME EASIER.

LIKE A LITTLE BELL RINGING CONTINUOUSLY IN YOUR INNER EAR.

DO YOU LOVE ME SOMEWHAT?

FLOAT A LOAN   ---   FLOAT ALONE

BOW-TIE DADDY   ---   POP ARCHITECTURE

THE ANSWERS ARE IN….<u>THE YELLOW PAGES!</u>

KEN AND BARBIELAND

PINK, BABY ANCHOR BOLTS

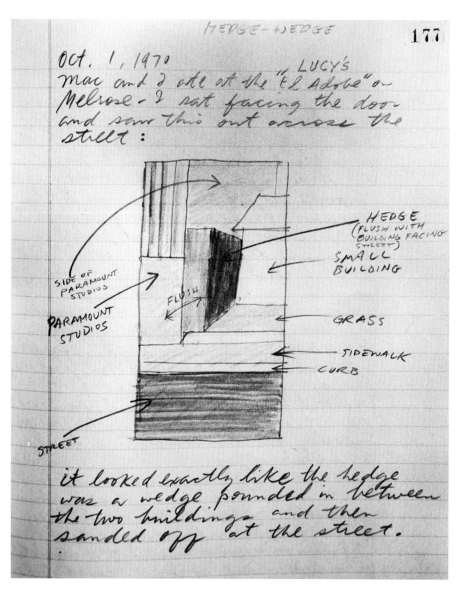

October 1, 1970.

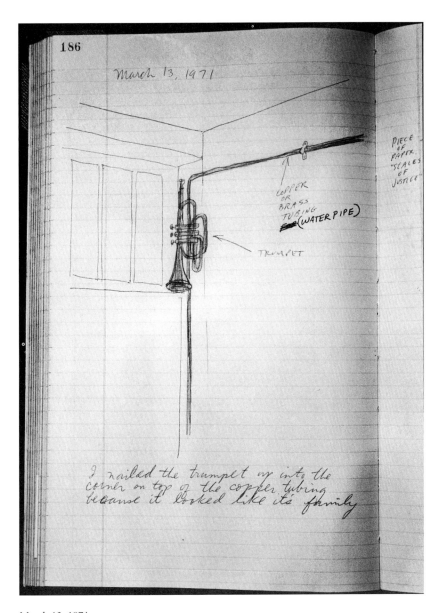

March 13, 1971.

NOTES

1

Eventually published as *Every Building on the Sunset Strip,* 1966.

2

Other artists contributing to this article: Carl Andre, Jo Baer, Walter Darby Bannard, Billy Al Bengston, Rosemarie Catoro, Rafael Ferrer, Donald Judd, Irving Petlin, Richard Serra, Robert Smithson, Lawrence Weiner.

3

On August 11, 1965 two officers with the Los Angeles Police Department pulled over a young black male named Marquette Frye near his home in downtown Los Angeles. Frye, accused of driving drunk, supposedly resisted arrest, claiming that his case was another example of the *LAPD*'s abuse of power within the urban, black community. A scuffle resulted, drawing the attention of Frye's family and neighbors, who were subsequently arrested, and as word of the arrest spread, rioting began. Five nights of chaos ensued, claiming the lives of thirty-four and injuring over 1000.

4

In 1957 Ruscha spotted Johns's *Target with Four Faces* (1955) in *Print Magazine.*

5

Other participants: Lawrence Alloway, Bruce Boice, Don Celender, Eric Fischl, Clement Greenberg, John Jacobus, Joseph Kosuth, Donald B. Kuspit, Elizabeth Murray, Carter Ratcliff, Larry Rivers, Peter Schjeldahl, Tony Shafrazi, Frederick Wight.

6

Words Going Round #1 (1985).

7

Coplans is referring to *Various Small Fires* (1964).

8

Ed Ruscha Books and Prints, Minneapolis Institute of Arts, April–May, 1972.

9

A proposed sketch for a work that was never executed.

10

The article in *Camera* was a reprint of John Coplans's interview for *Artforum,* v. 5, February 1965, reprinted in this volume, pp. 23–27.

11

New Painting of Common Objects was organized by Walter Hopps for the Pasadena Art Museum in 1962. Exhibited artists included: James Dine, Robert Dowd, Joe Goode, Philip Hefferton, Roy Lichtenstein, Ruscha, and Andy Warhol.

12

See this volume, pp. 64–72.

13

Ruscha is referring to *Sonsbeek 71.*

14

The Ferus Gallery was founded in 1957 by Edward Kienholz and Walter Hopps. Irving Blum was its director during the late '50s and early '60s.

15

Ruscha may be referring to Rauschenberg's *Odalisk,* 1955–1958.

16

Ruscha is referring to the *War Babies* exhibition at the Huysmans Gallery, Los Angeles, May 29 to June 17, 1961.

17

The Works of Edward Ruscha, San Francisco Museum of Modern Art, San Francisco; traveled to Whitney Museum of American Art, New York and Vancouver Art Gallery, Vancouver, Canada, 1982–1983.

18

Riko Mizuno owned and operated the Riko Mizuno Gallery for contemporary art.

19

Alloway describes this group as "Eduardo Paolozzi, the Smithsons [Alison and Peter], Nigel Henderson, Reyner Banham, Richard Hamilton, John McHale, and myself," Lawrence Alloway, "The Development of British Pop," chapter 1 in Lucy R. Lippard, *Pop Art* (New York: Frederick A. Praeger, Inc., 1966), p. 31.

20

Ibid., pp. 31–32.

21

Karlstrom is referring to the drawing *Made in U.S.A.* (1976), Pepto Bismol on paper.

22

Seventeen Painters of the Sixties: The Museum as Site; Sixteen Projects, organized by Maurice Tuchman, Los Angeles County Museum, July 21 to October 4, 1980.

23

Karlstrom is again referring to Ruscha's 1982 San Francisco Museum of Modern Art retrospective.

24

Susan C. Larsen, "Los Angeles Painting in the Sixties: A Tradition in Transition," *Art in Los Angeles: Seventeen Artists in the Sixties* (Los Angeles: Los Angeles County Museum of Art, 1981), pp. 19–24.

25

Christopher Knight, "The Word Made Flesh: L.A. Pop Redefined," *Art in Los Angeles: Seventeen Artists in the Sixties* (1981): 25–28.

26

Karlstrom here refers to the September 1981 issue of *Art in America,* which was devoted entirely to the subject of realism in contemporary painting.

27

Withdrawal from Dunkirk (1940), by Richard Eurich (British, 1903–1992). Ruscha first encountered this work many years ago in *What is Modern Art?* by Alfred H. Barr, Jr. (Introductory Series in the Modern Arts, New York: The Museum of Modern Art, 1946).

28

"They Shoot Corners, Don't They?" *Esquire,* v. 87, January 1977, pp. 89–93.

29

Karl G. Pontus Hulten was the director of the Museum of Contemporary Art, Los Angeles from 1981 to 1985.

30

In 1974, Norton Simon successfully instigated a coup at the financially beleaguered Pasadena Art Museum by offering to combine his personal collection with that of the museum. The conditions of his proposal were that the museum should agree to allocate seventy-five percent of its space to Simon and reduce the board of trustees from thirty-five to ten, reducing the number of Pasadena-based board members to three. Karlstrom refers here to a May 1980 incident when Simon chose to sell many of the Pasadena Art Museum's contemporary pieces at auction, without the approval of the trustees, among whom was Robert Rowan, the original donor of the auctioned works.

31

X, a Los Angeles punk band, rose to cult status with its documentation of the decay of Los Angeles in the late 1970s and 1980s.

32

In ". . . A Kind of a Huh?" an interview with Edward Ruscha by Willoughby Sharp (*Avalanche,* n. 7, winter–spring 1973, pp. 30–39, reprinted in this volume, pp. 64–72), Ruscha said, "I realized that for the first time this book [*Twentysix Gasoline Stations*] had an inexplicable thing I was looking for and that was a kind of a 'Huh?' That's what I've always worked around. All it is is a device to disarm somebody with my particular message."

33

Ruscha is referring to the project that would become *Hard Light* (1978).

34

Berman first exhibited in the Ferus Gallery in 1957, a show that led to the arrest of the artist on charges of "displaying lewd and pornographic material." He was subsequently found guilty and fined $150, which was paid by friend and actor Dean Stockwell. Berman later moved north to San Francisco where he continued to print *Semina,* a beat journal that contained poetry by, among others, William Burroughs, Robert Duncan, and Allen Ginsberg, as well as visual work by local artists.

35

Lawrence Dietz, "Mixed Media: Some Words on Ruscha," *Rolling Stone,* December 6, 1973, p. 88.

36

Dave Hickey, "Available Light," in *The Works of Edward Ruscha,* intro. Anne Livet, foreword by Henry T. Hopkins (New York, Hudson Hills Press, 1982), p. 21.

37

David Bourdon, "Ruscha As Publisher [Or All Booked Up]," *Art News,* v. 71, April 1972, pp. 32–36, 68–69, reprinted in this volume, pp. 40–45.

38

Joan Cosademont, "Ed Ruscha, Leo Castelli Gallery," *Artforum,* December 1980, p. 81.

39

Linda Cathcart, in *Paintings, Drawings and Other Works by Edward Ruscha* (Albright-Knox Gallery, Buffalo, NY, 1976), p. 4.

40

Dave Hickey, "Available Light," in *The Works of Edward Ruscha,* intro. Anne Livet, foreword by Henry T. Hopkins (New York, Hudson Hills Press, 1982), pp. 18–29.

41

Henri Man Barendse, "Ed Ruscha: An Interview," *Afterimage,* February 1981, p. 9, reprinted in this volume, pp. 210–219.

42

Ruscha played a supporting role in the film *Choose Me* (1984), directed by Alan Rudolph.

43

This became part of the painting *Do AZ I Do* (1988), in which the phrase is superimposed over an image of clouds.

44

This project, a catalogue raisonné of paintings, will be published by Gagosian Gallery (ed. Pat Poncy).

45

The exhibition *Edward Ruscha: Paintings/Schilderijen,* organized by the Museum Boymans-van Beuningen, Rotterdam and the Centre Georges Pompidou, Paris; toured Europe and the United States, 1989–1991.

46

The film *Stranger Than Paradise* (1984), directed by Jim Jarmusch.

47

This would become the "O Books" series (c. 1992–1997).

48

Ruscha's *Chocolate Room,* which he made for the thirty-fifth Venice Biennale, 1970, was refabricated and reconstructed in 1995 for the exhibition *Reconstructing the Object of Art: 1965–1975,* presented by the Museum of Contemporary Art, Los Angeles, October 15, 1995 to February 4, 1996, and was shown as part of the exhibition *Edward Ruscha: Editions, 1959–1999* at the Walker Art Center, Minneapolis, June 12 to September 5, 1999.

———

ADDITIONAL SOURCES

A number of additional interviews and statements by the artist, not included in the present volume, are listed here in chronological order.

"Artists Share House," *Oklahoma City Times,* December 16, 1958.

Edward Ruscha, "The Information Man," October 2, 1971, *Los Angeles Institute of Contemporary Art Journal,* n. 6, June–July, 1975, p. 21. Reprinted in *Artweek,* v. 22, June 6, 1991, p. 20; exhibition brochure, "The Books of Ed Ruscha," Harvard University Graduate School of Design, October 4–29, 1993; and Siri Engberg, *Edward Ruscha: Editions, 1959–1999,* Minneapolis: The Walker Art Center, 1999, pp. 55–56.

[John Coplans,] "Ed Ruscha (Rew-shay)," *Camera,* v. 51, n. 6, June 1972, pp. 34, 43. Reprint of Coplans, "Concerning 'Various Small Fires': Edward Ruscha Discusses His Perplexing Publications," *Artforum,* v. 3, February 1965, pp. 24–25. Reprinted in this volume, pp. 23–27.

Lawrence Dietz, "Mixed Media: Some Words on Ruscha," *Rolling Stone,* December 6, 1973, p. 88.

Barbara Radice, "Interview with Ed Ruscha," *Flash Art,* n. 54–55, May 1975, p. 49.

Barbara DeZonia, "Ed Ruscha on Various S-Subjects," *Stuff Magazine,* n. 24, 1976, n.p.

Marshall Berges, "Home Q&A: Edward Ruscha," *Los Angeles Times House Magazine,* March 28, 1976.

Carol Nuckols, "Artist World Made of Carrot Juice," *Fort Worth Star Telegram,* December 11, 1977, p. 51.

"Important Talent—Artists Making Mark on Art World," *Berverly Hills People,* February 15, 1978.

"Caviar and Gunpowder," *New Zealand Herald,* August 23, 1978, sec. 1, p. 3.

Michael Tennesen and Richard B. Marks, "'Local' Art Hits the Big Time," *Los Angeles Magazine,* February 1980.

Ruthe Stein, "Ruscha, the Artist Who'd Rather Not Talk Art," *San Francisco Chronicle,* March 26, 1982, p. 43.

Susie Kalil, "Straight Talk from Pair of Hard-working Artists" (interview with Ruscha and Billy Al Bengston), *Houston Post,* December 12, 1982, p. 20F.

Daniela Morera, "Edward Ruscha," *Vogue Italia,* n. 427, October 1985, pp. 325–329.

Peter Plagens, "Ruscha's Landscape," *Vanity Fair,* v. 49, n. 2, February 1986, pp. 88–95, 119.

Barnaby Conrad, Jr., "Los Angeles: The New Mecca," *Horizon,* v. 30, n. 1, January–February 1987, pp. 21–30.

[Bernard Blistène], "Born to Watch Paint Dry," *American Way,* March 1, 1991, pp. 60–64. Reprint of Blistène, "Conversation with Ed Ruscha," *Edward Ruscha: Paintings/Schilderijen.* Rotterdam: Museum Boymans-van Beuningen, 1990: pp. 126–140. Reprinted in this volume, pp. 300–308.

Dave Hickey, "Available Light," in *The Works of Edward Ruscha,* introduction by Anne Livet, foreword by Henry T. Hopkins (New York: Hudson Hills Press, 1985), pp. 18–29.

Barbara Isenberg, "Ed Ruscha: Variation on a Theme for Summer," *Los Angeles Times,* May 29, 1994, special section, p. 8.

Hunter Drohojowska-Philp, "Rancho Ruscha: The Artist's Los Angeles Residence," *Architectural Digest,* v. 51, August 1994, pp. 64–70, 138.

Giulia D'Agnolo Vallan, "Edward Ruscha," *L'Uomo Vogue,* September 1996, pp. 382–385.

Ludwig Seyfahrt, "Die Plastikeite des Lebens: Bilder des Amerikaners Edward Ruscha in der Galerie Jürgen Becker," *Hamburger Rundscau,* n. 13, March 20, 1997, pp. 50–51.

Suzanne Muchnic, "Updating the Getty," *Los Angeles Times,* September 12, 1997, p. F1.

Lyn Kienholz, "Interview with Ed Ruscha and Ed Hamilton," California/International Arts Foundation, www.netropolitan.org, c. 1998.

Edward Ruscha, Statement in "The New Season/Art: Looking Ahead; Delacroix to Degas, Hot Tubs to Fairies," compiled by Elizabeth Hayt, *New York Times,* September 13, 1998, sec. 2, p. 107.

Mary Abbe, "Ruscha is the Word in Cool Walker Show," *Minneapolis Star Tribune,* June 18, 1999, p. 1E.

Dennis Hopper and Ed Ruscha, "The Pop Fathers," *Independent* (London), April 30, 2000, p. 1, col. 5.

Jo Ann Lewis, "Ed Ruscha, Getting beyond Words: At the Hirshhorn, the Painter Who No Longer Spells Out His Affinity for Conceptual Art," *Washington Post,* July 2, 2000, p. G1.

―――――

CREDITS

WRITINGS AND INTERVIEWS

Every effort was made to locate the owners of copyrighted material and to make full acknowledgment of its use. Errors or omissions will be corrected in subsequent editions if notification in writing is received by the publisher. Grateful acknowledgment is made for permission to include the following material.

Henri Man Barendse, "Ed Ruscha: An Interview." Reprinted by permission of *Afterimage* and Henry Barendse.

Tracy Bartley, "Seeing Things Age Is a Form of Beauty: A Conversation with Ed Ruscha." Reprinted with the permission of the J. Paul Getty Trust.

Thomas Beller, "Ed Ruscha." Copyright © 1989 by Tom Beller.

Bill Berkson, "Ed Ruscha." Reprinted by permission of Bill Berkson.

Bernard Blistène, "Conversation with Ed Ruscha." Reprinted by permission of Bernard Blistène.

Fred Fehlau, "Ed Ruscha." Reprinted by permission of *Flash Art*.

Jeffrey Hogrefe, "Confession in Chelsea." Reprinted by permission of Jeffrey Hogrefe.

Walter Hopps, "A Conversation between Walter Hopps and Edward Ruscha." Reprinted by permission of Walter Hopps and Edward Ruscha.

Chris Hunter, "Rebel with A Canvas." Reprinted by permission of the *Palm Beach Daily News*.

Reed Johnson, "From Ruscha with Light." Reprinted by permission of the *Daily News of Los Angeles*.

Paul Karlstrom, "Interview with Edward Ruscha in His Western Avenue, Hollywood Studio . . ." Reprinted by permission of the Archives of American Art.

Victoria Lautman, "Hot Property." Reprinted by permission of Victoria Lautman.

Lewis MacAdams, "Catching Up with Ed Ruscha." Reprinted by permission of Lewis Mac-Adams.

Kristine McKenna, "The Sentimental Musical Tastes of Ed Ruscha," and "Lightening Up the Getty." Reprinted by permission of *Los Angeles Times*. Copyright 2001, *Los Angeles Times*.

Trina Mitchum, "A Conversation with Ed Ruscha." Reprinted by permission of Petrine Mitchum.

Suzanne Muchnic, "Getting a Read on Ed Ruscha." Reprinted by permission of *Los Angeles Times*. Copyright 2001, *Los Angeles Times*.

Howardena Pindell, "Words with Ruscha." Reprinted by permission of *Art in Paper*.

Joan Quinn, An Excerpt from "Art: L.A.R.T.: Edward Ruscha." Originally published in **INTERVIEW** Magazine, Brant Publications, Inc., March 1984.

Steven Rosen, "Panoramic Art at Library Elusive But Impressive," and "Library Muralist Slow to Praise...." Reprinted by permission of the *Denver Post*.

Ralph Rugoff, "Ed Ruscha: Goodbye to Vistas and All That," "The Last Word," and "Collecting Our Thoughts." Reprinted by permission of Ralph Rugoff.

Edward Ruscha, Statement in "The Artist and Politics: A Symposium." Reprinted by permission of *Artforum*.

Edward Ruscha, Statement in *50 West Coast Artists: A Critical Selection of Painters and Sculptors Working in California*. Reprinted by permission of Henry Hopkins.

"Picasso: A Symposium," Comment by Edward Ruscha. Originally published in **ART IN AMERICA** Magazine, Brant Publications, Inc., December 1980.

Edward Ruscha, Proposal in *Projects pour la Défense,* 1974. Reprinted by permission of Edward Ruscha.

Edward Ruscha, "A Proposal by Edward Ruscha for the Archway Lunettes of the Second and Third Floors of the Miami-Dade Public Library." Reprinted by permission of Edward Ruscha.

Edward Ruscha, "A Proposal by Edward Ruscha for the Circular Ring and for the Lunettes of the New Miami-Dade Public Library." Reprinted by permission of Edward Ruscha.

Edward Ruscha, Statement in "What Artists Like About the Art They Like When They Don't Know Why." Reprinted by permission of Paul Gardner.

Edward Ruscha, Statement in "'West Coast Style': Something about Los Angeles." Reprinted by permission of Henry Hopkins.

Edward Ruscha, "The Witness." Reprinted by permission of Edward Ruscha.

Vicki Sanders, "A Few Words with Ed Ruscha." Reprinted with permission from The Miami Herald Publishing Company.

Diane Spodarek, "Feature Interview: Edward Ruscha." Reprinted by permission of Diane Spodarek.

Jana Sterbak, "Premeditated: An Interview with Ed Ruscha." Reprinted by permission of Jana Sterbak.

Susan Stamberg, "Profile: The Paintings of Ed Ruscha." © Copyright NPR® 2000. The news report by NPR's Susan Stamberg was originally broadcast on National Public Radio's "Morning Edition®" on July 11, 2000 and is used with permission of National Public Radio, Inc. Any unauthorized duplication is strictly prohibited.

BITS AND PAGES

All "Bits" and "Pages" are used with permission of Ed Ruscha.

ILLUSTRATIONS

Photographs appear courtesy of the photographer unless otherwise noted in caption.

———

Index

Page numbers in italics refer to illustrations.

Abstract Expressionism, 118, 131, 138, 146–147, 160, 177, 251, 255, 262–263, 291, 326, 329, 358

Absurdity, concept of, 10, 19, 31, 65, 82–83, 153–154, 211–212, 227, 280, 297, 303–305, 311, 323, 370

Alanis, Art, 49

Alexander, Peter, 179

Ali, Muhammed, 285, 347

Alloway, Lawrence, 142–143, 148, 431n5, 433n19

Altoon, John, 115–116, 132–133, 174–175, 228

Antin, Eleanor, 77, 219

Antonioni, Michelangelo, 38, 196

Apollinaire, Guillaume, 120, 208

Arnoldi, Chuck, 178

Atget, Eugène, 49

Avedon, Richard, 197

Baargeld, Johannes, 127, *128*

Baechler, Donald, 325

Baker, Chet, 272

Baldessari, John, 218

Balla, Giacomo, 370

Ballard, J. G., 255, 278, 298

Baltz, Lewis, 218

Barney's Beanery, 132–133

Barragán, Luis, 318

Basquiat, Jean-Michel, 298

Batterton, Wally, 228

Beiderbecke, Bix, 273

Bell, Larry, 71, 82, 111, 130–131, 134, 168, 179, 228, 233, 236, 334

Bengston, Billy Al, 53, 82, 108–109, 113–114, 132, 134, 143, 145, 195, 228, 232, 334, 431n2

Bereal, Eddie, 130–131, 178, 228

Berman, Wally, 114, 217

Bertelli, R. A., 58, *59,* 120

Bing, Leon, 71

Black and white paintings. *See* Strokeless paintings

Blackwell, Patrick, 48, 49, 107, *110,* 130, 228

Blum, Irving, 131, 135, 138

Bochner, Mel, 374

Bonaparte, Bob, 98

Bosch, Hieronymus, 91

Bow Wow Wow, 273

Brady, Mathew, 49

Branca, Glenn, 273

Brown, Jerry, 87

Brushless paintings. *See* Strokeless paintings

Buehler, Herbert (Ruscha's cousin), 100, 119

Burgin, Victor, 251

Byrne, David, 273

Cage, John, 167

Captain Beefheart, 207–208, 273

Caravaggio, 351

Cars and car culture, 105, 161–164, 180, 213–214, 228, 243–244, 252, 304, 316

Cartoons, 86, 98–99, 102–103, 326

Castelli, Leo, 68, 125–126, *181,* 298

Catholicism, 11, 93–99, 227, 238, 344, 348

Celmins, Vija, 175, 178

Centre Georges Pompidou (Beaubourg), 288, 298

Cézanne, Paul, 380

Choose Me (film, dir. Alan Rudolph), 277, 435n42

Chouinard Art Institute, 11, 103, 105–118, 225, 227, 230, 301, 362

Clark, Candy, 195

Cohen, Aaron, 111

Collage, 313, 357, 378

Conceptual art, 36, 63, 129, 144, 146, 248, 281, 373

Conner, Bruce, 367

Conservation of works of art, 355–360

Corcoran, James, 310

Cornell, Joseph, 324

Crosby, Bing, 273

Crown Point Press, 366

Crumb, Robert, 102

Cubism, 268

Dada, 127, 208, 323, 378

Dalí, Salvador, 58, 304

Dark paintings. *See* Strokeless paintings

Darling, Lowell, 87

Davis, Ron, 182

Davis, Stuart, 124

Dean, James, 310, 335

Défense project, 6–7, *8–9. See also* Ruscha, Edward, works of, *234 Things*

de Kooning, Willem, 117, 323, 378

DeLillo, Don, 278

Denver Central Library, 336–340 (*337*)

Diebenkorn, Richard, 176

Dill, Laddie John, 179

Disney, Walt, 103, 106, 228

Domokos, Attila, *70*

Dove, Arthur, *13,* 19, 324, 332

Duchamp, Marcel, 57, 65, 116–117, 120, 215–216, 228, 302, 324–332, 371. *See also* Readymade, concept of the retrospective, Pasadena Art Museum, 57, 116, 331

Dwan Gallery, 179

Dylan, Bob, 335

Eakins, Thomas, 351

Eggleston, William, 218

Eilshemius, Louis, 325

Ensor, James, 332

Eurich, Richard, *188,* 189, 433n27

Evans, Walker, 126, 214, 250, 262, 318

Ferus Gallery, 40, 113, 130, 132, *135,* 137–138, 176, 225, 432n14

Films and filmmaking, 11, 38, 73, 79, 166–172, 196, 245, 255, 277–278, 291, 307, 357

Flynn, Errol, 174

Food, works made with. *See* Organic materials

Ford, John, 250

Foster, Gus, 56

Foulkes, Llyn, 228

Frank, Robert, 317

Frankenheimer, John, 38

Frizzel, Lefty, 273

Futurism, 370

Ganzer, Jim, *80*

Geldzahler, Henry, 131, 226

Gemini G.E.L., 365–366

Gernreich, Rudi, 71, 233

Getty Museum. *See* J. Paul Getty Museum

Getz, Richard, 101

Glass, Philip, 273

Goode, Joe, 49, 86, 105, 107–108, *110,* 112, 130, 133–134, 137–139, *173,* 195, 227, 232, 334

Graham, Don, 107

Graves, Michael, 338

Guggenheim Museum, 258

Gunpowder drawings, 155, 231, 292

Hall, Su, 230

Hamilton, Richard, 121, 143

Heath, Bryan, *70*

Hefferton, Philip, 142

Herms, George, 114, 175

Hickey, Dave, 153, 227, 251, 334

Hirshhorn Museum and Sculpture Garden, 298, 379–381

Hockney, David, 105, 149, 174

Hoffmann, Hans, 299

Holzer, Jenny, 263, 299

Homer, Winslow, 126, 351

Hopkins, Henry T., 49, 130–131, 135

Hopper, Dennis, 323

Hopper, Edward, 127, 285, 306, 351

Hopps, Walter, 130–131, 135, 138, 144, 198, 312–328, 331, 373, 432n11

Huelsenbeck, Richard, 323

Hulten, K. Pontus, 199, 433n29

Huston, John, 255

Hutton, Lauren, 196

"Information Man," 46

Irwin, Robert, 107–108, 132, 179, 228, 262, 349–350

Jazz. *See* Music

Johns, Jasper, 11, 36, 116–118, 120, 124, 167, 216, 228, 230, 320, 324, 378, 431n4

Jones, Spike, 11, *271, 272,* 370

J. Paul Getty Museum, 345–354

Karp, Ivan, 36, 126

Kauffman, Craig, 133, 179–182

Kerouac, Jack, 114

Kienholz, Ed, 109, 113, 132, 135

Kline, Franz, 114, 117, 267, 316–317, 323, 333, 378

Knight, Christopher, 182–185

Kosuth, Joseph, 36, 325, 373

Kruger, Barbara, 263, 299

Kubrick, Stanley, 38

Lane, Fitz Hugh, 351

Language and words, 23, 57, 150–157, 191–193, 221, 231, 234, 247–248, 262–267, 270, 281, 286–290, 298–299, 301–303, 311, 319, 333, 339, 378, 380

Last Poets, 273

Lawler, Louise, 263

Leaf, Monroe, 91, 102

Léger, Fernand, 124

Lichtenstein, Roy, 36, 126, 138

Lippard, Lucy, 143

Liquid works ("romance with liquids"), 57, 157–158, 231, 320–322

Los Angeles art scene, 3, 29, 148–150, 198, 212–213, 220–224, 239–240, 243, 263, 297, 309, 331, 334, 343, 373–374

Los Angeles County Museum of Art, 113, 138, 142, 174–187, 199–201, 262

Lovich, Lene, 273

Lugosi, Bela, 47

Luminism, 182–184, 351

Lustig, Alvin, 19

Lyons, Lisa, 347–348

Lyotard, Jean-François, 266

Magritte, Rene, 58, 304, 324

Mapplethorpe, Robert, 344, 348

Marinetti, Filippo Tommaso, 370

Mastroianni, Marcello, 38

Matisse, Henri, 306, 326

McCracken, John, 179

McGuane, Tom, 278

McLaren, Malcolm, 273

McLaughlin, John, 176, 262

McMillan, Jerry, 49, 105, 107–108, *110,* 112, 130, *173,* 178, 228

Meier, Richard, 347–348, 353

Metropolitan Museum of Art, 126

Miami-Dade Public Library, 14–17, *256, 257*–258, 269–270, 294–295, 360

Millais, Sir John Everett, 375, *377*

Minimalism, 372

Miyashiro, Ronnie, 130–131

Mizuno, Riko, 135, 432n18

Modernism, 120

Monahan, Leo, 109, 111

Mondrian, Piet, 375–378

Monet, Claude, 146, 170–171, 319

Moore, Don, *110,* 228

Moses, Ed, 133–134, 334

Motherwell, Robert, 326–327

Museum of Contemporary Art, Los Angeles, 199–203

Museum of Modern Art, New York, 84, 126–127, 258

Music, 207–209, 267–268, 272–273

Nauman, Bruce, 52

Nelson, Rolf, 135

Norton Simon Museum, 201–203, 434n30. *See also* Pasadena Art Museum

Notebooks, 185, 276

Oldenburg, Claes, 32, 185, 367, 418

Organic materials, 30–33, 85, 154–157, 226, 231–232, 264–265, 359, 365, 371–372

Pasadena Art Museum, 63, 116, 138, 199, 201–203, 315, 331

Performance art, 241

Phillips, Michelle, 233

Photography, 23–29, 36, 41–54, 61–62, 84–85, 214–217, 284, 292, 305, 317–318, 320, 357, 369, 374–375

Photorealism, 187, 327

Picabia, Francis, 120

Picasso, Pablo, 12, *13,* 120, 127, *188,* 189, 306

Politics, 4–5, 87, 239

Pop Art and artists, 63, 121, 129, 138, 144–150, 160, 182, 190, 254–255, 263, 297, 299

Postmodern art, 263

Powell, Earl A., III, 176

Premeditated image, concept of the, 11, 117, 184–187, 228–230, 253, 263, 291, 302, 323, 326, 363

Presley, Elvis, 114

Price, Kenneth, 114, 132, 134, 232

Price, Monroe, 135

Prince, Richard, 299

Prints and printmaking, 35, 55–63, 87–88, 274, 362–369

Process art, 118

Projets pour la Défense. See Défense project

Quinn, Jack, 135

Ramos, Mel, 142, 145, 177

Rauschenberg, Robert, 116–118, 120, 121, 167, 432n15

Ray, Man, 116, 120, 318

Raysse, Martial, 179

Readymade, concept of the, 26, 215, 253. *See also* Duchamp, Marcel

Reichline, Neil, *70*

Rockwell, Norman, 102–103

Roeg, Nicolas, 79

Rosenquist, James, 230

Ruben, Richards, 108

Rubin, Marvin, 107

Ruscha, Danna Knego (Ruscha's wife), 142, 232, 259, 261

Ruscha, Dorothy Driscoll (Ruscha's mother), 93–98, 119, 318

Ruscha, Edward

books, 3, 23–29, 38–54, 64–72, 74–77, 168–170, 210–219, 230, 250, 252–254, 267, 292, 303, 325, 372, 374–375

early life and work (1937–1960), 11, 86, 92–106, 213, 225, 227, 232, 242, 250, 290, 300–301, 312–318, 336, 339

education (art school) (*see* Chouinard Art Institute)

Europe, trip to as student, 58, 118–125, 251, 313, 320

exhibitions, solo and group

Ed Ruscha, 379–381

Ed Ruscha Books and Prints, 56, 432n8

Edward Ruscha: Editions, 362–369, 435n48

Edward Ruscha: Paintings/Schilderijen, 289, 298, 309, 435n45

Frederick R. Weisman Foundation Collection of Contemporary Art, 269

New Painting of Common Objects, 63, 138, 144, 315, 432n11

Seventeen Artists of the Sixties, 174–187, 207, 239, 433n22

Six More, 142

Sonsbeek 71, 34, 76, 432n13

The End, 339–340

The Museum as Muse: Artists Reflect, 361

The Works of Ed Ruscha, 203–207, 225, 289, 298, 432n17, 433n23

Three Catholics, 344, 348

War Babies, 130

family life of, 194–195

work habits of, 90–91, 142, 194–195, 247–248

works of

234 Things, 6–7, 8–9

A Few Palm Trees, 47, 168, 233

Actual Size, 183, 262, 315

Adios, 153, 157, 320

Ancient Dogs Barking—Modern Dogs Barking, 171, 206

Annie, Poured from Maple Syrup, 231

Another Hollywood Dream Bubble Popped, 221

Automatic, 289

Babycakes, 47, 211

Bamboo Pole, 206

Banks, Tanks, Ranks, 61

Bengstonland, 195

Bicycle Sign, 123

Blue Collar Tires, 327

Blue Collar Tool and Die, 327

Boss, 176, 264

Boulangerie, 320

Box Smashed Flat, 315

Bronson Tropics, 221–223, 222, 233

Brother, Sister, 333

Business Cards, 47, 52, 82

Chain and Cable, 276

Chatanooga, 290

Chick Unit, 276

Chilly Draft, 151

Chocolate Room, 372, 435n48

Christ Candle, 278, 279

Colored People, 61, 64, 66–67, 69, 74, 76

Crackers, 47, 52, 71, 73, 82–83, 168–169, 212

Cut, 320

Do AZ I Do, 286–287, 435n43

"Domestic Tranquility" series, 236

Dublin, 290, 313

Dutch Details, 34, 47, 76, 211

Eat, 264

España, 320, *321*

Every Building on the Sunset Strip, 43, 52,
  67, 76, 84, 168, 170, 233

Eye, 157, 320

Five Past Eleven, 293–294, 298

Hard Light, 215, 434n33

Heaven, 274

Hell, 274

Hollywood, 157, 248, 251, 290, 379

Hourglass, 275

I Don't Want No Retro Spective, 361

I Live Over in Valley View, 223

Insect Slant, 236

It's a Small World, 195

Joe, 195

Johnny Tomorrow, 323

Large Trademark with Eight Spotlights, 60,
  159, 221, 230–231, 236, 290–291, 322

Los Angeles County Museum on Fire, 45,
  60, 131, 236, *377*

Metro, 320

Mint, 157, 320

Miracle (drawings), 221, 348

Miracle (film), 79, *80,* 81, 172, 233, 238,
  349, 357

News, Mews, Pews, Brews, Stews & Dues,
  31, 154, 232, 240–241, 365, 372

Nine Swimming Pools and a Broken Glass,
  43, 47, 60, 66, 233

Noise, Pencil, Broken Pencil, Cheap Western,
  207

Norm's La Cienega on Fire, 153

O-Books series, 322, 435n47

Parking Lines, 128

Pepto Bismol, Made in U.S.A., 156,
  433n21

Picture Without Words, 345–354 (*346*),
  356, 359–360

Pontiac Catalinas, 235

Pool, 320

Premium, 37, 52, 62, *70,* 71–72, 81, 83,
  169, 233, 357

Rancho, 157

Real Estate Opportunities, 44, 47, 211, 214

Records, 47, 212, 233

Rooster, 289

Royal Road Test, 29, 47, *48,* 52, 60, 167,
  211

Scratches on the Film, 339

Securing the Last Letter, 231

Sin, 344

Smash, 158, 264

Some Los Angeles Apartments, 47, 49, 168,
  211, 368

Squeezing Dimple, 231

St. Crosses Ave., 377

Stains, 32, 56, 154, 322, 365, 371

Standard Station, 364

Standard Station, Amarillo, Texas, 153,
  157–159, 177, 196, 223, 236, 291, 352,
  380

*Standard Station, 10¢ Western Being Torn in
  Half,* 25, 223

Standard Station at Various Times of Day (unfinished), 170

Steel, 157

Study of Friction and Wear on Mating Surfaces, 253

Su, 229, 230

Sweetwater, 131–132, 313, *314*

Telephone, 327

The Back of Hollywood (Hollywood Rear-View Mirror), 163

The Catholic Church, 238

The End, 338–339

Thirtyfour Parking Lots, 43, 47, 84, 211, 233

Twentysix Gasoline Stations, 23–25, 29, 41, 47, 64, 71, 75, 168, 210–211, 214, 218, 226, 233, 239, 368, 434n32

Various Cruelties, 154

Various Small Fires, 42, 47, 52, 60, 168, 368, 432n7

Vaseline, 289

Vicksburg, 290, 313

Western with Two Marbles, 157

Words Going Round #1, 432n6

Words Without Thoughts Never to Heaven Go (mural), 14–17, *256,* 257–258, 269–270, 294–295

Ruscha, Edward III (Ruscha's father), 93–99, 102–103, 106, 318

Ruscha, Edward V. (Ruscha's son), 142, 232

Ruscha, Paul (Ruscha's brother), 94, 119

Ruscha, Shelby (Ruscha's sister), 94, 103, 318

Russian Constructivism, 262

Sabol, Audrey, 364

San Francisco Museum of Modern Art, 203–207, 225

Schwitters, Kurt, 267, 324, 332, 358, 378

Serial imagery, 100, 170–171, 275

Shakespeare, William, 14, 99, 257–258, 269–270, 294

Sheeler, Charles, 126

Shore, Stephen, 218

Siegel, Don, 38

Siegelaub, Seth, 77

Silhouette paintings. *See* Strokeless paintings

Sloan, John, 126

Smith, Alexis, 353

Smithson, Robert, 308, 373, 431n2

Smothers, Tommy, 71–72, 233

Snow, Hank, 273

Southern California art scene. *See* Los Angeles art scene

Stein, Gertrude, 208

Still, Clyfford, 114

Sting, 273

Strokeless paintings, 267, 274–276, 283–285, 293–299, 333

Surrealism, 208, 349

Syrop, Mitchell, 299

Tamarind Institute, 364–366

The Byrds, 272

The Doors, 272

The Eagles, 272

Thiebaud, Wayne, 142, 144, 177, 350

Tinguely, Jean, 357

Tuchman, Maurice, 175–178

Turrell, James, 349–350

Vaisman, Meyer, 325

Valentine, DeWain, 175, 179, 199, 203

Vega, Alan, 273

Vermeer, Johannes, 66

Visconti, Luchino, 38

Voulkos, Peter, 114

Walsh, John, 345–354

Warhol, Andy, 71, 138, 144, 171, 212, 255, 344, 348, 366, 380

Wayne, June, 367

Weiner, Lawrence, 36, 78, 215, 251, 325, 373, 431n2

West coast art scene. *See* Los Angeles art scene

Westerman, H. C., 182

Whitney Museum of American Art, 126, 258

Wilder, Nick, 135

Williams, Hank, 273

Williams, Mason, 52, 71–72, 73, 101, 105, 142, 167–168, 227, 232, 234, 312

Woelffer, Emerson, 107

Wolverton, Basil, 102–103

Words in Ruscha's art. *See* Language and words

Wright, Frank Lloyd, 109

Wyeth, N. C., 126

X, 209, 433n31

Young, Faron, 273

Zak, Ed, 125

Zammitt, Norman, 180

Zappa, Frank, 207–208, 234

DATE DUE

OCT 8 2004			
NOV 2 8 2012			
3/12			
OCT - 1 2013			

Demco